THE BEAGLE

POPULAR DOGS' BREED SERIES

THE

BEAGLE

Thelma Gray

POPULAR DOGS
London Melbourne Sydney Auckland Johannesburg

Popular Dogs Publishing Co. Ltd
An imprint of the Hutchinson Publishing Group
3 Fitzroy Square, London W1P 6JD

Hutchinson Group (Australia) Pty Ltd
30–32 Cremorne Street, Richmond South, Victoria 3121
PO Box 151, Broadway, New South Wales 2007

Hutchinson Group (NZ) Ltd
32–34 View Road, PO Box 40–086, Glenfield, Auckland 10

Hutchinson Group (SA) (Pty) Ltd
PO Box 337, Bergvlei 2012, South Africa

First published (*as The Popular Beagle*) 1963
Second edition, revised 1970
Third edition, revised 1975
Fourth edition, revised 1980

Printed in Great Britain by The Anchor Press Ltd
and bound by Wm Brendon & Son Ltd
both of Tiptree, Essex

ISBN 0 09 140420 7

This book is dedicated to the grandfather I never knew—Sir David Evans, K.C.M.G., late Master of the Surrey Farmers' Stag Hounds, lover of Beagles. From my modest study of the laws of heredity, I believe he started all this.

ACKNOWLEDGEMENTS

We are indebted to Mr Arthur Dalgety, M.H.,
for his substantial contribution to the chapter
on the Hunting Beagle. Also to Mr Gerald
Massey for allowing us to reproduce the
photographs of pictures by Harry Hall, John
Emms, and Maud Earl, all from his collection.

CONTENTS

ILLUSTRATIONS

ILLUSTRATIONS

Ch. Rossut Foreman, *owned by Mrs C. G. Sutton*

Am. Ch. Bravo of Sun Valley, *owned by R. and J. C. Doyle*

Between pages 128 and 129

Am. Ch. Rozavel Ritter's Sweet Sue, *owned by the author*

Aust. & Am. Ch. J. Dons Salt of the Earth of Rozavel, *owned by the author*

Ch. Tavernmews Ranter and Ch. Tavernmews Bonnett, *owned by the Misses J. Whitton and J. Siddle*

Rozavel Beagle puppies, *owned by the author*

Ch. Rozavel Elsy's Diamond Jerry, *owned by the author*

Rozavel Crystal Gift, *owned by the author*

Aust. Ch. Rozavel Circle the Earth, *owned by the author*

Ch. Beacott Buckthorn, *owned by Mr P. J. Tutchener*

IN THE TEXT

AUTHOR'S PREFACES

THE panel of dog-show judges approved by the Kennel Club includes a number of experts who undertake the judging of all breeds. They often accept appointments to judge the mixed companies known as Variety classes, many of which are open to any kind of dog, and all have to be compared and finally placed in order before prizes are awarded to the first four or five. Persons outside the world of dogs are often mystified as to how one can possibly choose between, say, a Great Dane and a Pekingese and decide which of the two is the better. In fact, since there is a Standard of Points for each breed it is merely a question of deciding which of the animals is the one that is closest to its list of desirable breed points—in simple terms, which is the better specimen of its breed. And this is not difficult if one has studied the breeds concerned, even though they may be utterly unalike in almost every respect.

Because the author has bred and kept a considerable number of breeds which bear little resemblance to one another, people often ask, wonderingly, how it is possible to have a particular liking for dogs that vary so greatly in type, size, purpose, etc. The breeds in question, it is conceded, do not have a lot in common. Starting with a large kennel of Alsatians (German Shepherd Dogs), and passing on to the building-up of what was the largest and most successful kennel of Welsh Corgis (Pembroke), the Rozavel kennel also housed Welsh Corgis (Cardigan), Chihuahuas, English Setters, Smooth Fox Terriers, Welsh Terriers, Greyhounds, Rottweilers, Dachshunds, Schnauzers, Toy Poodles—and Beagles.

The first four named above, and the last, are still kept, and the kennel houses approximately a hundred dogs, about a third of which are the little hounds.

The two varieties of Corgis share certain similarities, both being cattle dogs, while the Alsatian is basically a sheep-herding dog. The

Chihuahuas are a unique breed, possessing many admirable and completely fascinating qualities in an incredibly small compass. The Beagles are different again—but how fascinating! Their balance, their beauty of outline and colour, the sturdy soundness of their limbs, the sweetness of their faces—no other breed compares with them. Their appeal lies in their natural beauty, shall we say—in their complete lack of exaggeration or weaknesses. And we love their sterling character, their jolly, carefree natures. Certainly they are mischievous, but this is true hound character and who would have them otherwise? They are so good-natured, so affectionate, so clever, and such sterling little hunters.

As the dedication shows, the love of hounds and hunting seems to be an inherited characteristic of ours. We have enjoyed following Beagles from our early teens, and, even earlier, riding to hounds. An early reminiscence is the floods of tears we shed when the hound puppies we 'walked'—Languid and Languish—were returned to the pack.

And now we are, literally, knee-deep in Beagles, with never a dull moment. We recommend this attractive breed for sport, for the family, for showing, for friendship—and for fun.

1963   T.G.

In this second edition I have largely rewritten Chapter IV and where necessary amended the text elsewhere. The appendices have been brought up to date, and one of the photographs has been replaced.

1970   T. G.

For this third edition I have brought the appendices up to date once again and included the latest Kennel Club standard of the breed. Some minor revisions have been made to the text and three of the photographs replaced.

1975   T.G.

In this fourth edition I have again brought the appendices up to date and included the current Kennel Club standard of the breed. A few minor revisions have been made to the text; two of the photographs have been replaced and two have been added.

1980   T.G.

CHAPTER I

ORIGINS OF THE BEAGLE

THE Beagle is probably one of the oldest hounds of the chase—the hounds that hunt by scent—as distinct from the 'gaze-hounds'. The former classification includes such well-known breeds as the Basset hound, the Foxhound, the Harrier, and the Bloodhound. The second category includes the Greyhound, together with the Saluki or Gazelle hound, the Afghan hound, and the Whippet, all breeds dependent on keen eyesight when hunting for their prey. There are certain similarities shared by the hounds which hunt with their noses, too obvious to need much emphasis, and possibly all have connections in the dim past.

Undoubtedly hounds of these and other mixed types existed many, many years ago. Archaeologists in various parts of the world have discovered wall-paintings and carvings in which hunting scenes are clearly recognizable, and in which hounds of various shapes feature. Many of these possess characteristics we can recognize in some of the pure breeds with which we are now familiar. Lovers of particular breeds are a little addicted to wishful thinking and seek to add lustre to the history of their favourites by proving their antiquity. To this end they claim to recognize them in the murals and tablets, though, if we are honest with ourselves, we have to admit that it is the type of dog, rather than the breed, that is recorded for posterity. However, even if separate breeds cannot be truly identified, we do know that hounds of very much the same stamp as our present-day varieties were used, both for sport and for the more practical issue of procuring food, many hundreds of years ago.

Man from time immemorial has had hounds with pendant ears, short hair, and sickle tails. Furthermore, it appears that however wide the range of sizes may have been, some were small. Facts relating to the very early stages are scarce and it is not easy to guess

how much these resembled the modern Beagle, but as far back as the
reign of King Henry VII (1457–1509) we begin to find references to
little hounds actually *called* Beagles. There is no particular reason
to suppose that they were a novelty then; they probably existed long
before that time. The fact that we have no earlier records does not
necessarily mean that they were not known by that name.

Hounds of Beagle type have been known to exist in the British
Isles for centuries. It has also been authoritatively stated that it is
more than likely that the ancient Greek hounds, used for hare
hunting by Xenophon about 350 B.C. (descriptions of which have
appeared in his famous essays 'Cynegeticos'), would be of the type
known as Beagles today.

Two celebrated Greek writers, Oppian and Arrian, have described
the hounds of their day. Oppian lived in the latter part of the second
century A.D. and was a poet of Cilicia. Arrian, born about A.D. 100,
was a noted historian. Both writers accurately describe the Agaseous,
or Beagle, Arrian telling us that: 'In pursuit, these give tongue with a
clanging howl, like the yelping Carians, but are more eager when they
catch the scent. Sometimes, indeed, they gladden so outrageously,
even on a stale trail, that I have rated them for their excessive
barking—alike on every scent whether it be the hare going to form,
or at speed.'

Arrian's remarks could have applied to the Beagle, or, to be fair,
to another small hound of the time, the Segusian, known to have
resembled a small Basset hound.

Oppian, in a poem attributed to him, refers to small hounds
peculiar to the ancient Britons, thus:

> 'There is a kind of dog of mighty fame
>   For hunting, worthier of a fairer frame
> By painted Britons brave in war they're bred;
>   Are beagles called, and to the chase are led.
> Their bodies small . . .'

In the forest laws of King Canute (994–1035) certain dogs were
prohibited from entering the Crown forests. Special exemption was
granted to the Velterer, 'which the English call Langehren [long-
eared] for, manifestly, they are too small to do any harm'. Harm,
that is, to the King's deer.

This interesting fragment could, it is thought, refer only to the

Beagle or to a drop-eared terrier breed. If, however, we delve into the histories of our pendant-eared terriers, the Bedlington, Dandie Dinmont, Fox Terrier, Airedale, and the like, we find that they are believed to have attained that very feature from a hound cross, and all these breeds are of more recent manufacture.

King William the Conqueror—we will not mention the date since it is certainly the one we all know—brought the Talbot hound to these islands. The Talbot, scarcely known today, though immortalized by numbers of inns which bear its name and sometimes its portrait on the signs, was a large, predominantly white hound, thought to have been used in the production of the old Southern hound, of which we will hear more later in this book. It is fairly certain that our modern Beagles are descended from the Southern hound, and after such recurrent references to the 'small' hounds from various sources one cannot help speculating on the possibility of the Talbot blood being the cross that eventually resulted in an increase in the size of some Beagles.

There is plenty of evidence to show that the first Prince of Wales, afterwards King Edward II, was very fond both of dogs and of hunting. Letters from him, written in 1304 and 1305, when he was in his very early twenties, read: 'I am sending some of our bow-legged hare-hounds of Wales who can well discover a hare if they find it sleeping; and some of our running dogs who can swiftly chase it.'

Can we assume that the first reference is to Bassets and the latter to Beagles? Or were the 'running dogs' Greyhounds?

Chaucer, towards the latter part of the fourteenth century, makes references to hounds in his various writings, and among his most often-quoted lines are those from *The Canterbury Tales*. When speaking of a lady dog-lover he writes: 'Of smalle houndes hadde she, that she fedde ... But sore wept she, if on of them were dedde.'

Another author, contemporary with Chaucer, was Edmund de Langley, who wrote *Mayster of Game*. He referred to a type of hare-hunting hound as 'the Rache', a word that was also used by that great authority on hunting, Dame Juliana Berners. Juliana was an Englishwoman, said to have been Prioress of Sopwell Nunnery, St Albans, though some doubts have been expressed about this. She was the reputed author of *The Boke of St Albans*, printed in 1486–96, 'a rimed treatise on hunting'. Dame Juliana does not include either Beagles or Harriers by such names in the list of breeds of dogs that she published, namely:

'The names of divres manere of houndes.
These ben the names of houndes:
Fyrste, there is a Grehounde, a Bastard,
a mongrell, a Mastife, a Lemor, a Spanyell,
Raches, Kennetty's, Terours, Butcher's houndes,
Dunghill dogges, Tryndel tayles, and Pryckered
Curres and smalle ladyes Popees that bear away
the fleas and divers small fawlis.'

The Greyhound, the mongrel, the Mastiff, and the Spaniel are all easily identified. The 'pryckered curre' may have been our popular Welsh Corgi. Terours one assumes to be terriers. We would love to know what Tryndel tayles looked like. Perhaps they were the Spitz type of dog with tightly curled tails. But what were Dunghill dogges? Some writers believe that the 'raches' may have been harriers, so perhaps the 'kennetty's' were Beagles?

One Walter William Skeat, a well-known English philologist and writer born in 1835, refers to the word Beagle as appearing in *The Squire of Low Degree*. The word 'Kennetty's' or 'Kenet' is given in Wright and Thomas's *Dictionary of Obsolete and Provincial English* as meaning 'a small hound', so it would therefore apply to the Beagle.

There are records of some revealing regulations appertaining to the household of King Henry VIII, including an interesting note to the effect that dogs kept outside the court must be kept 'sweete, wholesome, and cleane'.

In His Majesty's Privy Accounts appear various items which include 'colars and mosulles', their diet of 'mate', and disbursements made to Robert Shere, 'Keper of the Begles', also for the care and feeding of 'buk hounds'.

There is an entry referring to the sum of three shillings paid for the hire of a cart for the King's hounds to be transported from 'Newelme' to 'Wodstock', and seven shillings and sixpence for 'canvas to cover them with'. Presumably a part of the same enterprise, a man by the name of Humphrey Raynesford collected five shillings for ten elles of canvas to cover the cart, and sixpence for three hundred nails used in the making of the awning.

One of the earliest experts on dogs emerges in Dr Johannes Caius, also referred to as John Keys or Kays, for he produced a complete classification of breeds, published in 1570 and entitled *De Canibus Britannicus*; it was written in Latin. Dr Caius, who was born in

1510, and died at the age of sixty-three, was Physician-in-Chief to Her Majesty Queen Elizabeth I, and became the second founder of Gonville and Caius College, Cambridge. An edition of his book was translated into English by Abraham Fleming and published in 1576. It was entitled: *Of Englishe Dogges. A short treatise in Latine by Johannes Caius, drawne into Englishe by Abraham Fleming.* According to Caius, there were sixteen breeds of dogs at that time, or, more correctly, sixteen types, for it is doubtful if pure breeds as we understand them today existed in those days. He wrote of the Levararius: 'The dog that wins by scent and is always swift, is unusually keen in following up the trail; this dog we call Sagax. Its hips protrude; its ears hang forward towards its mouth; it is of moderate size.'

Shakespeare, in *A Midsummer Night's Dream*, tells us:

> 'My hounds are bred out of the Spartan kind
>   So flewed, so sanded and their heads are hung
> With ears that sweep the morning dew.'

This could, of course, be a description of any of the hounds that hunt by scent, but although it might well apply to the Basset, it has been suggested that the lines may have been penned about the old Southern hound, a breed, as we already know, that was certainly used in the evolution of our present Beagle.

King James I was yet another of our monarchs distinguished by his great affection for, and interest in, dogs, and for his love of hunting. Born in 1566, this son of the ill-fated Mary, Queen of Scots, whose pet dogs followed her to the scaffold, is perhaps an early example of something we know well—that a liking for dogs frequently runs in a family.

James was addicted to expressions of endearment that seem to us both original and expressive. He called his Queen his 'deare little beagle'. His friend Robert Cecil, Earl of Salisbury, was also addressed as 'my little beagill'.

The King was devoted to his dogs. On one occasion, during a storm at sea, the ship appeared to be sinking. In the moment of crisis His Majesty was heard to shout: 'Oh! Save the dogs and Colonel Churchill!' He was known to refer to himself as his Beagle's 'deare dadde'.

One of King James I's letters reads:

'Sweet hairte blessing blessing blessing on my sweet tome badgers hairte rootes and all his, for breeding me so fyne a kennell of young howndes. Some of them so faire and well shaped and some of thaime so fine prettie litle ones as thaye are worthie to lye on Steenie and Kate's bedde; and all of them run together in a lumpe, both at scente and vewe . . . the bearer will tell you quhat fyne running we had yesterdaye.'

It is round about this time, in 1560 to be exact, that Johannes Stradanus depicts in print a small pack of Beagles killing rabbits.

In the very early seventeenth century, a foremost zoologist named Edward Topsell, B.A. Cantab, wrote two books on animals. He made free use of the works of Dr Caius and Abraham Fleming, and borrowed much of his material from the labours of a Swiss doctor, Conrad Gesner, also an authority on livestock.

Topsell writes about 'terriars or Beagles, called in the German tongue Lochundle', and he also refers to them as 'smelling dogs'.

It is a modern writer, however, Sir Arthur Bryant, who gives us insight into the pastimes of yet another King of England, for in his *Life of Charles II* he tells us that the merry monarch frequently hunted hares with Beagles on Newmarket Heath. King Charles II was born in 1630 and died in 1685.

On a more fanciful scale the poet Dryden, born in 1631, makes the following allusion in one of his fables:

'The graceful goddess was array'd in green
About her feet were little Beagles seen,
That matched with upturned eyes the motions of their Queen.'

Pope, born in 1688 and considered by some to be the greatest of our English poets, writes:

'To plain with well-bred Beagles we repair,
And trace the mazes of the circling hare.'

The Earls and Dukes of Bedford kept hounds at Woburn Park in Bedfordshire. The accounts have survived the years, and an item dated 1644 is of interest to us. It reads:

'Paid for biscuit, broken bread and chippings, for barley, graves, and other provisions bought for the beagles and spaniels, £29 7s. 1d.

To the huntsmen upon their bills and for some other necessary expenses about dogs, with £2 3s. 8d. for 30 pair of dog couples—£6 5s. 10d.'

We pass from one century to another and still we find the royal connexions with our little hounds. King William III (1762–1830) kept a pack of Beagles during his lifetime.

William Somerville, writing early in the eighteenth century, described the characteristics of the Cotswold Beagle of his day and relates how he bred some of his best harriers by crossing this type of hound with the old Southern hound. Some other seventeenth-century writers also mention a North Country Beagle, said to be faster and more slender in outline than the Cotswold type.

Peter Beckford, perhaps the greatest authority on hunting we have ever known, was the author of that great classic *Thoughts on Hunting*, written about 1750. He wrote that 'the Fox-Beagle was exceptionally lively as well as light and fleet of foot' and he explains how he crossed this type of hound with his harriers in order to produce a hound with more dash and drive.

Reverting to the Royal Family—King George IV is known to have kept a pack of Beagles, and is said to have endeavoured by selective breeding to reduce them in size, but without very great success. He was very much attached to his little hounds, so much so that he had them included in one of the best portraits of himself, and the artist has depicted him surrounded with them—a merry little pack and very typical.

A Colonel Thornton hunted with these hounds on the downs at Brighton, Sussex, and expressed himself surprised at the pace they could go. We do not know the exact size of these hounds, but it is thought that they were certainly not 'pocket' Beagles. Possibly they measured from 11 to 12 or even 13 inches at the shoulder.

Another immortal writer, Sir Walter Scott, mentions Beagles, his lines reading:

'If they rob us of name and pursue us with Beagles
Give their roofs to the flames and their flesh to the eagles.'

Some poetic licence here, we feel sure. We cannot imagine that Rob Roy would flee from Beagles! Either Sir Walter was mixing them up with Bloodhounds—and surely he, who was a close friend of that greatest-ever painter of dogs and hounds, Landseer, would know better—or he could not find any other word to rhyme with eagles!

Sydenham Edwards's famous, and now scarce, book *Cynographia Britannici*, published in 1803, prints a coloured plate showing Beagles, and it is most interesting to note that in type they are not at all dissimilar to the type of little hound that has persisted throughout the ensuing years.

In the following year Reinagle, in the *Sportsman's Cabinet*, indicates that Beagles existed in several sizes, a point worthy of note in view of the recurrent present-day controversy on the subject of height. Reinagle tells us that:

'Packs of Beagles were frequently seen in the possession of gentlemen whose age or infirmities prevented their enjoyment of sport of a different description; but in proportion to the improvements made in the different kinds of hounds (according to the different chases they were intended to pursue) the former attachment to Beagles has been observed to decline. They are the smaller of the hound race in this country, are exquisite in the scent of the hare and indefatigably vigilant in their pursuit of her.'

He goes on to say:

'Though wonderfully inferior in point of speed yet equally energetic in persevering pursuit, they follow her through all her windings, unravel all her mazes, explore her labarinths, and by the scent alone trace and retrace her footsteps to a degree of admiration that must be seen to be properly understood, during which the soft and melodious tone of their emulous vociferation seems to be the most predominant inducement to the well-known ecstatic pleasure of the chase.'

George Stubbs, celebrated artist most famed for his paintings of horses, also depicted Beagles. He was born in 1722 and died in 1806.

It is another artist, however, J. F. Herring, who was privileged to undertake a portrait of Prince Albert and his Beagles. An engraving of this attractive picture appeared in *The Sport Sketch Book*, edited by J. W. Carleton, in 1842. The hounds in this painting are definitely very small. The text tells us:

'In the course of last year, ten or a dozen of the most perfect Beagles that could be procured in England were brought to Cumberland Lodge for His Royal Highness Prince Albert. For this unique little pack, one of the most elegant kennels our sporting architecture boasts has lately been completed in Windsor Home Park. The lodge is of the Gothic order, replete with all possible appliances . . . and is frequently honoured by visits from Her Majesty.'

Another exceedingly attractive picture, by the Barraud brothers, shows Maynard with Queen Victoria's Beagles—again very tiny hounds, about pocket size. One imagines that the little hounds shown in this picture are very likely the descendants of the other Beagles pictured in Herring's portrait of the Prince Consort, which can be dated some ten years earlier.

As can be expected, a writer such as 'Stonehenge', the pseudonym that shrouded the identity of J. H. Walsh, one of the most outstanding writers on the canine race, and a world authority on dogs of every known breed, had quite a lot to say about Beagles, especially in his book published in 1879. He says:

'Any English hound less than 16 inches in height is ordinarily called a Beagle, but in reality there is as great a difference between a dwarf Harrier or Foxhound and a true Beagle, as between a Bloodhound and a Foxhound.

'A true Beagle is a miniature specimen of the old Southern hound, except that like almost all moderately reduced dogs as to size, he possesses more symmetry than his prototype.

'Where, however, this reduction is carried to extremes in order to produce a little hound capable of being carried in the pocket of a shooting jacket, and slow enough to allow of his followers keeping up on foot, there is generally a loss of symmetry and of its ordinary accompaniment, a hardy constitution.

'For this reason it has been found impossible to keep up a pack of Beagles less than 9 or 10 inches in height. Mr Crane, of Linthorn House, Dorset, for some years maintained one kept exclusively for hunting rabbits . . . Mr J. Grimwood, of Stanton House, Nr Swindon, has a beautiful little pack of somewhat larger size, averaging nearly 12 inches, and usually hunting hare; while Sir Thomas Lloyd, of Carmarthenshire, breeds to a still higher standard. For many years Lord Caledon was famous for his Beagles, with which he hunted hare in Tyrone, and they were said to be of the purest old blood. Mr Everett, of Abingdon, has been the most successful on the show bench and has attained a high reputation in the field, his little hounds being able to account for sometimes a brace of hares in the day, after showing a good run with each.

'Some twenty years ago Mr Honeywood hunted over the Essex marshes on foot with Pocket Beagles, very little above Mr Crane's height limit, but these tinies were often unable to get up the banks of the drains when the water was low, and frequently required assistance to save them from drowning.

'Foot Beagles, generally hunting "drag", sometimes hare, were kept by subscription throughout the country, in almost every populous parish, for the purpose of giving exercise to, and educating to the sport, the rising generation. But,' laments Stonehenge, 'since the coming in with a rush of lawn-tennis, they have gone out of fashion for this purpose and very few packs are now kept except by those who love the chase pure and simple, irrespective of the exercise it gives.'

A writer of an article in *The Dogs of the British Islands* describes the pack known as the Southover Beagles as 'perfect in symmetry, excellent in nose and intelligence, not exceeding 9 inches in height, and all of them model miniature hounds'.

Dalziel in his book *British Dogs*, which appeared in 1888, remarked that 'it is to be regretted that the Beagle is not more encouraged by committees of shows, and that when a class is made for them, all sizes are lumped together'. He also says, 'Not only in the time of Elizabeth (I) but in our own, there has been an occasional rage for the very diminutive Beagles and much emulation in producing the most perfect Lilliputian hound.'

There are other writers of distinction, such as 'Idstone', the Rev. Thomas Pearce (what a fashion there was at that time for the pseudo-modest custom of writing under nom de plumes!), who were prolific spokesmen on canine matters. 'Idstone' also refers to Mr Crane's little hounds, saying that they have 'never been excelled for excellence in the field and beauty on the show bench'. He has

'. . . seen them on a cold, bad scenting day work up a rabbit and run him in the most extraordinary manner. Mr Crane's standard is 9 inches and every little hound is absolutely perfect. I saw but one hound at all differing from his companions, a little black-tanned one. This one on the flags we should have drafted, but when we saw him in his work we quite forgave him for being of a conspicuous colour. "Giant" was perhaps the very best of the pack, a black, white, and tanned dog hound, always at work and never wrong. He had a capital tongue and plenty of it. A bitch, Lily, had the most beautiful points. She is nearly all white, as her name implies. Damper, Dutchman, Tyrant are also, all of them, beautiful models. The measurement of Damper was:

> Height—9 in.
> Round the chest—16 in.
> Across the ears—12 in.
> Extreme length—2 ft 4 in.
> Eye to nose—$2\frac{1}{8}$ in.

Mr Crane's standard is kept up with great difficulty. He has reduced the Beagle to a minimum . . . but all are models of symmetry and power and are as accomplished and steady as Lord Portsmouth's hounds. The Southover Beagles are as small as it is possible to breed them (in sufficient numbers to form a pack) without losing symmetry, nose, intelligence, and strength.'

'Stonehenge' wrote in *The Field* in 1855, and describes the Beagle as 'a model of a foxhound—a "pocket lexicon" '. He says:

'The small Beagle is hardly ever used for or with the gun. It is kept for hunting, a pack of six couples of not more than 9 inches in height.
'Hounds of this size must be powerfully made to get through thick furze brakes and to keep up their work from eleven to four o'clock.'

Mr Crane died in 1894, and most of the sayings we have recorded here were set down in writing round about 1850. He is said to have kept a few of his favourites until his death, some two years before which his pack was decimated by distemper. It may well be because, by this tragedy, the best of them were wiped out, that shortly after this, Pocket Beagles began to be very scarce.

Poor Mr Crane, his last days saddened by the knowledge that his carefully built-up and cherished pack was dwindling away. Perhaps he found some small measure of comfort in the memories of the wonderful sport he had enjoyed in their company, and he may have felt the blow less since it was coupled with the growing realization that advancing age was making it well-nigh impossible for him to hunt them as of old.

It was a few years later that Rawdon Lee wrote in his book *Modern Dogs* that had Mr Crane but lived a few years later he might have been able to obtain some new blood, for, says Lee, 'just now our little Rabbit Beagle, Pocket Beagle, Dwarf Beagle, or whatever you like to call him—and name him anything but toy—has quite an increasing number of admirers'.

From time to time there were records of wire-coated Beagles, but this variety never became either very numerous or very popular.

In 1892 a *Stud Book of Packs of Beagles* was published by Waterlow's as part of the stud book for Harriers. The first volume listed twelve packs (although there must have been a great many more in existence) which purported to be foundation stock. But it was said that the entries were not of such untarnished breeding as they should be, and some sceptics of the times did not set too much store by the particulars given of a good many of the entries. No show hounds were included, although it was said that these were probably of much purer breeding.

For a good many years it has been known that a majority of Masters of Hounds have been prejudiced against dog shows, and their attitude appears to date back even to those far-off days, when it seems that the best-looking hounds were seen more frequently on the bench than in the field.

Rawdon Lee remarks that, according to the *Rural Almanack* hunt tables, as shown at the turn of the century, there were about forty packs of Beagles hunting in various parts of the country, some of which no doubt had more than a dash of harrier blood in their veins.

This, however, is the background of the Beagle as we see it today. For hundreds of years it has been loved and carefully bred by kings, queens, and commoners, indeed by sportsmen in all walks of life—and, latterly, by you and me.

CHAPTER II

THE DEVELOPMENT OF THE HUNTING BEAGLE, AND PACKS

ALTHOUGH the Hunting Beagle and the Show Beagle were at one time almost indistinguishable, there is now a gulf between the two. Show Beagles have become more standardized, and there is less tendency to breed from immediate pack-bred stock, since there are now plenty of show-bred hounds available, most of which are likely to breed more true to type than the pack hound. As a whole, these Show Beagles are found to be shorter-coupled and more compact, better in skull, foreface, and expression, and frequently superior in reach of neck and lay-back of shoulder.

The Hunting Beagle, however, has not altered greatly in recent years, except in size. Whereas, taken overall, the Beagles were predominantly small at the end of the last century, now, in order to suit modern conditions and tastes, the larger Hunting Beagle is in the ascendant.

We have read in Chapter I about the beautiful miniature hounds kept and hunted by the eighteenth-century sportsmen, but, alas, in these days we know of no 9- or 10-inch packs in this country. Among the present-day packs of smaller Beagles, the Pipewell has always been noted for its diminutive size, and Mr Dalgety's were under 13 inches until fairly recently, when a change of country resulted in a move to raise the height.

It is easily understandable that little hounds can be fast over downlands and fields, but on rough, ploughed earth, or in thick, deep heather, a longer-legged and larger hound clearly has the advantage. Far more land is under the plough since the last war, when so much rough land was reclaimed and brought into production, and the science of grassland management and crop rotation has reached a higher level; but when Mr Thornton, Mr Crofton, Mr Lord, and Mr Crane were hunting with 'pygmy' packs there were great areas of uncultivated land. It is this change in terrain that has come about in recent years that is largely responsible for the increase in size.

Colonel Thornton, writing about his own pack of Beagles more than 160 years ago, said:

'Here I must observe that the Beagle, in point of height, should be regulated by the country in which he is to hunt; but he ought at any rate to be very low. In a dry country, free from walls, the Beagle cannot be too low; but where there are such impediments he should be larger, to prevent being stopped by fences; as also, when the water is out, he is better calculated for swimming.'

Mr Crofton, the enthusiast who resided at Totton, Hants, during the late nineteenth century, certainly appears to have had a good deal of fun and some excellent sport with a lively pack of really tiny hounds. These were described by a contemporary writer as 'extremely dainty creatures, well made, full of muscle as a rule, and hardy'. Of them it was said:

'He prefers them 10 inches or as much under as he can get them. His earliest hound was picked up in Winchester, an almost perfect little fellow. He always had a few couples of hounds not exceeding 10 inches, and his smallest were a couple which did not exceed 8 inches. It is said that one of the 8-inch hounds was presented to a lady who resided in London, and that it even contrived to find material to hunt in Kensington Gardens. It went away on the line, throwing its voice merrily, much to the amusement of everyone.'

Mr Crofton found his little favourites quite hardy, well able to stand up to severe work, and not more liable than other dogs to disease.

He considered his smallest hounds the best workers, and the most intelligent, pleasant companions. They must have been versatile too, for he used them for rabbit hunting, rabbit shooting, and an occasional drag hunt.

Rawdon Lee, in his book *Modern Dogs*, published 1897, writes:

'Perhaps there is a future for these miniature hounds, especially as the Beagle Club is encouraging them. Previously they were heavily handicapped in the show ring by having to compete against larger hounds. Still, there is a quaintness and a character about these Rabbit Beagles which I greatly admired, and their merry movements and silvery cry delighted me very much.'

One wonders upon what grounds the present-day Beagle Club seeks to discourage the restoration of these attractive, sporting little hounds.

Another quote, this time from Youatt:

'There are many pleasurable recollections of the period when the good old English gentleman used to keep his pack of Beagles or little harriers, slow, but sure, sometimes carried to the field in a pair of panniers on a horse's back; often an object of ridicule at an early period of the chase, but rarely failing to accomplish their object ere the day closed. It was seldom, in spite of her speed, her shifts, her doublings, that the hare did not fall a victim to her pursuers. The power of scent in these little hounds is remarkable and they hardly ever seem to tire; the densest cover has no terrors for them, whether brambles, fern or furze. . . .'

Mr Mills in *The Sportsman's Library* says:
'Beagles to be very choice can scarcely be bred too small. The standard of perfection is considered to be from 10 to 11 inches and the latter should be the maximum height. Although far inferior in speed to the harrier, the sense of smelling is equally, if not more, exquisite in the Beagle. In pursuing the hare, he exercises the indefatigable vigilance, energy, and perseverance, every winding and double is traced with a degree of exactness which must be seen to be enjoyed and justly estimated, and his cry loads the air with unequalled music.

'Nothing can be more melodious and beautiful than to hear the pygmy pack open at a hare, and if slow, comparatively speaking, in running her, should the scent be good, she stands but little chance of escape from them in the end.

'The Pocket Beagle must not exceed 10 inches. These are greatly valued for rabbit shooting, as they can follow wherever bunny leads, and try to drive him out to face the guns. In a suitable country they are capable of affording much sport in connexion with hare hunting, for although the actual kills may be few, those who find keen enjoyment in seeing hounds can watch every yard of the run even if they have passed the best milestone on life's journey and will find these miniature hounds at least as keen and full of music as their larger brethren.'

According to Rawdon Lee, Mr Lord's 11-to-12-inch Beagles hunted the large, uncultivated areas of moorland near which he resided. His popular meets were held every Saturday, from November to April.

It is Lee who tells us that:
'Greater attention appears to have been given to the Beagle in the South of England than elsewhere and the County of Sussex has usually been noted for them.

'Indeed, the handsome blue-mottled specimens were at one time known as Sussex Beagles; and I fancy from this county first sprang the variety with a wire-haired coat, not unlike a miniature otter hound or Welsh hound in appearance.'

A Mr H. P. Cambridge of Bloxworth was said by 'Stonehenge' to have had a pack of 13-inch Beagles in which there were some rough hounds. One of his best rough-coated members of the pack was a tri-colour, secured from the Cranbourne, Dorset, district.

It seems that the wire-coated Beagle fell from favour, however, for a few years later we find a reference to its being 'not much in evidence', and it was said that 'few seem to care for them'.

Probably one of the last to keep a pack of this variety was Mr G. H. Nutt. It has been suggested that there was more than a sus- picion of a terrier cross to bring about the wiry coats, and this was supported by the fact that these Beagles tended to be deficient in voice, which doubtless caused them to become unpopular.

One rough-haired pack, however, was said to be entirely free from terrier strain. It was owned by Mr Gwynne of Sussex, whose foundation stock had, it was thought, been produced through a remote cross with an otter hound. Mr Gwynne kept it chiefly for rabbit shooting and said that individually they were wonderful workers. He had some seven or eight couples of adults, and aimed at a height of 13 inches, though some were an inch or two less and others an inch over his standard.

Long before Mr Gwynne had his little hounds, a farmer near Chiddingly, Sussex, had a few couples of wire-haired Beagles. These stood about 14 inches and bore a reputation for 'always being able to kill the hare however bad a scenting day it was'.

Rough-haired Beagles were thought at one time to have become extinct, but the Catterick had a couple of bitches named Blue Bell and Buttercup on parade at Peterborough show in 1969. They also have a dog hound, so are apparently planning to revive this rare variety, said to have come from an old Welsh strain.

There seem to have been several varieties of the Beagle, not only the one with which we are most familiar, the smooth-coated, and the rough- or wire-haired hounds, but also a black-and-tan breed. In 1851 a writer named Richardson told of the Kerry Beagle, 'a fine, tall, dashing hound, averaging 26 inches in height, and occasionally 28 inches'. The Kerry 'Beagle' has 'deep chops, broad, pendulous ears, and when highly bred is hardly to be distinguished from an indifferent bloodhound', and this same author says that they were used to hunt deer and that there were, at the time of writing, 'two packs in the neighbourhood of Killarney'.

But even so long ago as 1847 the so-called Kerry Beagles were said to be declining in popularity and numbers. Fifty years later the 'Scarteen' was the only pack in existence, and the Kerry Beagle was being spoken of as 'becoming extinct'. These hounds were said to have been remarkable for their tongue, which was 'rich and wonderfully sweet . . . their noses very keen, and their work true and persevering'. Formerly restricted to hare hunting, the last surviving pack had to fall back on deer as their quarry when hares became very scarce in Ireland.

However, from the description given, it is very doubtful if the Kerry Beagle was a Beagle in anything but name. Its size and its predominantly bloodhound characteristics, including colour, suggest it was completely foreign in appearance to the Beagle of its own time and of today.

In 1910 we hear tales of the beauties to be found in the Halstead Place pack, the Master, Mr James Russel, having produced at the hound shows some Beagles that were considered to be the best of their time. Perhaps his most remarkable was Halstead Place Searcher, described as being 'under 14 inches high' and as 'the most marvellous little hound in the world'. Mr Russel must have been a proud man, for he bred Searcher himself, from his Solomon out of Gracious, the latter being by Lord Ducie's Trumpeter. There can be few Beagles today which do not carry the blood of Halstead Place Searcher. Some hounds have ten or more lines to him.

Another excellent pack was the Leigh Park, owned by Sir Frederick Fitz Wygram. Other owners of good-looking, good-working hounds were Mr E. F. Goff, the Master of the Woodvale, and the Marquis of Linlithgow.

These owners were noted exhibitors at the hound shows at Peterborough and at the old Crystal Palace, many years later destroyed by fire. A contemporary writes:

'What must have struck anyone who saw these Beagle shows of 1906, was the obvious unanimity of breeders in the matter of type. There were no outsiders, if one may use the term. All were as much like Searcher, Fulmen, Primrose, Dorothy, and Dutchie as possible, without being quite their equals, and this speaks volumes for the

breed as, excepting in long existence in the hands of private individuals for their own use and pleasure, they have not been the
medium of public competitions for many years.'

The Dutchie referred to was a bitch owned by the Marquis of
Linlithgow, and is described elsewhere as 'a little gem', while
Primrose was a lovely little lemon-pied, owned by Mr Goff. Dorothy
was a daughter of Thorpe Satchville Bellman, and was said to
be 'as handsome as a picture'; she belonged to the Leigh Park
pack.

It was Mr Otto Paget who started the Thorpe Satchville in 1890,
and he was a great authority on hunting, not only in his time but of
all time. His book *Beagles and Beagling*, published in 1923, is still
regarded as one of the finest works of its type. It has been out of
print for many years, and second-hand copies, being scarce, command high prices when available. Otto Paget's pack began with a
limit of 14 inches, was soon reduced to 13 inches, and before World
War I he had a noted pack of 12½-inch Beagles. They accounted
for eleven to fifteen brace of hares in a season. He used to point out
that to kill a number of hares with such small hounds, every member
of the pack had to be first-rate workers kept in tip-top condition.
By never checking, or at least by never losing a moment at a check,
such hounds would make better time than faster hounds that waste
several minutes at every turn the hare makes. The war, however,
ruined Paget's efforts, and when he re-formed his scattered pack
after the Armistice, good tiny Beagles were scarce. He did, however,
manage to get together a pack measuring 13 inches.

The Bronwydd and the Royal Rock were both formed in 1845,
and although the former was dispersed in 1915, the latter is still
hunting and must be the oldest pack in existence. The Bronwydd's
Merryboy won the Champion Cup at Peterborough in 1894, as
did their Nigel in 1892, but Nigel was drafted because of his squeaky
voice. The Master, Sir Marteine Lloyd, was a stickler for hunting
qualities. Mr Otto Paget bought most of the Bronwydd Beagles
when they were sold, including Merryboy which he exported to the
U.S.A. Sir Marteine, during his breeding experiments, made use of
some harrier sires, and was later obliged to make use of some very
small Beagle stock to reduce the size again. At one time the Royal
Rock were said to measure from 14 to 17 inches.

All through the formative years of this pack many purchases were

C. M. Cooke

The author with Aus. Ch. Rozavel Diamond Star

Mr Crane's Beagles Giant and Ringlet. From *The Dogs of the British Islands*, by 'Stonehenge', 1882

The Beagle; engraving on wood by T. Bewick, 1790

'The Merry Beaglers', coloured mezzotint engraving by J. Harris
after a painting by Harry Hall, 1845

Pocket Beagles, and under-13-inch Beagles, at the Ladies' Dog Show, 1899
Thomas Fall

Beagles and Huntsman,
by John Emms, *circa*
1880

Beagles. Colour print
by Maud Earl, 1906

made, and eventually the blood of a number of the other best-known strains had been introduced. Some of their most successful hounds were bred as a result of securing fifteen couples from the Ulverstone Beagles, and this remarkably large addition did a great deal to improve the Royal Rock pack. Efforts were made to keep up a 16-inch standard, and consequently many smaller hounds were drafted, some of which proved excellent foundation stock for other breeders.

The North Worcestershire pack was started in 1877, being founded mainly on acquisitions from the Decker Hill and Rochford Beagles. Mr E. H. Humphreys became the Master in 1882, and he was also the inaugural Honorary Secretary of the Beagle section of the Harrier and Beagle Association. He gave up his hounds in 1898. North Worcestershire Ploughman was a notable ancestor of Halstead Place Searcher—the great-great-grandsire, to be exact. Ploughman was a blue-mottled hound, a colour rarely seen today. Otto Paget wrote that this colour was 'almost invariably accompanied by a good nose and sterling qualities in the field', and that although, unfortunately, it was not fashionable, he thought it a great mistake to try to breed it out. The best of the North Worcestershire stock eventually passed into the ownership of Mr Allen Turner, who added them to the Surbiton.

Mr Thomas Johnson hunted a pack near Whitchurch, Salop, about 1883, largely composed of stock acquired from the Bronwydd and the Royal Rock. He bred some fine Beagles, including one named Monarch, a badger-pied hound which won the Champion Cup at Peterborough on three occasions. Mr Johnson was one of the few breeders of his time who genuinely tried to improve the type and appearance of his hounds.

The Surbiton started in 1882, and its neighbouring pack, the Worcester Park, was formed in 1886. Those of us familiar with the area over which these packs hunted read of them with both astonishment and nostalgia. The part of Surrey that once resounded with the bell-like voices of the Beagles is scarcely more than an appendage of London, a maze of streets and houses, its busy roads roaring with the noise of traffic by day and by night. Eighty years ago it was a beautiful country made up of fields and woods, farmland, and parkland.

The Worcester Park standard, in 1891, was 16 inches. It was after Mr Jameson took them over in 1908 that they became so successful at Peterborough, where Worcester Park Lucifer won the Cup in 1911. A fair amount of their country was heavy ploughed land, but

even so, Otto Paget criticized their adherence to size. He remarked
that he felt sure that on a fair scenting day their pace would be such
as to preclude followers from seeing much hunting.

The Surbiton eventually merged into the West Surrey and, under
Mr Allen Turner, had some successes at Peterborough. The addition
of a couple and a half of bitches by the North Worcestershire Nigel
from a dam of Royal Rock strain was of considerable value where
the breeding operations were concerned, but in fact Mr Turner's
wins at the show were all with stock he had bought in. He never
succeeded in winning there with his home-bred entrants, but then
he had the pack for only eight years.

Stoke Place is a famous name in Beagle history. This pack was
founded in 1895 by Mr Howard Vyse, with a collection of 12-inch
hounds, but when the Stoke Place were disbanded in 1917, the
average height was nearer 15 inches. At that time they were spoken
about as one of the best-looking packs in the country, and Mr Vyse's
wins with his hounds confirm that this must have been true. A
number of the best Stoke Place Beagles went to America, but some
went to augment the Ampleforth pack and were responsible for their
Beagle winning the Champion Cup at Peterborough in 1923.

The Ampleforth have always been a noted pack of small- to
medium-sized hounds. The writer was fortunate enough to acquire
a 12-inch bitch named Ampleforth Duchess, which bred for the
Rozavel kennel its first Challenge Certificate winner in Beagles.

The Aldershot, another old-established pack, were in operation
at the end of the nineteenth century, and, unlike so many which have
passed into oblivion, are still being energetically hunted at the
present time, together with the Sandhurst.

Mr Allott's pack was recognized in 1899, and measured about
13¼ to 13½ inches. They hunted the country surrounding Louth,
Lincolnshire, and were reputed to show excellent sport. Mr Allott
was still hunting his Beagles when he was over seventy years of age!
He also won the much-prized Peterborough Cup in 1899, with a
hound named Rummage which he bought from Otto Paget, who
had, in turn, got him in a draft from the North Worcestershire.

The history of the Halstead Place pack is brief, but it could also
be described as glorious. Founded in 1904, it was disbanded in 1915,
but in that short space of time the number of major successes at
Peterborough were remarkable and almost, if not quite, unpre-
cedented. Apart from Searcher, four other hounds won the Cham-

pion Cup, three of these being Searcher's grandchildren. The Halstead Place hounds won the Cup for the best three couples on several occasions—in itself a memorable feat—which meant that the pack could boast of overall excellence not confined merely to just one or two outstanding good-lookers.

Otto Paget describes Searcher as being an example of strength with quality and soundness, and balanced overall. He criticizes his head only, which he considered to be rather longer in the foreface than was thought desirable.

Mrs Price's Beagles were an under-13-inch pack which hunted round Brockenhurst, in the New Forest, Hants. They joined the Association in 1903, about two years after they first got going. Mrs Price did some excellent winning with her hounds at Ranelagh, Richmond, and Peterborough, and when this select little pack was dispersed, some of its hounds were bought by Mr Day, who hunted them as the New Forest Beagles until the war broke out in 1914. The Royal Flying Corps purchased them then, and their other packs at Uxbridge and Cranwell subsequently benefited from the strain.

In 1906 a Mr George Miller, with Mr Cecil Nickalls, started the Springhill at Rugby, hunting in North Warwickshire. This pack made a reputation for itself in a remarkably short time (for it was dispersed in 1914) and it was noted both for its looks and for its work. Much of its merits were derived from the number of good small hounds acquired from Mr Russel.

The Eton College pack—so well known to all of us—were a recognized pack in 1858, and enjoyed considerable prosperity until World War I. During that period the unsurmountable difficulty of feeding the hounds caused them to be dispersed, but they started up again in happier times, however, and are a thriving pack today. The name appears in a great many pedigrees of hounds both in hunting and show-bench circles.

The Oxford packs, the Christchurch and the Magdalen and Exeter, not only provided much local sport, but also produced some Peterborough winners. Courtier, said to be over 16 inches in height, won the Cup in 1893, and later Ranger and Boaster each carried it off. The Trinity Foot Beagles existed in 1864. They were also Cup winners in 1904 and again in 1908.

The Chilmark, with Mr C. Hardwick as M.H., have a great name in the field and a long list of successes on the flags, as have the Farley Hill.

CHAPTER III

HUNTING

BEAGLING has been, very properly, described as one of 'the purest forms of sport'. The primary object of the beagler is to watch hounds at work. Beagling calls for a certain standard of physical fitness, but happily the habits of the hare and the speed of the hounds —in particular those packs which hunt the smaller Beagles— combine to enable even older enthusiasts to enjoy this wonderful sport. The quarry is usually the common brown hare (*Lepus europoeus occidentalis*). There are, in the British Isles, other varieties such as the Blue or Mountain hare (*Lepus variabilis* or *timidus*) and the Dublin variety of the Blue hare (*Lepus timidus lutecens*).

A Meet of Beagles may be held at a cross-roads, upon a village green, or in front of any hospitable inn or private house. Nowadays hounds often arrive in a motor-van, and after the traditional 'cup', Master, whippers-in, Field, and hounds proceed on foot to the first draw of the day. Hounds spread out fanwise in front of the Master, the whippers-in in line, while the Field, if they are behaving themselves, align themselves behind. Hounds put their noses to the ground, casting about for that illusive treasure-scent, and the Field marches forward, everyone using their eyes and hoping to spy a squatting hare.

As soon as hounds hit off the line, all sterns begin waving in that exciting, agitated manner known as 'feathering'. All noses search the ground busily, until one or more members of the pack begin to whimper. The pack will 'hark' to them, exhibiting gathering excitement until loud cries break forth, and all are speaking along a line. Suddenly the hare is seen, off like a streak, with every hound screaming with joy as they course her. Probably she will vanish through the nearest hedge, and then all the Beagles' heads will be glued to the ground again.

The hare usually tends to work round in circles unless diverted

36

from its natural course. But it may double back along its line, it may spring sideways and squat until hounds have passed, it may run along a road where scent holds badly, or even swim across a stream; many are its stratagems.

When the hounds are puzzling out a line, the Field must be careful not to press forward, and, in particular, must stand still and keep quiet when hounds check. It is when this happens that one is able to study the hounds at work. They will range about for a while until one gives a shrill cry, then the feathering of the sterns starts again, and the merry Beagles are on the line once more. Away they stream in full cry, and over the plough, through the barbed wire, climbing the five-barred gate (over the hinged end only, *please!* say the farmers) go the Field, young and old thrilling to the sound of hounds and horn. If anybody opens a gate the last man through shuts it.

If there is a kill it is a short and sharp affair. If there is not, the Field has still had an enjoyable day. Many think it is a blood-lust that urges folk to follow hounds, but most enthusiasts love to watch hounds at work, and often the question of a kill is the one farthest from their minds.

But those who love the joys of the chase, and others who long to know of them, should turn to a Master of Hounds, someone with a lifetime's hunting to look back on with nostalgia and gratitude. Someone who knew hunting in 'the good old days', and who still enjoys it in this modern age. Let us see what Mr Arthur Dalgety, M.H., has to tell us.

'It was on my fiftieth birthday that, in order to get new interests, I went out and bought a pack of Beagles. I have learned what I know about them too late in life; but having already hunted Foxhounds for upwards of a quarter of a century, and Deerhounds for seven seasons, I did start my learning on foundations that were not built upon sand.

'It has been said that the things one learns when one is young one learns easier and remembers longer. The latter, being controlled by the laws of nature, is undoubtedly true. The former may be true for academic subjects, but I do not think it applies in this case.

'For instance, without the background, it would be impossible to assert the true statement that the Beagle is more intelligent than the Foxhound.

'Apart from the production of a "straight" Beagle—i.e. a Beagle with straight legs instead of crooked forelegs like the Basset—the Beagle has altered very little over the years.

'There has not been a demand for greatly increased speed as with the Foxhound. The Beagle does not have to keep out of the way of a hundred horses, consequently he has not had to submit to the lengthening of his legs, the flattening of his ribs, or the spoke-shaving of his underline.

'The job of the Beagle remains the same; it is the true *hunting* of his quarry as opposed to the *chasing* of it. He does not have to submit to being "lifted" and galloped about and interfered with to anything like the same extent as the Foxhound, for his is a pedestrian accompaniment that must perforce go at a slower pace and cut corners to survive.

'Many Beagle packs, however, do suffer a disadvantage in the number of whippers-in with which they have to contend.

'Press photographs often show as many as five, which is undoubtedly three too many. A pack that is always being whipped-in soon learns to answer the rate of the whipper-in instead of the call of the huntsman.

'In all forms of dog control the control is best administered by one individual, and even he should not be garrulous. Hounds soon cease to listen to and respect a garrulous huntsman. Probably the best trained of all dogs are the Scottish Sheepdogs, seldom spoken to at all. When their master speaks to them it is a brief message, spoken like a telegram, and its meaning precise.

'The huntsman should at all times keep himself apart from everyone, so that he can be seen by his hounds. This is most important, for hounds will take their direction from which way their huntsman is looking, pointing, or running, even though he runs only a yard or two in indication. He is like the conductor of a band, he must be visible.

'The importance which is attached to clothes is not generally known. Dogs take great notice of clothes. When I was at school, against all rules, I had a dog. He was looked after for me by a policeman, of whom the dog was rightly most fond. When out with me he never saw a policeman, even in the distance, without wishing immediately to go and find out if it was "his" policeman.

'Having also a pack of Foxhounds, I have always found it convenient to use a red, pink, or scarlet coat for beagling—call it what you will, the colour is the same. It has undoubted merits over the green coats which form most Beagle liveries, and it is surprising from what distance hounds will recognize it.

'Hounds should not be regimented too much of the time. So long as they are not doing any harm they should be given times of freedom. Of course it is most important that Beagles should be well disciplined, especially on the road. They rely on their huntsman for their food and their safety, and with regard to the latter, the roads are so dangerous today that great care must be taken. In today's circumstances I think it is a mistake to get hounds over to the side of the road immediately one sees a motor-car approaching. By so doing it encourages the motorist to think all is safe for him to pass at speed, and it only needs a hound to side-step out to meet with death. It seems to me better to wait until the motorist has perforce slowed down before getting hounds over to the side of the road. The purpose of safety is better served in this way.

'It is a common device of the wily hare (perhaps that is why the hare is always referred to as "she", the name being taken from the wiles of women?) to run roads and tracks that very often leave no scent. It is a great advantage when casting in such circumstances to train the pack so that half of them will try one side and half the other. This is usually much more easily accomplished by having both lots off the road altogether, through their respective road hedges, and running parallel with their huntsman till the line is hit off. If you try to accomplish this manœuvre inside the road hedges you will find it well-nigh impossible.

'Should you be possessed of one or two good road-hounds they may solve the problem for you without the necessity of dual casting at all.

'In this age of ley farming where the plough is so regularly taken round the farm in rotation, the very small Beagle is at a disadvantage. This is a great pity as he had every advantage in a grass country, being nearer the scent, more suitably paced to his followers, eating less, taking up less kennel room, and being more easily transported. The plough has forced up the size of Beagles as has also the big stone walls in some of the northern counties, but it would be a great pity if the maximum of 16 inches were ever to be increased.

'To the student of hunting, beagling is most likely to remain the truest form of sport. The Beagle is naturally a diligent hunter, relying less on his eyesight than other hounds, and more on his acumen and his nose.

'Furthermore, there is not the impatience shown to Beagles, as it is well known by the followers that the quarry may well have zig-zagged or squatted. Some Beagles acquire a most useful trait—that of always, after casting themselves, returning to the spot where they last had the scent. When they have lost the scent it is highly desirable that they should cast themselves in an endeavour to recover it, but it is then of inestimable value to return to the last known spot for a more concentrated local investigation. If it is thought that a hare may have squatted, it seems to me wrong to work upon that assumption before first ascertaining that she has not gone on. After all, if she has squatted she will still be there when your first investigation has concluded, but if the process is reversed a great disservice will have been done.

'The size of the field following a pack of Beagles has a great effect upon the sport that can be shown. A crowd of followers undoubtedly disturb a lot of fresh hares that might otherwise never have made a nuisance of themselves. I suppose it can be said that the largest factor of preventing a successful conclusion in hare-hunting is the appearance of too many hares upon the scene. Every endeavour should be made therefore to avoid disturbing a lot of fresh ground by the letting loose of pedestrians in an uncontrolled manner.

'There are distinct advantages in hill-tops as viewpoints where followers can congregate to watch the proceedings. They, at least, are not disturbing fresh ground in the process. All such things as these help the Beagles and should be encouraged. There is usually only one form of riot that has much consequence with Beagles and that is the rabbit. I have not ever had the good fortune to find any solution to end this diversion other than the activities of the whipper-in. This noisy necessity must, I think, be tolerated for this purpose. It is not so bad when hounds have a hare on foot, as they can very often be taken from what is wrong to what is right, but when there is no hare afoot there can be no holloa, and no doubling of the horn, and no correct hound music to bring them to. In such circumstances I always get the impression that hounds look on me as a spoilsport, for it seems to me that whereas they do not resent being stopped off, for instance, a running pheasant, they do in a way resent being stopped off a rabbit, the sight of which, and, for all I know, the smell also, may to their senses be almost identical with that of the hare.

'If hounds are carried to the Meet in a van, it is better that the square tail of it should not be slatted because of the exhaust. It is best to carry them in a trailer as this gives more space for the car exhaust to become dispersed and diluted. Hounds are very susceptible to exhaust fumes, and they readily sneeze to be rid of it if it is inflicted upon them.

'Three of the greatest merits of the Beagle are not visible to the human eye. They are: nose, tongue, and drive. All that can be done about the nose is to encourage lines of blood that are possessed of wide, open nostrils. I have noticed that in gun-dogs and in hounds the little nostrils that are small and shut-in are not to be recommended. As for the tongue, the neck should not be too thin and wasted; and as for drive, it is impossible to find a signpost except that sleepiness, over-indulgence, and general laziness are almost sure to rule it out.

'Beagles seem more readily to overcome lack of blood than Foxhounds. They are perhaps more eternally optimistic, and they do not appear to become depressed by their inability to kill their hares sufficiently often. There are, of course, good beagling countries and bad ones. Too much wood in a bad scenting country is a great disadvantage. Just as in Foxhound countries, beagling countries have their tally in the same way as grouse moors (for instance), also have their well-defined "bags" within certain defined limits. There are countries, too, where scent and sport are consistently good, but which do not kill a lot of hares by reason of, for example, large areas of deep heather.

'In circumstances such as these, hounds are deprived of many tired hares that pass close to them and would be killed for certain if they could be seen. Unfortunately, there is no such thing here as running from scent to view. There is never any view, and it is a great disadvantage to the Beagles.

'Luckily for them they are happy little people, joyous to an extreme and apparently inexhaustible. It is no wonder that they are so much in demand and so popular as pets, especially in America. They seem capable of more love to the cubic inch than any other breed of dog.

'It is good to have some light-coloured hounds in the pack. They are easy to see, and this is appreciated not only by the followers, but by the Beagles themselves. Hounds with white markings also show to advantage.

'When you come to think of the small distance that a Beagle's eyes are from floor level, it is marvellous how much it sees. You have only to lie down flat on the ground and see how your vision is curtailed to understand the disadvantage the Beagle is put to. But perhaps it is not altogether a disadvantage as it has caused them as a breed to become more dependent upon their noses.

'It is very important that Beagles should be biddable, and with this in view, I contend that the horn should be used sparingly and precisely, and never superfluously. What is blown upon it should be correct for the purpose. It is quite possible to play upon the horn so much that it loses its merit, and ceases to be listened to, just as one ceases to listen to a talkative person after a very short while. If the voice and horn are properly and realistically used, and the pack of Beagles given sufficient range and freedom, then it should be perfectly possible to hunt without a whipper-in at all, and to have greater control of the hounds than that brought about by whippers-in and whip-cracking. Speaking of whip-cracking, this is a thing that should be used only in an emergency, such as stopping hounds off a railway line or a busy main road. Once you have used that resort you have used up all your reserves anyway, so it is as well to keep it for emergencies only.

'Nor do Beagles like being rated and having whips cracked at them. Such methods may produce the pack to the huntsman, but it produces them in the wrong frame of mind altogether to get the best results out of them. There is a psychology in dogs just as there is in human beings, and it deserves far more study than it gets.

'The hazards of hunting today are very great to a pack of hounds. The greatest hazard of all in some countries is the electric railway line, and it is more deadly to Beagles than Foxhounds by reason of their small size. I can remember being out foxhunting in the early 1930's on the top of the South Downs, and Joe Mackerness, my first whipper-in and kennel huntsman, pointing out to me the first trial train going down the line between Lewes and Eastbourne. The electric current had only been switched on for a few days, but already the linesmen had found several dead foxes, badgers, and otters upon it. The foxes were clear of the live rail, but several badgers were partially on it, having taken the shock on their full stomachs while scrambling over it. The otters were killed underneath it, in the process of creeping under. Nowadays, I believe, the casualties of these wild animals are very rare, for the word has gone round amongst them of the danger. I have never heard of a hare being amongst the casualties. There is no doubt that the word "danger" gets bespoken in wild life.

'I remember once pressing a fox on to the embankment of the electric line half a mile north of Hassocks station. We just succeeded in stopping hounds, but the fox dare not stop. He ran the embankment all the way back to the station, where he made his exit off the platform in the approved manner.

'So far as the Beagles are concerned, I believe the busy roads are almost an equal hazard in England today, but in spite of everything there is no doubt that the popularity of beagling is greater than ever.

'Mine is a private pack of Beagles, and at the very beginning you might say that it was only a bare nucleus, when I hunted it for my own amusement on my farms in Sussex. I was at that time Master of the Southdown Foxhounds, thereafter in succession I took the Beagles to follow my fortunes as Master successively of the Meynell, the Isle of Wight, and now the Hursley Foxhounds. I have thus hunted Beagles in only four counties, and of the four I would say that the Isle of Wight is the best beagling country of the lot. On much of the island there are too many hares, but if the Meets are carefully chosen they are ideal for beagling. Moreover, it is a "killing" country, inasmuch as the hares on the low ground are comparatively soft compared to those on the mainland. It is a rewarding country in which it is possible to kill a sufficient tally of hares to satisfy huntsman and his hounds.

'It has always been unfortunate that my other commitments have prevented me from beagling more than one day a week. This is not really ideal from the hound point of view. They would do better to hunt twice a week and would be that much fitter. However, one day a week is better than none, as is half a loaf than no bread. My successor, Mr Denys Danby, who hunts the Beagles in the Isle of Wight now, is similarly placed and can afford the time to hunt only once a week, but he loves his beagling and will, I am sure, agree with me as to the great merit of the country he hunts. Mr Danby is a beagler, who, like myself, thinks that the not-too-large Beagle is the type with which to show the best sport.

'The only time I ever got a hare to ground was in the Isle of Wight, and it happened in this way. We had got a hare tired, so that she squatted for what I verily believed to be the last time. Hounds had brought her round in such a way that I had been able to see her squat. I was standing twenty yards from a gate, with a hedge between her and me; she had squatted some fifty yards out in the next field. Hounds ran her line, after about three minutes, up to the place where she had squatted, then cast themselves round the field unsuccessfully. Then one of the hounds came back to the place where she had last had the scent, and became very busy with her local searching. The rest of the pack came back to her, having learned to trust her, and were in view of her when she jumped up this tired hare. The hare made straight for the gateway that was twenty yards from me, but, to my surprise, she never came through it. The whole pack arrived there, and cast themselves in a frenzy on both sides of the gate unsuccessfully.

'They were greatly puzzled, as indeed was I. After a while I thought of the drain across the gateway. I went down on my stomach and looked through it, and, sure enough, there was the hare in the middle of it. I thought that when I indicated this to the pack they would mark the ground like a pack of Foxhounds, but no such thing could I induce them to do. They thought I was mad; and I thought they were! I have often wondered, if this ever happened again, if they would remember and mark, but so far it never has, and now there are only a few of those hounds left to tell the tale.

'If the pack consists of fifteen to eighteen couple of Beagles in the field they will form a fine sight in action. There may be a temptation to draft young hounds much too readily at the end of their first season for some fault that does not please you. I have made this mistake several times and have learned not to do it now. Beagles "enter" much more slowly than Foxhounds, and a dog that does not please you in his hunting during his first season may well be a topper in his second season. With Beagles I have noticed that young hounds hunt for a bit, then come back to heel, then perhaps join in for a minute or two once or twice during the day. I would now be very chary of parting with them. On balance, I think that the hound that enters perfectly, straight away and with great enthusiasm, is likely to be the less worthy of the two in his second season. If a hound gets cunning and starts to skirt, it may well mend altogether by a change of kennel and different country. I have known many instances of this, as also have I known a bitch mended of her bad habits of jealousy by letting her have a litter of pups, even though there be no intention of keeping them.

'I persevered for the whole of a season (1928-9) with the Vine

Hounds, with a young dog called Champion. He never did anything but follow my horse around, but I wanted to keep him very badly because of his line of breeding. He was whole-coloured and tan, and became jokingly known as "the Master's Airedale". When I went to the Southdown at the beginning of 1929–30 I took him with me, thinking that a change of country and the sight of foxes on the Downs would mend his ways, but it did not do so.

'Harry Buckland, then Master of the Ashford Valley, took on the mastership of the Llangibby that season. He liked the look of this dog, so I gave him to him. Harry Buckland had hunted hounds the whole of his life, and he told me afterwards, not once but many times, that the best Foxhound he ever had was Champion—so he proved himself well named after all. I was very pleased because I knew Harry Buckland to be as good a judge of a working hound as he was an expert show-jumper when he rode the horses of the late Mr Walter Wynans.

'The Greyhound may appear fleet of foot, as indeed it is, nor is that surprising from its make and shape. What is surprising is the "dynamo" that works the Beagle, for that little creature can run clean away from a human being in any terrain you care to choose. It is just as well that he can, because if it were otherwise the temptation to interfere too often with the pack would be very great indeed. It does not do much harm at all to edge them on, that is a very different thing from lifting them.

'Say that you know where they last had the line, and that they have only just lost it. Say that you know where the hare is now, but that you do not know how she got there. Is it not much better to try to let the Beagles sort it out than to lift them straight away? The thing which is called "getting hounds heads up" is a thing that is very easily accomplished. Getting them down again is not so easy. It would seem far better to edge the pack forward in an unobtrusive manner, and it may well be that they will hit the line for themselves long before they reach the known place. In this event they believe they have done the job themselves, and that is all to the good.

'To see sport with Beagles it is not necessary to run all the time. The canny followers soon make up their minds whether the hare is on a right-hand or a left-hand circuit, and cut the corners accordingly, from one vantage point to another. Much sport is seen in this way— in fact, very little is seen in any other way after the first hour. The scent given off by individual hares varies considerably, and because hounds hunt one hare it does not necessarily mean that they will be able to hunt another. It has always been my hope early in the season to hunt leverets as much as possible, yet it is surprising how seldom this *does* prove possible. It seems that the adult hares protect them by jumping up first, and have probably instructed their young in the part to play. Taken all in all, it is a pretty well-organized game on the part of the hares. It is the relay-race policy that saves their lives —and they know it.

'The pack instinct in Beagles that are properly bred is very pronounced. There are fewer rogues than amongst Foxhounds, and less jealousy. Great fun can be had in pursuit of them, and their music is a joy to hear!'

Mr Dalgety's word-pictures are vivid ones, and we can almost hear the cry of his beautiful little hounds.

Many of us are already enthusiastic supporters of the sport. Others would like to follow Beagles, but are not sure how to go about it.

Most packs are mentioned in local newspapers, which give the time and place of the forthcoming Meets. A card to the hunt secretary will bring the season's programme. All Meets may be attended by subscribers, or if you prefer not to pay the subscription but to pay a 'cap' instead, this is permissible. A minimum sum—often five shillings—is dropped into the secretary's cap before hounds move off to the first draw.

If there is difficulty in getting the above information, a card to the secretary of the Association of Masters of Harriers and Beagles, asking for names and addresses of nearest packs, will usually solve the problem. The secretary is: Mr J. Kirkpatrick, Rissington Manor, Cheltenham, Glos.

Even so, there may still be some of us who live too far away from a pack to be able to get to any of the Meets, or even those of us who would like to hunt our own hounds and have few opportunities of doing so.

Where a farmer friend, or any interested landowner, will give permission for Beagles to hunt on private ground—and of course if such land is not already the official country of a local pack of Beagles —it is not difficult to train the little hounds. It is naturally easiest if there are hares around, and if these are uncommon the only solution is a drag.

A drag is a false trail, made by an individual dragging a 'lure' over suitable country, preferably varying the route and making turns and artificial 'hazards', such as lifting the lure for a few yards before trailing it again, thus imitating the sudden diminishing scent which can occur when Beagles follow their live quarry, the hare.

The drag itself, ideally, can be a fresh-as-possible dead hare. Failing this, a piece of rag or a hare-skin soaked in sump-oil to which has been added a large spoonful of aniseed oil. The Beagles should find a reward at the end of the trail—a fresh hare-skin, hunk of meat, or paunch. To begin with the trail should not be too long, and this can be increased and additional 'hazards' introduced as soon as the hounds are hunting well and learning to puzzle out the line.

Naturally a drag hunt is poor sport compared with the real thing, but it is better than no hunting at all. It does give owners of show hounds a chance to see how their stock works, and it is always fascinating to see and hear the Beagles as they get on the scent.

Happily, the newly formed Beagle Association is alert to the importance of preserving the working qualities of the breed as well as encouraging the breeding of better-looking Beagles, and this go-ahead society has already begun organizing drags, etc., in the Surrey and Sussex counties, which enable many of us to see what our show hounds can do under conditions which we would find difficult to imitate at home, especially those of us who live in the more urban areas.

The Beagle Club has also arranged, on one or two occasions, for its members to hunt their hounds with the North Warwickshire Hare Hounds in the Birmingham area, and drag hunts in other parts of the country.

Let us hope that we can bridge what gaps there are between the Show and Hunting Beagle, by promoting the working qualities of the one and the good looks of the other, with a beautiful, capable little hound as our joint aim.

CHAPTER IV

THE DEVELOPMENT OF THE SHOW BEAGLE

(including Standard of Points)

THE early history of the Show Beagle is shared with the pack hounds. Show and working hounds were once indivisible, for the better-looking members of the Hunting Beagles were, in fact, those seen in the ring. The gulf between the show and working types scarcely existed, and certainly it was not ever-widening as seems to be the case today.

The breed standard was drawn up originally with the intention of giving a word-picture of a small- or medium-sized hound, rugged, workmanlike, bright, and merry, in every way equipped to hunt the hare with skill, diligence, and endurance.

This same standard is in use today, apart from an alteration to the size, and it is used by breeders who aim to produce bench winners but who are, at the same time, anxious that the working qualities of the breed may be preserved as much as possible.

In our modern age, with its encroaching urban development and motor-packed, lethal roads, very few owners have opportunities of hunting their hounds. For scarcely any of us are 'landed' in the true sense of the word, and would soon be in double trouble if we allowed our Beagles to range on neighbouring properties.

This means that, apart from an occasional drag, the Show Beagle cannot exercise its qualities of scent, though these lie dormant and will spring to life when circumstances are propitious. The love of the chase and the ability to scent and track a hare has been bred into the Beagle for hundreds of years. To try to eliminate these special characteristics, merely because the chances of making use of them are few, would be a crime. Rather should the Beagle's unique qualities be nurtured and fostered, and to this end a new breed association has come into being, which includes among its activities the arranging of facilities to enable owners of show hounds to work and hunt them.

It is the fear that show-bred hounds are not good for hunting that has caused so much animosity over the years on the part of some

Masters of Hounds, who despise the Beagles bred primarily for the bench. We have every sympathy with their fears that the breed may lose its ability for work, and since we have applied our own theory to whatever breed of dog we have kept—that, however beautiful, no dog is worth keeping unless it possesses the temperament, brains, and the ability to do its natural task—we like to think that all serious breeders of Beagles will always bear this maxim in mind.

A dislike of dog shows does not mean that the hunting fraternity eschew their own hunt shows. These are held regularly, and the judging procedure is rather different from the way in which affairs are conducted under Kennel Club rules. The hounds are shown off leads, in a flagged, enclosed ring, and are well trained to stand and show. A scrap of biscuit may be used as 'bait' to encourage them to keep their sterns up and to move smartly.

One of the most celebrated hound shows is held at Peterborough, where the classes are hotly contested by entrants out of packs from various parts of the country.

Certain packs have especially high reputations as successful exhibitors at these shows, and are consistently high up among the prize-winners. Hound shows help to keep some uniformity of type among Pack Beagles, otherwise, with the accent on work alone, the Beagle could easily become completely divorced from the breed standard of points. Nevertheless, although entries are accepted only from recognized packs, criticism is made that, in order to win prizes, some masters may be tempted to keep back handsome hounds that are not good workers, when without the lure of the shows the skirters, babblers, and others would soon be drafted.

Although Kennel Club registered hounds may not compete at hound events unless they are also members of a pack listed by the Association of Masters of Beagles and Harriers, conversely a pack hound may be registered and shown under Kennel Club rules.

As a matter of fact one not infrequently hears of hounds bred from pure 'show' strains entering packs and proving themselves valuable workers. Certainly, in the past, breeders often secured drafted hounds from packs and used the best-looking for breeding and showing. This happens less frequently now, because the quality of the average show hound has lately surpassed that of its bred-mainly-for-work counterpart, and it has to be an exceptional pack-bred hound to go straight into the Championship show ring and beat the band.

But, even so, breeders are alive to the advantage of blending some of the best working strains with selected pure 'show' bloodlines, and this is frequently done with excellent results.

At one time it was customary for Masters of Hounds to draft hounds only to other registered packs, or occasionally to a home as a pet or with a breeder, when the pedigree was invariably withheld. All in all there are welcome signs of a slight change of heart on the part of the hunting folk, possibly due in the first instance to the economic necessity of selling any good young hounds that have to be drafted. Many packs find it increasingly difficult to make ends meet, and if surplus hounds can be sold it helps hunt funds. It is seldom possible to get a decent price for a Beagle without a pedigree, and thus the rule that papers should be withheld is largely disregarded.

We have gathered from Chapter I, devoted to the origin of the Beagle, that the present-day breed must be regarded as a standardized blend of original Beagle blood, plus Harrier and/or small Foxhound strains, and even a dash of Basset or terrier. The latter perhaps not so heinous as it seems at first glance since early historians think that the original small Beagle hound was the ancestor of the terrier.

In making this admission we are not suggesting that the Beagle is less of a pure-bred variety than all the other recognized breeds of dogs. It is really only since the Kennel Club came into being that its register resulted in dogs being bred with unimpeachable pedigrees.

Before that breeders often experimented with crosses intended to enhance certain points or eliminate others, or to introduce something completely fresh into a strain. Most breeds have been produced by mixing types or varieties of canines, and in general we think that the Beagle, admittedly a recognizable type of small, pendant-eared hound for centuries, is probably more worthy of the title 'pure bred' than many others.

Some of the very old prints of the Beagle show a slightly built, sharp-nosed hound, while others depicted verge on coarseness, with distinctly 'throaty' necks. So it is obvious that many different types have existed, and over an extended period, too.

The attempt to standardize a type has been gradual. It probably accelerated over the past fifty or sixty years, until the post-World War II period brought a surge of popularity that enabled existing breeders to redouble their efforts and which also attracted others to the breed. During these few busy years the Show Beagle improved out of all recognition, and began to breed very true to type, throwbacks to less typical forebears becoming comparatively scarce.

It is towards the latter part of the nineteenth century that we first begin to hear about dog shows; and, among other breeds, Beagles were exhibited.

Our own Kennel Club was formed in 1873, following which shows were held regularly and began to be held in high esteem. Before the Kennel Club control, shows were shady affairs supported by dubious personalities, and respectable dog-owners would have nothing to do with many of them. In particular, it was not at all the thing for ladies to frequent these affairs, and for some time women exhibitors were greatly outnumbered by men. The early shows were small, and drew comparatively few entries.

The Beagle Club was founded in 1890, and announced that its aims were to welcome Masters of Beagle hounds, the shooting man who used his Rabbit Beagles with the gun, the drag-hunter, the dog-show exhibitor, the pet owner and all with an interest in the breed. The club ran its first breed show in 1896, since when it has held numerous other shows. The present Beagle Club show, restarted after a rather long interval during which it ran no shows at all, appears to have become an annual event. In spite of this support, Show Beagles were never really numerous before World War II, and the breed received Challenge Certificates at only very few shows in a year.

In 1927, for instance, a total of seven Beagles were registered at the Kennel Club, and there were only two shows with Championship status for the breed—at which the average open class entry was two! The following year was no better, for although eight Beagles were registered in 1928, only one show at which Challenge Certificates were up for competition is recorded, at which three hounds were exhibited—all owned by Mr Oliver Jones, whose prefix at that time was 'Crymmych', the name of the village where he resided in Pembrokeshire.

It is of interest to note that this gentleman turned his attention to other breeds, notably Welsh Corgis (Pembroke) with which he had considerable success, but that in 1961 he reintroduced Beagles into his kennel. His present prefix is 'Pantyblaidd', so perhaps we will see this represented in the Beagle ring, since there appears to be scarcely anybody else breeding Show Beagles today who can claim to have been interested in exhibiting them over such a long period.

The breed went from bad to worse in 1930, in so far as there were no Beagles entered at the Championship shows in Beagle classes. Yet there were no fewer than twenty-one registrations.

Perhaps the revival had started, because 1931 not only produced twenty-seven Kennel Club registered Beagles, but four shows offered Challenge Certificates and, what is more, they had the surprising average entry of twenty. And there were better things to come, because the breed had Championship classes at six shows in 1931, supported by an average entry of thirteen.

Registrations, as can be seen in the table in Appendix B, continued to fluctuate for the next eight years, never falling below twenty-four, but never rising above sixty-three.

Nineteen-forty-one was a very bleak year for the world of dogs, when the war became a grim reality. Only seven Beagles were registered, and under current handicaps there were other breeds suffering numerical setbacks. Still, some other members of the Hound Group did not do so badly, since 399 Dachshunds (Standard Smooth-haired) were registered, 96 Elkhounds, and 46 Whippets. It is clear from these figures that Beagles were still a very long way from being a popular breed, although they had made some progress in the previous ten or eleven years.

Among the early exhibitors were the Marquis of Linlithgow, showing hounds with the prefix 'Hopetoun', and Mrs H. G. Beaumont with the 'Bilton' Beagles. A little later Mrs C. R. O'Halloran was winning, and Mrs Elms, with her famous 'Reynalton' Champions, made a most considerable impact at the shows.

All the breeds re-established themselves at the end of the war. Some had increased their popularity and attracted a great many new breeders and exhibitors who had come into dogs during hostilities (and by no means all of these stayed the course, many drifting away as things got back to normal). It was clear that certain breeds had emerged in a better state than others, and that Beagles in packs had suffered badly and had dwindled greatly in numbers. The lack of kennel help and the acute difficulty in feeding hounds meant that some packs had been disbanded; others had been reduced to a few couples, and only the most stalwart enthusiasts had managed to keep beagling going at all.

British dog breeders had taken many hard knocks, but are always capable of rising to any occasion, and they had no intention of letting a wonderful old breed diminish further for lack of support. It was not long before lovers of the Beagle were relieved to note that packs were being re-formed and built up, and that some useful show stock was appearing on the bench.

By 1950 there were four sets of Challenge Certificates on offer for Beagles, with such winners as Mr J. K. Dryden's Ch. Acregreen Wellbred, and that other noted stallion hound, Grady O'Grady, owned by Mr J. S. Stewart, M.R.C.V.S. Another veterinary surgeon, Mr W. R. Anderson, was also exhibiting and winning. It was apparent that a small band of enthusiasts were putting in some hard work for the Beagle because there were no fewer than eight sets of Certificates in 1951, and among the competitors many new names were to the fore. These included Miss Wilmshurst, Mr Douglas Appleton, Mrs Spowart, Miss Brucker, and Miss Whitton. The last-named was doing exceptionally well with her bitch East Nene Brides-maid, one of a number of ourstanding hounds sired by that pillar of the breed, United Pack Bellman, from whom so many good-looking Show Beagles and more than a few excellent workers have come.

There was a slight decline in 1952, when there were seven Championship shows for the breed instead of eight. Winners included Lindsey Makeway, owned by Miss P. Clayton and bred by Mr Dryden from his Ch. Acregreen Wellbred, out of East Nene Bluebell. Bluebell was a sister to Miss Whitton's Bridesmaid, and a host of winners have come down from these bitches.

There were ten Championship shows for Beagles in 1953, and another to share the prizes was Mr Wright, whose 'Rytow' prefix is well known; his hounds are hunted, as well as shown. Mrs Y. Oldman, who in recent years has been concentrating on her splendid Bloodhounds under the prefix 'Barsheen', was at that time interested in Beagles. She still judges the breed occasionally.

Mrs Parker, of the 'Towpath' prefix, began to do well, as did Mr Stephen Young from Scotland. His Ch. Wellshot New College and Magdalen Gesture lived up to her impressive name.

Mrs Ellis-Hughes had acquired Lindsey Makeway, and if ever there was a wise purchase it must have been this one. From her she bred the beautiful Ch. Wytchend Melody and Ch. Wytchend Linkella.

There were again ten shows in 1955, and at least two famous names in Beagle history claimed attention, Mrs Clayton hitting the headlines with Ch. Barvae Paigan, and Mr Watson with Ch. Barvae Statute. Both these grand hounds were born in 1954, thus making that year quite a milestone on the road of progress. Both hounds did a great deal of winning, and both made substantial impressions upon the breed, Paigan especially proving himself a remarkably successful sire. Apart from his five Champion offspring, he appears over and over again in pedigrees. Ch. Barvae Statute is one of the history-makers in that he is the first Beagle to win Best in Show at an all-breed Championship event. His lovely daughter, Ch. Derawuda Vixen, came close to eclipsing his achievement when she was chosen as the Best Bitch at Cruft's, on the first day of the show, 1959.

Mrs Macro began to win with Stanhurst Rachel, destined to be the dam of her lovely Champion Deaconfield Rebecca, in turn the mother of the 1962 Cruft's Challenge Certificate winner, Deaconfield Ripple.

Nowadays we associate the name of Mrs D. F. Whitwell with outstanding Greyhounds and Whippets, and excepting that she is sometimes persuaded to judge for us we might forget that she was also an exhibitor of Beagles. Her Vanda of Scarlac did well.

Mrs Ellis-Hughes had parted with the Wytchend Champions to Mrs Crowther-Davies of Wolverhampton, and they were the firm foundation upon which the Cannybuff Beagle kennel was built. Many winners came from this kennel—indeed, they are still coming—including that multiple Challenge Certificate winner, Ch. Cannybuff Clipper; also Cannybuff Barvae Playful, a lovely Champion bitch. At the 1962 Cruft's Championship Show, Cannybuff Barvae Pryor was awarded the prize for Best of Breed and also won the Hound Group.

Nineteen-fifty-seven brought further names to the fore, and how well known to us all they are! Mr and Mrs Herrick with their hounds bearing the 'Elmhurst' prefix; Mrs Wilmshurst with her 'Stanhurst' hounds continued to do well, and Miss Whitton and Miss Siddle had firmly established the 'Tavernmews' family on very sound lines. Another partnership active at this time was that of Mrs V. Collins and Mr Stephen Young, who together owned a number of the Wellshot Beagles. Unfortunately it was deemed necessary to disband the kennel, though both the owners remain actively interested in the breed and are popular Championship show judges.

Beagles had definitely arrived in 1958, an important year since no fewer than fourteen Championship shows had Certificates for them. Mr Allpress had Kirtlington Minstrel, and Mr and Mrs Graham their Ravold Beagles, while the small hounds from the Letton and Rozavel kennels made an appearance. This was a memorable year, during which the first American imports were released from quarantine. Mrs Beck and the writer had purchased Am. Ch. Renoca's Best Showman, a tiny $12\frac{1}{2}$-inch hound which had had a very successful show career in America, where he had become one of the youngest Champions. Am. Ch. Rozavel Ritter's Sweet Sue, a $12\frac{1}{2}$-inch daughter of Am. Ch. Thornridge Wrinkles, and her daughter by Am. Ch. Johnson's Fancy King, the 12¾-inch Am. Ch. Rozavel Ritter's Miss Babe, joined the Rozavel kennels. Mrs. Beck brought over Am. Ch. Letton Wynnstay's Citation.

Those who import dogs know how many hazards there must be, and the Beagle breed had its setbacks as did others whose supporters sought to strengthen them by bringing in stock from overseas. All three Champion bitches were mated—to three different leading Champions—before shipment, the intention being that they would whelp in quarantine. At the time, adult dogs had to stay for a period of six months, but puppies whelped in quarantine could be removed when eight or nine weeks old. The litters were eagerly anticipated, but, in the event, only Sweet Sue produced. Citation and Miss Babe had both 'missed'. Of the six puppies born to Sue, one male and the only couple of bitches died. The survivors were Rozavel Mighty Dollar, Letton Rozavel Dwight, and Rozavel Little Dime, three stallion hounds-to-be which have proved themselves valuable assets to the breed, as have a number of dogs and bitches born to the imported Champions after their release from detention.

Miss Whitton's and Miss Siddle's Ch. Tavernmews Ranter, sire of Ch. Tavernmews Barrister, also started collecting a string of C.C.s. Another new 'face' to emerge was that of Ch. Joyful of Hileah, bred by Mr O'Hara, followed by Ch. Rozavel Texan Starlet, by Showman and Miss Babe's son, Rozavel Texas Star.

The other current American import was Mr Douglas Appleton's Appeline Dancer of Camlyn, a hound from the over-13-inch and under-15-inch category, with American field trial strains behind him.

Mrs Clayton acquired her import from Canada, Barvae Benroe Wrinkles, a son of the record-breaking Ch. Thornridge Wrinkles, sire of more than seventy Champions in the U.S.A. It was thought at the time that England was fortunate in having secured both a son and a daughter of this famous show Beagle and sire, and the wisdom that prompted the selection of the pair became clear as the worth of their respective progeny made itself known. Benroe Wrinkles was an over-13-inch-class hound himself, but in fact many of his best get have been medium-sized or small type.

Wrinkles has proved himself a most outstanding sire, producing numerous Champions. His immediate progeny and indeed all his descendants are easily recognizable, inheriting great quality, flashy colouring and markings, much style and showmanship, as well as other desirable attributes.

On the distaff side, Miss Hewan's Sal-let Little Dottie and Miss Curties's Am. Ch. Double-Jac Chirpette were notable imports from the U.S.A. Dottie whelped a good litter in quarantine, and Chirpette, mated to Mrs Beck's 12½-inch C.C. winner, Letton Yankee, produced some splendid puppies, three of which did well at shows. Unfortunately, Chirpette was killed when crossing a railway line or might have made an even greater impact. Most of the Stormerbanks Beagles have come down from Dottie, and are outstanding representatives of the small type.

Mr Douglas Appleton's Can. and Am. Ch. Appeline Top Ace sired some Champions for his owner, as well as adding his British title to his American and Canadian Championships.

Miss Curties brought in Can. Ch. Lees Glenrobin Little Buckaroo, a smart, well-bred small-type hound, currently making a name for himself through his son, Lees Aylesbury Blazer, and the excellent stock which Blazer sires.

The writer's lucky day was when Ch. Rozavel Elsy's Diamond Jerry was acquired for the Rozavel kennel. This Beagle had been described as the best bred on the West Coast of America for twenty years, and his breeders, Mr and Mrs Stanley Elsy, only parted with him because he grew to be 15½ inches—half an inch over the American limit but half an inch inside the British 16 inches! His show career was outstanding, but as a sire Jerry excelled. He won the Beagle Association's award for the Leading Stud Dog four years in succession, judged by his progeny. At one show 27 of his sons and daughters—many of them winners at the show—paraded with him.

More recently, Mrs Ireland imported Page Mill Playboy, and Mrs Pickthall Am. Ch. Colegreens Little Rebel of Clovergates and Am. Ch. Jojean Sunnymeade Bobby of Clovergates. These hounds bring us valuable new bloodlines, as does Appeline Validay Happy Fella, whose son Ch. Dialynne Gamble has sired several champions.

That the American imports have had an enormous impact on British Beagles is undeniable. In 1961, for instance, the most successful stallion hounds were all American bred, the Challenge Certificate-winning progeny of Barvae Benroe Wrinkles, Am. Ch. Renoca's Best Showman, Letton Rozavel Dwight, and Appeline Dancer of Camlyn being outstanding. Since then the American influence has continued. We congratulate the breeders who produced the hounds which are serving us so well, and we also mark our appreciation of the sturdy British strains which have produced many of the dams to whom we owe our top winners—and count ourselves fortunate that there have been so many 'happy marriages' between the imports and the native stock. We congratulate our breeders, too, on their skill and foresight, and count ourselves lucky to be able to make such good use of these bloodlines which combine so well. We hope to continue to keep the Beagle breed on a sound basis, always improving on one generation after the other, yet keeping it what it is now—one of the loveliest hounds in the group.

It can fairly be said that the 'boom' in Beagles which first became apparent in the early 1960s was largely brought about by the attractive imports and their get. Their arrival heralded a reduction in size, and there is no doubt that at that time there were some very large and ungainly hounds appearing at shows, some being criticized for a resemblance to Harrier, rather than true Beagle, type.

The American blood appears in the main to breed very true, producing a small or medium-sized, compact hound with a 'black blanket' set on rich tan markings, plus dazzling white trim. All very eye-catching, the colouring has great public-appeal. The American stock is usually distinguished for attractive, well-proportioned heads with deep square muzzles, wide, ample leathers, and nice dark eyes.

Most owners of under-13-inch hounds felt that it would be desirable if the sizes could be separated, as they are in the U.S.A. where they are shown under two headings—classes for Beagles not exceeding 13 inches, and for Beagles over 13 inches and under 15 inches. The two sizes are often interbred, so there is no great likelihood of the one size deviating in type or quality from the other, since the American Kennel Club has one registration for all sizes. Many judges have said that they find it unsettling or difficult to have to judge very large or very small Beagles in the same class.

Unfortunately, when a division of heights was proposed it did not receive the support of the Beagle Club. While there were—and still are—many notable personalities in the Beagle world who admire the small hounds, there is a hard core of individuals who wish to keep the breed at the upper limits of the British standard, which seems a pity since there is a demand for the tiny hounds and room for both sizes in dog show circles.

At the start, detractors of the little Beagles rumoured that they were poor in type, apple-headed, unsound, and generally possessed of almost every breed fault. In spite of this, owners of good little hounds continued to show them fearlessly against the big specimens,

for it is only fair to say that, although most of their supporters were
in favour of a separate classification for the tinies, some felt that it
was best for them to compete against the big Beagles if only to show
that they could hold their own in the show ring under unbiassed
judges. This might have worked out quite well were it not for the
fact that some judges were so patently determined to give the major
awards to the large hounds, although from time to time the best of
the small Beagles notched up really outstanding wins. They certainly
dispelled any idea that they lacked anything in the way of breed
characteristics and in some respects were better than their competitors.

Some of the smallest in the ring were beautiful, sound, active little
Beagles with pretty heads and sweet expressions, smart, gay, and
thoroughly appealing. The majority of these were American bred,
but among them were a very few under-13-inch hounds obtained
from packs, also with good conformation and capable of winning.

Show secretaries experimented with occasional classes for Beagles
not exceeding 13 inches. The first of such classes was scheduled at
Thame Open show towards the latter part of 1958, and it was won
by a 12¼-inch bitch out of Mr Dalgety's noted small pack—Rozavel
Ransom. Ransom was almost entirely Pipewell bred, with one
grandparent of Ampleforth breeding. The Beagle Club attempted to
prevent these special classes being scheduled but they were perfectly
allowable under Kennel Club rules and they continued to be well
supported. The exhibitors in these classes were greatly encouraged by
the very favourable comments made by the judges, who invariably
stressed that the quality was excellent and that the little hounds not
only compared well in looks and soundness with the bigger ones,
but, on occasions, excelled them.

Chagrined by the mounting success and rapidly increasing popularity of the little Beagles, their opponents sought further desperate
means to hamper their progress. To this end, a proposal was sent to
the Kennel Club requesting that an alteration be made in the breed
standard—the standard originally drawn up mainly by Masters of
Hounds at a time when there were numerous packs measuring less
than 13 inches as well as plenty much larger. This read, 'Height, not
exceeding 16 inches' and gave no minimum height for the very good
reason that Beagles of any size had their uses under differing conditions, and some had even measured about 8 inches and been able
to hunt rabbits if not hares. If any alteration had been made, it

should have imposed some check on very large hounds since it is difficult for any but the younger enthusiasts in the field to keep up with a pack of very large foot Beagles. However, the alteration that was made read 'Height 13 to 16 inches' and at the present time this still stands.

A breed standard is intended to be a guide for breeders and judges, rather than a set of inflexible rules. Therefore, the size definition does not bar the under-13-inch hounds from the shows, but merely makes diminutive size a fault, which it was never held to be previously. Small size became a 'manufactured fault' through a decision made by a small section of the Beagle community in the face of the strongest protests from others.

Not only the supporters of the little hounds but many long-standing lovers of the breed deplored this alteration to the standard which had served the Beagle so long and so well, especially as no valid reasons for the step were put forward. As they rightly pointed out, nobody was trying to turn the Beagle into a toy or to manufacture a dwarf variety that had never before existed. On the contrary, the more we delve back into Beagle history, the more we find that there were tiny hounds, specially bred and greatly prized for both their looks and their working abilities. It was the laudable wish to re-establish them when they became scarce through the introduction of Harrier blood that led their admirers to go to so much trouble and expense in bringing good small hounds from the U.S.A., a country where their progress had been carefully nurtured both in the show ring and the field.

All the evidence goes to show that these doughty lovers of the smaller Beagles continue to do their utmost to strengthen their strains and to go on breeding them in spite of efforts to hinder their progress. From time to time, lovely little Beagles are seen at the shows, some only measuring around the 10- or 11-inch mark, and the admiration they command encourages their supporters.

It might be as well if, at this point, we looked back on the Pocket Beagle as it was at the height of its popularity. The true 'pocket' does not exceed 10 inches in height, although the term is loosely applied to the under-13-inch hounds, if only because nobody seems able to find a better name for them. In the past they were referred to as 'rabbit Beagles', sometimes as 'toy Beagles', and the latter name is deservedly unpopular since it has never been suggested that these dwarf hounds were not exceedingly diligent and able little workers—certainly not 'toys' in the usual sense of the word.

We know that Mr Crane, who died in 1894, hunted a remarkable Lilliputian pack consisting mainly of 'pockets', and some of his good-looking midgets did well at shows. Just about the time he gave up his pack—and this was only just before he died—Mrs Oughton-Giles successfully exhibited a number of splendid little Beagles. *Our Dogs* published a supplement in 1898 which depicted a group of four of her little ones, and an illustration of a couple of them appeared in the August edition of the *Kennel Gazette*, in 1899. The latter were both bitches, named Dainty and Dot, litter sisters bred by Mr F. B. Lord and born in December 1896. Mrs Giles also owned another—Dolly—from the same litter and this couple and a half were entered for Crufts, held in February 1897, in a class for 'Beagles not exceeding 10 inches'.

Mrs Oughton-Giles exhibited on a number of occasions, all her hounds being very small indeed, and mostly born prior to 1898. Several were described as being 'under 10 inches' and others between 10 and 12 inches. In the period from 1899 to 1901 she was advertising a team at stud, the list including:

	Height	Fee	Colour
Benedict of Radnage	10 inches	5 gns.	blue mottled
Totteridge Cato	10 inches	2 gns.	
Rambler of Radnage	11½ inches	1 gn.	tri-coloured
Gaffer of Radnage	11 inches	1 gn.	white and lemon
Little Jack	11 inches	1 gn.	tri-coloured
Wellington	11 inches	1 gn.	tri-coloured

Appearing in the *Kennel Gazette* for February 1900 is a picture of a tiny hound belonging to the Earl of Hopetoun. Born in December 1896, this little fellow's name was Latchkey, and he was stated to be 8½ inches in height! He was also a tri-colour.

Mr Harding Cox, that great hunting man and hound expert, judged the Beagles at the Ladies Kennel Association dog show, a three-day event held on 29 and 30 June and 1 July 1899, in the Botanical Gardens, Regent's Park, London. Among the principal winners we note that Mrs Oughton-Giles was prominent, showing a number of very small hounds bearing the 'Totteridge' and 'Radnage' affixes. Also, a Mrs E. Chesshyre's Petticoat, Trawler, and Bracelet did well for their owner.

It was Mrs Oughton-Giles's Dot which won the under-10-inch class. The other classes appear to have been won by 11- and 12-inch hounds. Another exhibitor at this show was a Mrs Kellog-Jenkins, who showed a couple and a half of tiny blue mottles. According to the judge's subsequent report, 'These three made a lovely leash.'

Mrs Oughton-Giles later changed her name to Chapman. Her affix 'of Radnage' was registered in 1898 and continued in Mrs Oughton-Giles's name until 1902, when it was altered to read 'Mrs Charles Chapman', and it continued thus until 1935. However, the last entry relating to her Beagles was in the Kennel Club Stud Book, 1905, though subsequently she had several other breeds.

Another distinguished exhibitor of the smaller Beagle was Lord Gifford, and these were sometimes referred to as the 'royal Beagles'. He owned an especially beautiful 12½-inch bitch called Barmaid, which he presented to Mrs Chapman, who was living at Cheltenham at the time. There is an engraving of Barmaid in 'Stonehenge's' book *The Dog*, published in 1879. We know now, from what we have read in Chapters I and II, that the working and exhibition strains were one and the same at the turn of the century. We are also aware that about that time there were plenty of Beagles measuring under 12 inches at the shoulder, and quite a number even less, 10 inches and under. They hunted well and gave their followers good sport, the older members of the Field appreciating their rather slower pace, since it enabled them to keep up with the hounds and to enjoy watching their work. For they were game little hunters notable for powers of scent, drive and voice, and yet they and their close relations impressed the judges when they appeared in the show rings.

Somebody with just such a dual-purpose pack, described as 'tiny Beagles', was Mr Nutt. He showed them at the Alexandra Park, Muswell Hill, London, at the end of the nineteenth century. In order to demonstrate that they could hunt as well as win prizes on the bench, their owner arranged a drag in the grounds of the show! The little hounds quickly made out the line, and 'merrily throwing their voices gave us a pretty bit of hound work through the shrubberies' according to an eye-witness.

We are told that Mrs Reginald Mayhew's Blue Belle was one of the best of the 'rabbit Beagles' at about that time, and that 'she had such character. The best of legs and feet, a perfect body, loins, back, stern, and ears, and she was as merry as a grig and when on the line of hare or rabbit, as melodious as a peal of wedding bells'.

A little later, other exhibitors were Mr Crofton, who showed Opera and Prima Donna, a couple barely 10 inches in height, and Mr Lord whose Beagles were 11 and 12 inches. He had Robin Hood and Lignum, of which it was written 'they have never been excelled'.

Rabbit Beagles were said to 'weigh pretty heavily for their size', a remark which justifies the present-day belief that they were at that time by no means deficient in stamina, bone, or substance. The 8-to-10-inch were said to weigh about 9 or 10 lb. and 'such as were about 12 inches in height ran from 13 to nearly 17 lb. each'. The latter weights seem the more realistic to us, for the pockets must have been in very hard condition to scale so little, we think. In show condition, which admittedly means carrying more flesh than would be the case if hounds were hunting two or three days a week, our 12- and 12½-inch Beagles weight from 17 lb. upwards.

Having studied the progress of the Beagle in Britain, it is interesting to turn to the other country in which the Beagle has developed even more extensively and rapidly—the United States of America. Many agree that breeders on the other side of the Atlantic reached a perfection of type long before we could say the same stage had been reached over here. Yet Beagles were not indigenous to North America—the original foundation stock was secured from this country and was basically the same as our own.

The British, from time immemorial it seems, have been a nation of great dog-lovers. 'Love me—love my dog' is their motto, consequently it is not surprising that the early emigrants who sailed to settle in the New World took many dogs along with them.

We do not doubt that sentiment played its part when decisions to include canine travellers with the family were made, but at the same time the more practical chose breeds that would be useful for hunting and shooting, and as an aid to procuring food.

There is no reason to suppose that all these dogs were necessarily pure-bred, but it is believed that some were of definite hound type. Somewhere about the middle of the nineteenth century, before the American Civil War, they were hunting hare and other quarry with small hounds, some of which were called Beagles, though it is thought that the hounds so named were more like very tiny Bassets than Beagles as we know the breed today.

It was after the war that General Rowlett of Illinois imported some Beagles from the United Kingdom, and it is actually from his stock that many of the best Beagles in the U.S.A. have stemmed. General

Rowlett's Beagles appear to have been of exceptional quality and very superior in every way to the so-called Beagles already existent in the States at the time. The General seems to have been both clever and fortunate with his pack, in so far as they were noted not only for their excellent type and correct show points, but also for their prowess in the hunting field.

About the same time a Mr Turner and a Mr Elmore also imported some good Beagles, and their strains were carried on by two residents in the State of Maryland, Mr Doub and Mr Dorsey; both were, primarily, hunting enthusiasts. Some of the excellent stock emanating from General Rowlett's collection found its way into other parts of the North American continent, including New England; some even went to Canada.

The Royal Rock is famous as one of Britain's oldest packs, and it was from this source that a Mr Arnold of Rhode Island acquired a number of Beagles. Towards the end of the nineteenth century his hounds were extensively bred from, to the lasting benefit of the breed. We have mentioned Mr Crane's wonderful little hounds which he hunted in Dorset, and it was one of his very small Beagles that went to Pennsylvania. The Royal Rock have generally been on the larger side, so doubtless the little stallion which Mr Crane exported was useful in helping to keep the size down. A book published in the U.S.A. in the year 1891 refers to the growing popularity of the Beagle, so it is clear that the breed was becoming very well established there in a manner which more than kept pace with any progress it was making in Britain.

American field trials for Beagles were first organized in 1888, when the National Beagle Club was formed out there. Along with this awareness of our extraordinarily versatile little hound's usefulness as a hunting and gun-dog came a gradual appreciation of his qualities as a smart, eye-catching show-ring personality, and also as a companion for the family. It is not certain just why or how the American breeders managed to produce such a distinctive and definite type from what was exactly similar stock to that used to develop the breed in Britain. We more or less got off to an equal start, but experts who had the opportunity of comparing the overall quality in the U.S.A. with the average found over here thought it was clear that, at least so far as the show Beagle was concerned, the two countries had quite different types.

Opinions not unnaturally did not always coincide as to which type was best, or, perhaps to put it better, which of the two approximated most closely to the standard. Although one or two individuals among those travellers who had seen the best show stock on both sides of the Atlantic thought that the Americans had as many faults as we had here, albeit some were different failings, the majority agreed on one thing: taking it as a whole, the American stock was far more level overall, and it also possessed a greater share of that elusive thing we call 'quality'.

For a considerable number of years Americans have classified Beagles in the two size categories—under 13 inches, and over 13 inches and under 15 inches. Both the American and British standards are included in this volume and can be studied, but the greatest difference lies in height. Whereas the American Beagles may be any size up to 15 inches, the present standard in Great Britain reads '13 to 16 inches'. While we certainly see Beagles measuring 16 inches and over in the show ring (though admittedly there are nothing like so many oversized specimens as there were some years ago), the American hounds tend to come well within their standard height, many shown in the 15 inches class being very little over 13 inches. The American hounds are generally more compact and shorter in back; the heads are shorter with more distinct stops and a greater refinement and softer expression than we find in a good many of our Beagles bred from purely British bloodlines. Quite a lot of these hounds, but a few generations removed from pack-bred Beagles, have heads that are more like the Foxhound, longer in skull and foreface, showing less stop, and a flatter skull. Some of these Beagles are also proportioned differently, being longer in body and shorter on the legs.

Some difference in the colouring can be seen, for American-bred Beagles are usually possessed of 'black blankets', the term used to describe an all-black back, with tan head and back of neck, thighs and breeches, with, usually, flashy white markings on face, throat, chest and legs, and always on the tip of the stern. Some English-bred Beagles have similar markings, but often they are predominantly white with large, broken coloured patches.

However, the marked division between the pure American and the pure British bred Beagles has greatly diminished over the last ten years or so. A few kennels have 100 per cent American breeding. A few keep stock of the old original strains into which no imported blood has been introduced. Most breeders, however, have blended the American bloodlines with basic British stock, and the result has been good.

An opening Meet of the Brighton and Storrington Beagles. Sir Francis Samuelson (Senior Joint Master) moves off with the pack

Rozavel Texas Star

Ch. Rozavel Earring

Ch. Barvae Statute

Ch. Barvae Paigan

Ch. Deaconfield Rebecca

Ch. Cannybuff Clipper

C. M. Cooke

Harking back to the differences between our stock on either side of the Atlantic, one wonders how the difference came about. It seems certain that breeding to a set standard or pattern has been more widely practised over a longer period of time in the U.S.A. than has been the case here. The Beagle attained popularity there much earlier, and while it was being extensively bred as a show dog, our own breeders were few and far between and the Beagle in Britain was regarded in the main as a pack hound.

Undoubtedly the breed suffered greatly here through the two wars, when very little breeding was done. The shortage of young stock meant that not only were the immediate post-war winners few, but they came mainly straight out of packs and, in general, such packs had not been maintained to a high standard throughout hostilities. In any event, in the packs it was the working qualities that received prime consideration with looks taking second place.

In spite of this rather gloomy picture, however, there were some nice-looking hounds which found their way into the ring, and it is from their descendants that many of the best current exhibits have been obtained, plus the judicious mixing of such stock with American imports.

Certainly, the picture of the Show Beagle in Britain has undergone a marked change during the past few years. An improvement in type was gradually becoming apparent, but few will deny that it was the arrival of the American stallions and dams that really accelerated this progress. Already we owe much to them, and are now in a position to appreciate the full results of their prepotency and the dominant type, so easily recognisable, which they transmit.

We cannot say that the average pack-bred Beagle is any better-looking than an average pack-Beagle here. Nor would we care to say that the one was a better worker than the other, since conditions and methods vary, as does the quarry on most occasions. But, worker or winner, the Beagle has been produced in great numbers over that vast country, with no sacrifice of type or temperament. At one time, Beagle supporters in Britain were becoming dismayed at the rapid rise in the number of litters being bred to keep pace with the demand, but this appears to be settling down and finding its own level. All to the good, for other fashionable breeds have suffered through indiscriminate breeding to supply a rising pet market. So far our Beagle is unspoiled, unexaggerated, and sensible, holds its sporting characteristics, robust constitution and overall freedom from hereditary defects, and, with all this, is handsome and intelligent. What more do we ask of any canine?

It has been interesting to observe the progress made in other countries overseas. Australia, for instance, now has a large Beagle population, big entries at shows are usual, and imports from Britain —including some good hounds bred from American stock—have set Beagles going the right way down under. New Zealand has also fallen for the Beagle, and once more the British-bred foundation stock has given them the quality they need.

Ceylon has a relatively small doggy population, but Beagles are one of the most popular breeds out there. Most of the successful breeders have imported our stock and made good use of it. Some hunt their show Beagles, the quarry being a small type of deer.

South Africa, as well as Rhodesia, has its nucleus of enthusiastic Beagle breeders, and it may well be that in the years ahead we will hear more of these and other countries as they strive, with us, to better the Beagle breed.

THE BRITISH STANDARD

(Approved 17 April 1973 and reproduced by kind permission of the Kennel Club)

CHARACTERISTICS: A merry hound whose essential function is to hunt, primarily hare, by following a scent. Bold with great acitivity, stamina and determination. Alert, intelligent and of even temperament.

GENERAL APPEARANCE: A sturdy and compactly-built hound, conveying the impression of quality without coarseness.

HEAD AND SKULL: Head fair length, powerful in the dog without being coarse, but finer in the bitch; free from frown and excessive wrinkle. Skull slightly domed, moderately wide, with indication of peak. Stop well defined and dividing length between occiput and tip of nose as equally as possible. Muzzle not snipy, lips reasonably well flewed. Nose broad and nostrils well expanded; preferably black, but less pigmentation permissible in the lighter coloured hounds.

EYES: Dark brown or hazel, fairly large, not deep set or bulgy, set well apart and with a mild appealing expression.

EARS: Long with round tip, reaching nearly to end of nose when drawn out. Set on low, fine in texture and hanging gracefully close to cheek.

MOUTH: Teeth strongly developed. Upper incisors just overlapping and touching outer surface of lower incisors to form scissor bite.

NECK: Sufficiently long to enable hound to come down easily to scent, slightly arched and showing a little dewlap.

FOREQUARTERS: Shoulders clean and sloping. Forelegs straight and up-right, well under the hound, of good substance, strong, hard and round in bone. Not tapering off to feet. Pasterns short. Elbows firm, turning neither in nor out. Height to elbow about half the hound's height to withers.

BODY: Topline straight and level. Chest well let down to below elbow. Ribs well sprung and extending well back. Short between the couplings.

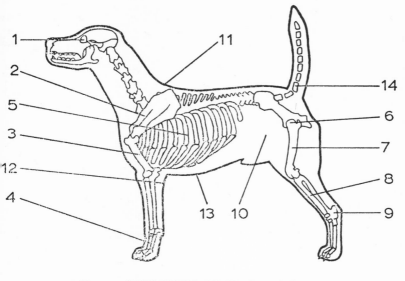

FIG. I. SKELETON OF THE BEAGLE

1. Skull and stop.	6. Pelvis.	11. Withers.
2. Scapula.	7. Femur.	12. Elbow.
3. Humerus.	8. Tibia and fibula.	13. Chest or brisket.
4. Pastern.	9. Hocks.	14. Stern.
5. Ribs.	10. Loin.	

Loins powerful and supple, without excessive tuck-up.

HINDQUARTERS: Very muscular about the thighs. Stifles well bent. Hocks firm, well let down and parallel to each other.

FEET: Tight and firm. Well knuckled up and strongly padded. Not hare-footed. Nails short.

GAIT: Back level and no roll. Stride free, long-reaching and straight without high action. Hind legs showing drive. Should not move close behind or paddle or plait in front.

TAIL: Sturdy and of moderate length. Set on high and carried gaily but not curled over back or inclined forward from the root. Well covered with hair, especially on underside.

COAT: Short, dense and weatherproof.

COLOUR: Any recognised hound colour other than liver. Tip of stern white.

WEIGHT AND SIZE: It is desirable that height from ground to withers should neither exceed 40 cm (16″) nor fall below 33 cm (13″).

NOTE: Male animals should have two apparently normal testicles fully descended into the scrotum.

The following definition was a part of the original standard and was deleted a few years ago:

CLASSIFICATION: It is recommended that Beagles should be divided at shows into rough and smooth with classes for 'not exceeding 16 inches and over 12 inches', 'not exceeding 12 inches and over 10 inches', and 'not exceeding 10 inches'.

Pocket Beagles must not exceed 10 inches in height. Although ordinary Beagles in miniature, no point, however good in itself, should be encouraged if it tends to give a coarse appearance to such minute specimens of the breed. They should be compact and symmetrical throughout, of true Beagle type, and show great quality and breeding.

The following height definition was official until altered in 1961: HEIGHT: Not exceeding 16 inches.

THE AMERICAN STANDARD
(Reproduced by kind permission of the American Kennel Club)

HEAD: The skull should be fairly long, slightly domed at occiput, with cranium broad and full.

EARS: Ears set on moderately low, long, reaching when drawn out nearly, if not quite, to the end of the nose; fine in texture, fairly broad—with almost entire absence of erectile power—setting close to the head, with the forward edge slightly inturning to the cheek—rounded at tip.

EYES: Eyes large, set well apart—soft and Hound-like—expression gentle and pleading; of a brown and hazel colour.

MUZZLE: Muzzle of medium length—straight and square-cut—the stop moderately defined.

JAWS: Level. Lips free from flews; nostrils large and open.

DEFECTS: A very flat skull, narrow across the top; excess of dome, eyes small, sharp and Terrier-like, or prominent and protruding; muzzle long, snipey or cut away decidedly below the eyes, or very short. Roman nosed, or upturned, giving a dish-face expression. Ears short, set on high, or with a tendency to rise above the point of origin.

BODY: Neck and Throat—Neck rising free and light from the shoulders strong in substance yet not loaded, of medium length. The throat clear and free from folds of skin; a slight wrinkle below the angle of the jaw however, may be allowable.

DEFECTS: A thick, short, cloddy neck carried on a line with the top of the shoulders. Throat showing dewlap and folds of skin to a degree termed 'throatiness'.

SHOULDERS AND CHEST: Shoulders sloping—clean, muscular, not heavy or loaded—conveying the idea of freedom of action with activity and strength. Chest deep and broad, but not broad enough to interfere with the free play of the shoulders.

DEFECTS: Straight, upright shoulders. Chest disproportionately wide or with lack of depth.

BACK, LOIN, AND RIBS: Back short, muscular and strong. Loin broad and slightly arched, and the ribs well sprung, giving abundance of lung room.

DEFECTS: Very long or swayed or roached back. Flat, narrow loin. Flat ribs.

FORELEGS AND FEET: Forelegs—Straight, with plenty of bone in proportion to size of the Hound. Pasterns short and straight.

FEET: Close, round, and firm. Pad full and hard.

DEFECTS: Out at elbows. Knees knuckled over forward, or bent backward. Forelegs crooked or Dachshund-like. Feet long, open, or spreading.

HIPS, THIGHS, HIND LEGS, AND FEET: Hips and thighs strong and well muscled, giving abundance of propelling power. Stifles strong and well let down. Hocks firm, symmetrical, and moderately bent. Feet close and firm.

DEFECTS: Cowhocks, or straight hocks. Lack of muscle and propelling power. Open feet.

TAIL: Set moderately high; carried gaily, but not turned forward over the back; with slight curve; short as compared with size of the Hound; with brush.

DEFECTS: A long tail. Teapot curve or inclined forward from the root. Rat tail with absence of brush.

COAT: A close, hard Hound coat of medium length.

DEFECTS: A short, thin coat, or of a soft quality.

HEIGHT: Height not to exceed 15 inches, measured across the shoulders at the highest point, the Hound standing in a natural position with his feet well under him.

COLOUR: Any true Hound colour.

GENERAL APPEARANCE: A miniature Foxhound, solid, and big for his inches, with the wear-and-tear look of the Hound that can last in the chase and follow his quarry to the death.

Scale of Points

Skull	..	..	..	5	Forelegs	.. ..	10
Ears	..	..	..	10	Hips, thighs, and hind legs		10
Eyes	..	..	..	5	Feet		10
Muzzle ..	..	..	5		Running gear		30
	Head			25			
					Coat		5
Neck	..	..	..	5	Stern		5
Chest and Shoulders		..	15				10
Back, loin, and ribs		..	15				
	Body			35		Total	100

CHAPTER V

CHOOSING A BEAGLE

BEAGLES are chosen, generally speaking, for any one of three principal purposes—for hunting, for show and/or breeding, or merely as companions and family pets. In a few isolated instances, perhaps, a little hound is required to fit all the above categories, but probably most people who read this book will be less concerned with the hunting side.

As there are some variations in the type of Beagle required, according to the reason prompting its selection, it is as well to examine the question in detail.

Taking hunting first, and properly so since the Beagle is a hound designed and bred for this sport, we must know that Masters of Hounds do not go to breeders of Show Beagles to augment their packs. Most of them breed their own replacements, and some of the old-established packs can trace back many generations. Occasionally they add to their packs by taking in hounds drafted from other hunts.

We know that the average person does not set out to buy a hound for hunting, indeed he is probably more concerned with finding one that will stay at home, since if it hunts it may well get itself into trouble with neighbouring landowners. This does not mean that owners of show-bred hounds never use them for hunting. Those with sufficient land, or with permission to hunt on adjacent paddocks or downs, frequently enjoy hare hunts and drags, and many show hounds work very well indeed.

Anyone whose ambitions incline towards starting a pack, and who resides in an area that is not already hunted, is advised to contact the Association of Masters of Harriers and Beagles, who will advise on procedure and customs. If hunting is the prime reason for selecting a Beagle or Beagles, then the best source is probably the packs that have stock for disposal. Here again the association may be helpful; sometimes drafts are advertised in *Horse and Hound*, too.

When getting together a pack it is usual to acquire hounds that are as nearly as possible of the same height. Beagles come in a wide range of sizes, the smallest around 10 inches and the largest standing as much as 16 inches at the shoulder. The type of country over which it is planned to hunt may be a decisive factor in selecting Beagles of one size or another. The smaller hounds provide plenty of sport on grassland, but are slower over heavy ploughed fields. Much greater areas of land are under the plough nowadays than when the country was farmed less intensively, so if the hunt will be largely over much cultivated acreage, hounds between 14 and 16 inches might prove the best, though these may also be faster, a fact which is not always popular with the older followers. Following hounds on foot is quite a strenuous sport albeit stimulating, health-giving, and very enjoyable. There are plenty of young people making up the Field in holiday times, but in term-time the bulk of the supporters, especially in some parts of the country, are on the elderly side, and these enthusiasts find the sport provided by the 12- or 13-inch hounds very much to their liking, for even these small hounds can keep up a cracking pace when in full cry.

Supporters of the anti-blood-sports movement appear to think that it is a lust for the kill that provides the urge to follow hounds, but this is seldom so, and never so where genuine hunting enthusiasts are concerned. Such followers find their greatest interest in watching hounds at work, seeing them puzzle out a line, lose the scent, find it again, cast around, and then fly down the hedgeside, their lovely cries ringing out as their gay sterns wave and flutter. To enjoy this to the full it is necessary to keep within viewing distance of the pack, and it is easier to do this when the hounds are smaller and not as swift as the bigger Beagles.

The question of size, therefore, needs careful consideration, but whatever decision is made, soundness is essential in the working Beagle, and extremes and exaggerations of conformation are to be avoided. A coarse, cloddy hound, or one that is shelly and lightly built, are both undesirable, the one because it is hampered by having too much unnecessary weight to carry about with it, the other because lack of substance is likely to be accompanied by a lack of stamina.

Very little attention is paid to colour. It is traditional that Masters of Hounds have always considered the blue mottles and the tan-and-lemon pieds to be especially good workers, and the lighter colours have some advantage over certain types of country—the dark brown earth of newly ploughed meadows, or thickly heather-covered land, for instance. In such cases there is something to be said for the light-coloured hounds and those heavily splashed with white, since they obviously show up better on dark backgrounds. Over downlands and similar terrain, however, the black-and-tan heavily marked hounds seem just as useful and popular, and although the liver, white, and tan hounds have never been liked, either for hunting or for showing, it is correct to say that a good Beagle, like a good horse, is never a wrong colour.

Apart from size and substance, character is also a primary consideration, and though frequently the cleverest and most dependable hounds in the hunting field come in various sizes, shapes, and colours, a bold, gay disposition usually accompanies their other qualities. Even the tone of voice is of some importance, a deep, bell-like cry being much sought after, and a squeaky bark or terrier-like yap being anathema to the purists.

Working ability is difficult to assess until a hound has been hunted on a number of occasions. Puppies naturally take a little time to learn the ropes and to come to their best, and, once entered, need time and patience to gain experience. Natural hunting instincts are ever dormant in the Beagle, and it needs only the right environment and opportunities for these to manifest themselves in some degree or another. But the hound must also learn pack discipline and obedience, know the sounds on the horn, the message of the crack of the whip, and so on. Sometimes it seems clear at the start that a few of the young entry show no signs of making the grade. Hounds may lack keenness, become discouraged, and fail to persevere, may be 'babblers' (the name applied to hounds that speak too easily and often take the whole pack off on what proves to be a false alarm) or skirters—these last being hounds that cut corners or run wide of the pack.

Hounds possessing these and other faults are often put down; those drafted are normally discarded for lesser reasons. Hounds required for hunting should, when possible, be drawn from a first-class pack, and at least be bred from parents known to be really good workers. Very few top-class hounds are drafted for any reason other than illness or advancing age, so it is likely to be difficult to obtain entered hounds of real merit, except when a pack is being disbanded.

The selection of stock primarily for show or for breeding, or both, is an entirely different matter requiring a different approach. When Beagles first began to attract breeders after World War II, much of the foundation stock was of necessity acquired straight out of packs. But at the present stage in the breed's history it is possible to buy good-looking hounds from kennels owning stock directly descended from several generations of show-ring winners, and these tend to breed truer to type than do the hounds from the packs. There is a deep chasm between the two sources of supply, since it has long been the custom for Masters of Hounds to transfer their surplus stock to other hunts rather than to sell hounds to individual breeders of Show Beagles.

In recent years Beagles have rapidly increased in numbers and in popularity, and there are many well-established kennels breeding beautiful hounds. While such kennels breed primarily for show, the best of them pay great attention to temperament and working qualities, some going to considerable lengths to hunt their Beagles in spite of the difficulties of encroaching on new housing estates and roadways, and the dearth of hares in parts of the country where they once were plentiful. Beagles from certain predominantly successful strains breed very consistently, and owners are unable to keep all the good puppies they breed. Consequently it should not be difficult for a new breeder to obtain high-class foundation stock.

For whatever reason we seek to obtain a Beagle, and whatever its ultimate destiny may be, there are a few basic characteristics to be considered, and even if we want nothing more than a pet we must not be ready to take anything we are offered. Clearly, we scorn any Beagle that is not healthy, sturdy, and obviously well reared. The eyes should be bright and clear, and the whites of the eyes free from any pinkish or yellowish discoloration. The skin must be free from blemishes, and the pelt should be supple and pliable, fitting loosely on the puppy. A tight-fitting skin, hard to grasp in handfuls, generally means an unthrifty puppy that is not in very good condition. The ears should be clean and sweet-smelling, and free from any dark brown discharge. The puppy should be plump, the bones of the legs straight and substantial, and the coat sleek and shiny. The general appearance of the little hound should be of solidity, and it must appear cheerful, lively, and keenly interested in everything, quick to notice unusual sights and sounds, and friendly without being gushing.

A dull, sulky puppy, one that runs away or hides, may grow into a nervous adult, or at best may require a good deal of special attention and training before it grows into a companion that is pleasant to have around. Health and temperament are the most important things when choosing a pet, for, apart from indulging in personal fancies regarding colour and size, it is a waste of time to bother over the many other finer points if it is certain that the little Beagle is never likely to be shown or used for breeding.

Many people choosing Beagles for companions fall for the flashy tri-colours, the bright tan, dazzling white, and heavy black markings being considered most attractive, especially when there is a 'black blanket'. This is the term used to describe a Beagle with an all-black back, when the head, sides of neck, flanks, shoulders, and upper parts of the leg are tan, as is most of the stern. The lower part of the legs and the feet, chest, and sometimes part of the neck, together with the tip of the stern, are white. Such markings are very popular. Less in demand are the pieds—the white hounds marked with various shades of lemon, tan, sable (the latter referred to as 'hare' or 'badger' markings), and there are also the whites irregularly marked and flecked with the above colours which are not actually pieds. The liver, white, and tan hounds are not very common, and their definite markings are quite smart. They almost invariably have the yellow eyes that is the usual accompaniment of liver colouring in dogs of any breed, and perhaps this is mainly the reason why this colouring is not very popular, because the actual combination of the three colours is quite pretty in itself.

The rarest of all the markings are the mottles, and, as the term implies, these consist of white portions profusely speckled with blue or tan flecks, the usual predominantly black markings being also present in most instances where these mottled hounds are still seen. The genuine blue mottles are even scarcer than the tans. They are an acquired taste. A few people, whether or not because the markings have a real appeal, or possibly because they regret the fact that these once common colours are rapidly vanishing from the show ring, aim to breed mottles. Most people, however, think that the pure white markings are the smarter. Mottles have always been popular in hunting circles, being said to be unusually good workers.

But colour should not be allowed to overcome other, far more important considerations, when the hound is chosen, and type and soundness, and even size, must be placed relatively high on the list of essentials.

The public appear to find that the small and medium-sized Beagles often make the best companions, and are more suitable as house dogs, especially in urban areas. Large hounds are also delightful, and many make good pets, especially in country homes, but they are in some cases inclined to be more headstrong, and on occasion they prove too much for the average pet owner to train and manage.

The little Beagles, those that mature to a height not exceeding 14 inches at the shoulder, are a very handy size. They are small enough to be carried up the steps of an omnibus, yet plenty big enough to be thoroughly tough, rugged little companions. They are not heavy, clumsy, or tiring to lead, nor are they rough with young children or rampageous in small houses. A little Beagle measuring from 11 to 13 inches is much sought after, and the near-pocket-sized specimens round the 10-inch mark, though rare, are greatly prized. In spite of being so tiny they are as sturdy and full of character as their larger brothers and sisters, and as there are a few breeders working to revive this once popular and now scarce variety, it may well be that in a few years' time they will not be nearly so hard to obtain as they are at the present time.

Obviously, if the hound is required to live in a small house or flat, and if a considerable amount of time cannot be devoted to giving it freedom and exercise, then obviously the smaller it is, under those circumstances, the better. There are people who feel that a Beagle should never be kept in a city environment, and that it does not 'look right' outside the rural areas. But the Beagle is adaptable, and it is also fun to own; those of us who are lucky enough to live in the country feel that it is quite bad enough to have to live in a town, without being denied the pleasure of owning a Beagle as well.

Taking all this into consideration, therefore, a decision as to the size of the stock acquired for breeding must be reached. Some kennels aim at breeding hounds all of a specific height, others breed large as well as small. Make up your mind on the size question, and then seek a reliable kennel known to breed the size of Beagle desired. The word kennel is used with a purpose, since it is always wise to go direct to a breeder and not to a dealer.

There are some reputable pet-shops, most of them well known, where care is taken of the stock offered for sale. Unfortunately there are also others of a different type, where dogs are just a marketable commodity, and at such places the welfare of dogs or the interests of buyers is seldom the prime concern. Even the best dog-shops only rarely breed their own stock for sale, usually buying in litters from small breeders. New breeders—the person with one pet bitch which produces a litter—may not always find it very easy to sell the puppies as soon as they are weaned. There are always such people who, for various reasons, are not in a position to keep the puppies long enough to place them in new homes one by one, and such persons often sell entire litters to dog-shops and dealers. Frequently the puppies are disposed of at low and very uneconomic prices, but the ultimate buyer will pay two or three times as much over the counter, for the dealer has overheads and expenses, so tries to make a substantial profit.

The larger kennels, and those small establishments which have built up reputations for breeding stock of fine quality, usually have a ready market for puppies and are unlikely to be tempted to pass them on to dealers at the small prices paid for re-sale. Therefore the really good stock seldom finds its way into the pet-shops, and more often than not the customer buys an ordinary puppy for a price that would purchase a really fine specimen in its home kennel.

Apart from anything else, a shifting population of puppies, brought in from various sources, and occasionally kept in surroundings that are far from conducive to good health, invariably end up diseased, and even if such a puppy looks well when taken away from the shop, it may develop an illness after it gets to its new home. This means veterinary surgeons' accounts, worry, and even loss, all of which could have been avoided had the dog been obtained from a more dependable source.

Let us not deny that a few dog-shops do sell good dogs, and many are well kept and make commendable efforts to ensure that the animals they sell are clean and healthy. But it is surely obvious that the very nature of their trade makes some risk of infection almost inevitable, so we advise the beginner to play safe and to visit a good kennel.

How are the good kennels located? Through advertisements in the weekly dog papers, the *Kennel Gazette* (which is the Kennel Club's official monthly publication and obtainable from them) or from the Kennel Club, which will supply addresses of breeders within a reasonable distance of the enquirer's home. Dog shows are among the best sources of contacts, for the leading kennels usually show their stock. The visitor can form his own opinion of the hounds on exhibition, note which do the winning, and ask about puppies that may be for sale.

Shows are held all over the country, often in a variety of different areas on the same day. Occasionally they take place in mid-week, in which case the town's early-closing day is chosen, but mostly dog shows are held on Saturdays. Unlike many other countries abroad, we in Britain rarely hold dog shows on Sundays. The Kennel Club rules discourage it. Show announcements are found in dog newspapers, advertisements in local periodicals, and they are sometimes advertised on posters displayed in shops and on hoardings, also on 'stickers' attached to the back windows of motor-cars.

Once a suitable kennel is contacted, an appointment should be made to call at a convenient time to see the stock for sale. As a matter of fact, many mutually satisfactory deals are concluded by telephone or through the post, and this must be done if it is not convenient to travel to view the hounds. There is nothing like seeing for oneself, however, and apart from the actual Beagle offered for sale it may be possible to see its sire and dam, and other relations: interesting even to the buyer of a pet, and invaluable assistance to the person acquiring stock from which it is hoped to breed.

Dog-breeders are invariably extremely busy people, and an appointment is much appreciated, so that when callers are expected the day's work can be arranged and the routine is not too upset by the time spent showing visitors round the kennels. People who drop in unannounced cause a lot of inconvenience, especially in the winter months when it is a rush to get done before darkness makes outside work impossible.

What does a good Beagle puppy cost? A really promising youngster, well reared and free from any glaring faults and bred from well-known parents, should not be considered expensive at £75–£100, although puppies are sometimes sold for less. Having regard to the escalating costs of rearing livestock, a breeder is likely to be very out of pocket on a youngster sold for less.

A puppy with some minor faults may be priced down to £40 or £50 and still be an excellent buy as a pet, but probably not as a proposition for showing or breeding.

When deciding on foundation breeding stock, age is the first consideration. A young puppy is bound to be a gamble. Although it looks very promising at a couple of months old, it may develop faults as it grows. On the other hand, it may have a small fault or faults which it will overcome with time. Although this does happen, it takes an experienced breeder to know which faults are likely to improve and which will remain or get worse.

Obviously, a semi- or completely grown Beagle is more of the finished article, and one can see what one is buying with such a hound. Buying a grown Beagle has two disadvantages. If it is a very good specimen it will cost more than a puppy—and we are thinking of buying it only because it is outstanding. Also, so many of us prefer to start with a youngster, training it and bringing it up ourselves.

It is natural that the adult costs more. After all, its breeder or owner has kept it longer, paid for its food, its injections, and so on. Furthermore, having taken a chance, as it were, in running it on, the breeder naturally wants a fair price, since it has turned out well. If, as could have been the case, it had not grown into a good specimen, it might have to be sold for a small price as a pet, far less than it would have fetched at eight weeks of age.

Many people, having kept a puppy to maturity, feel disinclined to part with it at all if it is turning into a first-class show specimen, so it is never very easy to buy outstanding adult show stock, though for various reasons adults are offered for sale at times. But if the young adult is exceptionally handsome, even promising to be of Championship show calibre, the buyer must expect to pay a substantial figure if it is to be charmed away from its owner.

When a litter of baby puppies is sold at a few weeks old, the buyer has a fair chance of drawing a prize in what is, admittedly, a lottery. While the expert eye can often grade the whelps accurately, the puppies do alter as they get older and there is scarcely a breeder who has not at some time or another sold, sometimes unintentionally, the best puppy in a litter, perhaps keeping another which eventually turned out nothing like so beautiful. Buying a puppy is, then, rather like taking a ticket in a raffle, but if it is a pup from a well-bred, even litter, our chances of a prize are very good.

What should we look for when we try to select a super-puppy? Compact build, for a start. No sign of a long back, no elongated, slab-sided body, but a chunky, cobby youngster with nicely rounded ribs, and plenty of strength over the loin. The stern should be well set, and nicely carried, never joined to a sloping croup and never tucked between the legs. On the other hand, it should not be very curly, nor laid flat on the back; the latter is known as a 'squirrel tail'.

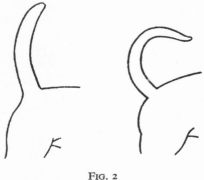

FIG. 2

Good, well-carried   Thin, gay
stern.   stern.

The front legs should be straight, with thick, strong bone. No knobbles or bumps, and running down to neat, thick, well-rounded little feet. Thin, flat feet, with wide spaces between the toes, and a long, hare-shaped foot, are all wrong. The elbows fit closely to the

 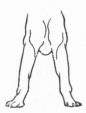  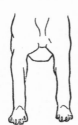

FIG. 3

Wide front.   Narrow chest.   Crooked front.   Good front.
Loaded   Weak front.   Weak pasterns.
shoulders.   Legs splayed.

sides of the brisket and should not protrude or wobble outwards when moving.

The head should be set upon a nice, reachy neck. A Beagle puppy is a chunky little fellow and the word 'elegant' is hardly applicable to him at a tender age, for elegance comes later, as he bids farewell

to puppy chubbiness. The generous reach of neck that is going to
be so desirable when he is the finished article will not be too marked
in the early stages, but a *very* short neck can usually be noted, and
may cause the hound to look 'stuffy' eventually. A 'stuffy' hound
does not look an aristocrat, so leave behind you the puppy with its
head set right down on its shoulders.

The head itself is going to have a great deal to do with the hound's
future, and must be carefully inspected. The skull should neither
be absolutely flat nor very round; the latter is referred to, in derogatory terms, as an 'apple-head'. The skull should be slightly domed,
and the leathers, as the ears are called, nicely set on the head. They
are not put on high, but set quite low, and this position of ears makes

FIG. 4

Typical head.
Good ears.

Short ears. Lack of
stop. Snipy muzzle.

Apple head.
Coarse muzzle.

such a difference to the expression as a whole. The skull is a moderate
length, from the top of the head between the ears to the stop, between
the eyes, and the muzzle is also medium long and never fine or snipy.
There is plenty of chin, hung with soft, slightly loose lips, and it is
square rather than pointed. The stop is quite clearly defined. Lack
of stop, that is a gradual slope between the eyes, completely spoils a
Beagle's head and gives the hound a sour and untypical appearance.

The nose should be black. Many baby puppies have dudley or
butterfly noses (i.e. noses that are checked pink and black, or noses
that are dark in places, shading to a lighter colour) and these usually
become wholly black in time. Few black-marked hounds fail to
have correctly pigmented noses, but some of the pieds, and the
whites with tan-and-lemon markings, have pale or light-coloured
noses. Liver- or chocolate-coloured Beagles almost invariably have
brown noses, and eye-rims to match.

Eyes have a very important bearing on any animal's appearance,
although, purely from the working point of view, the shape or colour

need not affect the utility of the hound. A show Beagle is much handicapped by light-coloured eyes, for only the brown eyes have that lovely, mild, innocent (yes, innocent, misleading though this may be!), pleading expression so absolutely typical of the well-bred Beagle. A false, foreign expression is also found in hounds which have very small eyes, even when they are dark, or large, round eyes of any colour.

Teeth are strong, white, and fit with a smooth scissor bite, the upper front set sliding down over the lower row. Teeth that are pitted with brown marks—caused by an illness—are often classed as faulty in the show ring although judges hold varying opinions

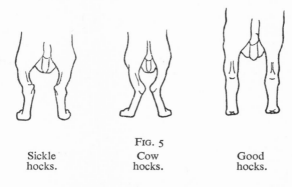

FIG. 5

| Sickle hocks. | Cow hocks. | Good hocks. |

on this subject, some contending that as the fault has been acquired and is not inborn it is of small consequence.

The young dog's hindquarters should be well boned, and the hocks well let down. This term 'well let down' is applied to the length from the point of the hock to the ground. If this part of the back leg is long, the hound is said to be 'straight behind', and will probably move with a choppy, stilted action. The hocks should not turn in or out, but be quite straight when viewed from behind.

When the puppy trots it should move freely, with plenty of drive. In a youngster we expect a somewhat looser and less co-ordinated gait, for the muscles are by no means fully developed. But even at an early age the puppy should not flop or waddle or roll as it moves, nor should it wave front or hind feet in various directions.

The coat should be smooth, flat, yet dense; not too fine, yet by no means harsh, wiry, or wavy. We know that many years ago there were, in fact, recognized varieties of wire-haired Beagles but these are rare and we are concerned only with the popular, smooth-haired variety.

As we have already noted, colour should not play too great a part when we make our choice, but if we buy a Beagle for showing or a male for stud purposes, there are just one or two facts to be considered. Unquestionably, the tri-colour Beagles with the 'black blankets' are eye-catching, and they seem greatly to appeal to the judges. Next come the irregularly marked tri-colours, and after them the various pieds, tans and whites, lemons and whites, etc. Livers are seldom seen at shows.

On the whole, the tri-colours sell best, and so most breeders prefer to use a tri-colour stallion. In a show kennel it is doubtful whether a lemon-and-white or tan-and-white male would be much patronized at stud, however good he was.

We know that absolute perfection is the livestock breeder's 'El Dorado'. But we also know that some faults are considered to be more deadly than others, and if we have to accept the fact that our puppy is almost sure to have a fault of some description, it is as well to be familiar with the failings that are best avoided. Which faults can we take a chance on?

Some faults are rated differently by individual judges. One judge will say, 'I never forgive a gay stern if I am judging', or, 'Under no circumstances will I put up a hound with bad feet'. Others attach great importance to ring manners and showmanship. Some will discard a plain-headed Beagle irrespective of the fact that it has many admirable qualities, while still more experts attach greater importance to sound movement, overlooking some faults that do not affect a hound's action and mobility.

Therefore there are few single faults that are, in themselves, complete disqualifications, and though one judge may ignore an exhibit because of its shortcomings, the next judge may think it excels in certain other respects to an extent which justifies overlooking the bad points. If all judges penalized faults and lauded virtues to an identical degree, placings at shows would certainly be consistent but they would also be rather dull, at any rate for the regular losers. As things are, a hound can win at one show and not at another, and although good exhibits are generally there or thereabouts in any line-up, it has to be a most outstanding model of the breed to keep at the top without an occasional tumble.

Still, we want a Beagle with as few defects as possible, so, keeping a mental picture of our ideal always in mind, we try to decide on faults to avoid, especially faults likely to remain constant from puppyhood onwards.

For instance, light eyes do not darken, and there is nothing that can be done that can make them look any better than they are. An over-long back or body will never get any shorter, but as the hound matures and thickens out it will certainly be less obvious. A moderate looseness of the joints of the front legs can often be corrected with proper exercise and judicious feeding, and the same applies to irregular hocks. The degree of improvement that can be expected or hoped for depends on how bad the irregularities are during the puppy's first few weeks. Very obvious unsoundness is unlikely to right itself completely, even though proper care can effect some improvement.

A too long, too short and stumpy, or very snipy head is never likely to improve to any extent that justifies such faults being over-looked in a prospective show dog.

A rather gaily carried stern occasionally straightens itself, but this is not always the case and in a few instances it actually becomes worse. There are some judges who treat a gay stern fairly leniently, provided it is only slightly curled, but a good many more regard it as a heinous fault, taking a cue from Masters of Hounds, who dub it a detestable fault.

Our budding Champion should be full of true Beagle character. Nervousness is to be deprecated. Certainly it is possible, by working hard upon a puppy, taking it into crowded streets and shops, etc., to get it out of its shyness, but it often takes a very long time. Is it worth it? Shy Beagles are uncommon, the majority are quite the reverse, being bold, cheeky, friendly, and inquisitive. There is nothing attractive in a hound that shivers and shakes, and the new-comer to Beagles is advised to start with a nice, cheerful puppy, fearless, gay, and nice to know.

CHAPTER VI

FEEDING AND GENERAL MANAGEMENT

A FIXED routine is really essential when it comes to keeping hounds in peak condition, this rule applying as much to a couple of Beagles as to a pack consisting of ten times that number. All breeds of dogs are the better for a regulated way of life, and although some people think that dogs know monotony, and go to great lengths to give them a varied time-table and diet as a relief from this, others do not believe this to be true and prefer to establish a system of regular habits for their hounds.

A dog will suffer a form of claustrophobia and frustration if kept confined and seldom given freedom; that is a form of ill-treatment that results in monotony of a kind we are not proposing to discuss here. But a properly balanced programme should be worked out, consisting of periods of free-range exercise, conducted walks, punctual mealtimes, and spells of rest. There is nothing dull about this, even if it is adhered to day after day. The work is simplified if ample runs and enclosures are available, and if there is someone in charge of the hounds who has plenty of free time to devote to their care. But although this is a highly desirable state of affairs, there is no reason why the kennel time-table should not be drawn up to dovetail in well with household duties and hours of meals.

One might, for instance, decide that it is nice for the hounds to have a brisk walk in the middle of the morning, but if this is constantly being cancelled because of domestic chores or visitors it is much better not to try to make it a regular feature, but to arrange the exercising period for some other part of the day when it will be more convenient and less liable to interruptions. For Beagles are creatures of habit. Sometimes one might almost suppose they read the clock, especially when they start a happy chorus half a minute before feeding time, or the moment one reaches for coat and scarf before taking them out. Regularity, therefore, means a lot to them and efforts should be made to feed punctually at the same time each day, and to take walks at regular intervals.

The following is a suitable time-table for a fair-sized kennel:

7.30 a.m.   All hounds turned into runs or yards.
             Breakfast served to puppies, brood bitches, and any show hounds requiring to put on weight.
             Water-bowls rinsed and filled.
             Kennel cleaning begun.
8.30 a.m.   Kennelmaids' breakfast.
9.30 a.m.   Kennel cleaning resumed. Runs cleaned. Stock-pot or copper put to boil.
             Breakfast dishes and jugs washed.
             Hounds go for short walk.
12 noon   Main meal for adults and puppies.
             Hounds turned into runs or yards, for a short spell only, then returned to kennels.
             Runs cleaned.
1 p.m.   Kennelmaids' luncheon.
2 p.m.   Grooming, including care of ears, teeth, nails.
             Lead training. Stud work. Visitors by appointment.
             Hounds go for long walk.
5 p.m.   Winter. Hounds kennelled up for the night.
             Summer. Hounds in runs or yards until dusk, then kennelled up for night.
             Water-bowls emptied and turned upside down.
9 p.m.   Supper for puppies and brood bitches with litters.

The above routine presupposes the services of a kennelmaid, or a full-time working owner, but naturally it can be modified according to the number of hounds kept and the amount of time that can be spared for their care. There are bound to be occasional interruptions which tend to disorganize matters. The visits from the vet, for instance, are sure to be unpredictable, and callers have a tiresome habit of dropping in to see the hounds without making an appointment; always, it seems, at awkward times. There is that other exacting time-absorber too, the telephone. Finally there are the in-whelp bitches, who invariably choose to have their puppies at the worst times.

The routine for one or a few hounds kept in the house is bound to be more elastic and less exacting, but, even so, life should tick over steadily and the day should include regular mealtimes and outings. Trouble arises when house-dogs are turned loose to wander off to exercise themselves. At best, they become adept at removing the lids of dustbins, growing fat and unhealthy on the garbage they scrounge. At worst, they walk over neighbouring flower-beds, get into trouble over poultry or sheep, and, most serious of all, find their way on to the roads with the almost inevitable disastrous result to themselves, motorists, or both.

If the garden is securely fenced, then the Beagle can stay outside in reasonably fine weather, but if it is not enclosed, the hound must be provided with a run of his own, or should be kept indoors between the spells of accompanied exercise that are so important to his well-being. It is not difficult to construct a run from strong, chain-link wire netting, on angle-iron stakes, nor is such a run very expensive since it does not need to be very large provided the hound will be properly exercised outside. If a small wooden kennel or lean-to is provided, the Beagle can always be left in safety and comfort. Attaching a hound to a kennel by means of a collar and chain is highly undesirable, and even the much preferred 'running chain' is not nearly as suitable as a run. A running chain is fastened to the collar, and by the other end, via a ring, to a length of wire. The wire is suspended, a few feet from the ground, between two strong posts. The dog is able to dash up and down, since the ring runs smoothly along the wire.

In any busy household where not more than a couple of hounds are kept, it is often found that an evening main meal is the most convenient for the Beagles, say at 6 or 6.30 p.m. The time does not matter much, so long as it is adhered to and so long as it is sufficiently early in the evening for any hound to have a good run to make himself comfortable inside before he and the family retire for the night.

Feeding Beagles is just about the easiest thing in the world, and one of the most rewarding. Beagles are energetic, healthy, greedy little creatures, whose busy, active life sharpens the appetites and they thoroughly enjoy their food. Faddy and finicky feeders, commonly a bugbear to many owners of other breeds, are practically unknown among Beagles.

Pack hounds are normally trencher-fed. The basic foods used are meat, meat offals, and 'pudding'. The pudding can be oatmeal, flaked maize, or barley, boiled in a copper with stock or broth until it is thick, then left to cool to a stodgy consistency. At this stage it can be hacked out in chunks, and put into the troughs. In addition to any meat or offals boiled with this pudding, some meat is almost always fed raw. The rations are tipped into the trenchers, and the hounds are turned into the yards. The slower feeders, or any hounds thought to be thin or light in condition, enter first, and after they have had a flying start the greedier and plumper members of the pack rush in to snatch a share. Hounds are not fed daily during the season, for it is usual to fast them the day before they hunt.

Communal feeding probably saves the pack kennelman a good deal of the trouble which handing out separate dishes to hounds in show kennels entails, but it is rather a hit-and-miss affair when it comes to keeping hounds just right in condition. It may not make all that much difference to the hunting hound if it is a few pounds too light, but it could cost the show hound its prizes. Individual feeding is generally the rule in a show kennel, and the habit of shutting up each hound in its house or its run, with its own dish containing the correct quantity of food, is the only sure way of maintaining a Beagle in top show form. It may be more bother but it certainly gives the best results. There is another point in its favour, too, inasmuch as it enables the person who does the feeding to notice if any of the kennel's inmates fail to clean up a dish of food. Something is wrong when this happens, but prompt action may mean that trouble can be averted. Obviously, if several hounds are all shut up together with their dinners, one may scoff its neighbour's ration and the fact that it is off its food and disinclined to eat can easily go unremarked. So many disorders can be checked if spotted in the early stages, but can lead to all manner of complications if neglected.

Basically, a Beagle needs a balanced diet of good-quality meat and cereals to keep it in vigorous health. Precisely the form taken by these items is largely dictated by the sources of supply. Most people who own show hounds find it convenient to feed proprietary brands of kibbled biscuit meal, or rusked brown bread. Wholemeal biscuit is always to be preferred to any of the meals baked from white flour. A portion of meat, or, when obtainable, bones, can be boiled to make a tasty soup, and this is poured, while still hot but not boiling, on to the biscuit, sufficient liquid being used to swell it to a crumbly moist consistency; it should never be sloppy or mushy. The advice to pour the warm soup on to the meal is given because broth at boiling point seems to make it pasty and unpalatable.

Puppies receive their meat minced or chopped, but it is best fed to adult Beagles in chunks. Hounds like to gnaw and chew, and it is good exercise for their teeth and jaws. Bones used for soup-making can be boiled to a chalky mush, and thus provide a form of calcium-containing bonemeal which the hounds enjoy. But bones should never be given half cooked or raw if at all likely to splinter. This is rather a controversial subject, for some owners do feed bones indiscriminately and profess to believe that they do no harm. Many others forbid them entirely; some compromise by excluding chop, poultry, and rabbit bones, but give large marrow bones to their hounds. Big bones are normally safe for puppies.

Most veterinary surgeons say that they are constantly being called to treat cases of dogs with the intestines perforated by small bones, or with the intestines impacted with a mass of pulverized bone, often with fatal results. There are also many cases reported of dogs getting bones wedged in throats or gullets. The large bones which do not splinter easily are by far the least risky, but even these can be broken up by Beagles which, as a breed, have very strong jaws. They certainly are a treat for the hounds, but there is always an element of risk when they are fed. They can be gnawed scores of times without any ill effects, but there can be the one isolated case leading to tragedy. Perhaps it is best to play safe, and not to feed bones to adults at all. Though much less exciting for the Beagles, the large, square dog biscuits made by most of the well-known canine bakers give hounds a lot of pleasure, and are perfectly safe and wholesome.

The precise quantity of food required is difficult to set down in print, since not only is there a very wide range of sizes within the breed, but even hounds of about the same measurement can need more or less food to be maintained in good condition. After all, we would not think of handing out an identical bowl of food to a 10- or 11-inch Beagle as we would to 'big brother' who stands 16 inches high. The meal that would just about satisfy the latter would blow the little fellow up like a balloon and make him far too fat in a very short time.

And, reverting to hounds of the same size, it is clear that the metabolism of the animal plays a big part in determining the quantity of nourishment it requires, for we all know human beings who eat all the delicious things they most enjoy, without putting on any excess weight, while others, alas, need to say 'No, thank you!' to cakes, sweets, potatoes, and other nice but fattening items. Otherwise their figures would bulge in all directions. It is just the same in the kennel. A couple of litter brothers may be kept on similar lines, fed identical quantities of the same foods, yet one will get too plump and the other may stay too lean. The amount of exercise the animal is given has, of course, a good deal to do with its food requirements, and there is quite an art in feeding show animals, adding a little to this one's bowl, cutting out some of the biscuit for the hound in the next run, stepping up the once-daily main meal by adding a milky breakfast when it is hoped to put extra weight on a show hound in a limited amount of time. No amount of trouble taken over individual diets is ever wasted. It will probably make all the difference between success and failure in the show ring.

An intelligent observer knows at once if a dog has had too much to eat. Its body looks distended, the tummy feels taut, and there are obvious signs of discomfort such as restlessness, grunting, panting, or even vomiting. Half a day or a day's fasting is recommended, and less food at mealtimes from then on.

We have already mentioned meat as being a most desirable part of the diet. The hound is a carnivore, a member of the enormous family of meat-eating animals, equipped by nature with sharp fangs designed to tear and masticate the flesh, and with a comparatively small stomach designed to digest a moderate amount of highly concentrated nourishment. Thus we know that dogs do not do well on bulky, predominantly starchy diets. They can and often do thrive on nothing but meat, but generally remain lean, and such a menu seldom gives them the well-rounded, well-covered appearance which is considered to be the best condition for the show ring.

There is another consideration, which is that meat is expensive, and many people would find it impractical to feed hounds on nothing else, even if it were especially beneficial to do so. Even paunches and tripes, at one time very cheap, have risen in price and though less costly than meat are quite expensive in most parts of the country. Many kennels pay 75p or more for a bullock's paunch, which once upon a time was obtainable for a few pence.

Tripes and paunches are regional, and some people seem to be able to get hold of as many as they require, while in other areas they are very difficult to obtain at all. They are nauseating to wash and boil, but the hounds love them, and they can be fed in almost any quantity. Although there are nutritional authorities who say they contain very little nourishment, the fact remains that a lot of kennels feed little else, and always have dogs in lovely bloom. It is customary in some kennels to feed tripes unwashed and raw, but they tend to have a laxative effect and it is really best to cook them.

Fish is also popular, but by no means cheap, and whereas hounds seldom if ever become indifferent to meat or tripe, a great many seem to get rather tired of fish. The most economical fish for hounds are herrings, and these are best beheaded and well boiled. A few hounds like them raw, but they sometimes make them vomit, so they must be indigestible. Fish flaps are also inexpensive, but need cooking until any bones are turned to a mush. Apart from the smaller herring-bones, all fish needs pressure-cooking or lengthy boiling. Spiky fish-bones can easily choke a dog.

Whale meat is not always obtainable, but when it is the price compares very favourably with ordinary fresh meat, and with whale there is no fat, bone, or waste. Hounds thrive on it, and as it contains oil it puts a shine on their jackets. It is fairly rich, and in general should not be generously fed. It is relished raw or cooked.

Adult hounds do not ordinarily need milk and are better without it, the exceptions being in-whelp and nursing bitches, or invalids or convalescents. It may also be given to any hound which is light in weight. Unless the vet advises otherwise, milk does most good and is most easily digested when given as a gruel, fortified with some kind of cereal. Thick oatmeal porridge, shredded wheat, corn flakes, flaked maize, barley flakes, rusked brown bread—all are suitable and highly recommended. White bread is not much good to hounds, and not even brown bread should be given in its ordinary form, since it often causes diarrhoea. Bread is best chopped into thick slices or cut into large cubes, and dried in a cool oven, with the door ajar, till dry and hard. The bottom ovens of the well-known solid-fuel cookers are perfect for this process.

Adults are generally fed once daily, a meal consisting of a well-balanced combination of starch (meal or rusks) and protein (meat, paunch, or fish). There is no rule about biscuits being fed dry or soaked in broth, it is a matter of preference and some dogs do better on the one than on the other. Dogs fed on hard, dry biscuit are sometimes lean, and while this may be all right for the hunting hounds or the companions, the show specimens need good bodies on them, and broth-soaked meal is more suitable for them.

If an extra milky meal is thought desirable it can be given as a breakfast, and the main meal can be handed out later in the day.

The puppies, of course, require a much more elaborate menu. From the day when they flop, spluttering, into their mother's bowl of gruel, and the time when the first taste of scraped raw meat is pushed into their reluctant little mouths, their appetites increase. They progress, from day to day, from a teaspoonful of meat to a dessertspoonful, then a tablespoonful, and finally a large saucer of the mince, and this can be offered once or twice a day. Four meals should be given, and the others can consist of gruel, and of puppy grade biscuit meal or rusks.

To begin with each puppy is fed separately, but once they lap milky mixtures and gobble meat from a dish they can all be fed from one, two, or three large dishes, according to the size of a litter. There needs to be sufficient dish-space to enable every puppy to secure a fair share for itself—otherwise the smaller ones will get pushed aside and will not do well in consequence.

It does no harm to allow the puppies to help themselves to some of the mother's breakfast, especially if she is served with a generous portion to allow the little thieves to take some without leaving her hungry. Supervision is necessary, however, at such a time, since even the most devoted mothers will sometimes snap at their offspring if they approach her dish. In any case, the dam's main meals are unsuitable for young puppies, for chunks of meat can make them sick or choke them, and terrier- or hound-grade biscuit meal is much too coarse for baby Beagles. The puppies should be fed separately, and their mother put out of sight until they have done.

The following time-table and diet have been found very suitable. It is assumed that the puppies have been hand-fed on scraped raw meat, and allowed to lap milky gruel, for a week or more, and they gradually get increased amounts until they are enjoying regular meals, thus:

7.30 a.m.   Milk, thickened with shredded wheat, or well-boiled oatmeal porridge.

12 noon   Raw meat, preferably minced, or at least very finely chopped.

4 p.m.   Puppy-grade biscuit meal, or rusked brown bread, soaked to a crumbly moist consistency with good broth. A little meat, raw or cooked, well-boiled tripe,

or carefully boned cooked fish, can be minced and stirred into the meal.

9 p.m.   As at 7.30 a.m. plus a hard biscuit for each puppy to take to bed.

Goat's milk has absolutely no equal for rearing puppies, and is to be preferred to milk in any other form. Unfortunately goats are not widely kept, so their excellent product is by no means easily procurable. The British Goat Society will recommend any members in a district, and it is always worth asking the dairyman if he sells goat's milk, since a few will supply it to order. As a last resort, why not keep a goat? They are delightful, entertaining animals, the nannies are spotlessly clean, free from odour, and very intelligent. They need to be carefully and well fed, and they have to be milked twice daily—but puppies thrive on the milk, and the household would enjoy it, too. If fresh cow's milk is used, only Channel Island grade is good enough for puppies. The fat content from goat's milk and from the Guernsey and Jersey cows is higher than any other, and approximates more closely to the rich milk of the bitch.

Dried milk, as sold for babies, is easy to mix, stores almost indefinitely, and produces good results. It should be mixed generously, using a rather stronger mixture with less water than is directed on the tins for human 'pups'. Powdered skim milk is sold in bulk for pigs, and some dog-breeders have experimented with this. We do not like it and do not think it is good enough for dogs of any breed. Condensed milk is favoured by a few, and it is also easily reconstituted with water. As directed for dried-milk mixtures, the resulting solution should be rich and never blue or watery.

Because the bitch's milk is the most suitable for puppies, nature decides that it should be creamy and nourishing, instead of bulky, to suit the small canine stomach. Puppies fed on poor-quality cow's milk have distended tummies, loose motions, and do not look plump and healthy.

It is most unwise to pinch pennies where puppy-rearing is concerned. Puppies require the best of everything if they are to grow on really well. Beagles make quite a lot of bone for their size, and if stinted of any essentials in the early all-important weeks they scarcely ever regain lost ground, no matter how lavishly fed they may be in later stages. While some people pay more than others for milk, biscuits, and meat, according to how lucky they are in finding local suppliers, well-done puppies have always cost money by the time they are a few months old. The task of rearing them is never cheap—it is either fairly expensive or very expensive, and that is all there is to it. If one is not prepared to lay out money in order to make a first-rate job of a litter it is better to leave dog-breeding alone, and try rabbits or cavies!

In addition to plenty of good, wholesome, fresh food, of good quality and carefully prepared, the puppies need some extras such as bone meal or calcium, cod-liver or halibut oil, Parrish's Chemical Food, or a comprehensive mineral supplement such as Minadex or Vionite. Any of these can be mixed with the food. Cod-liver oil and malt, Roboleine, or Virol are all regarded as a treat, and puppies will squabble and push among themselves to lick these toffee-like preparations off a spoon. Vetzyme yeast tablets are much liked by all hounds. They can be handed out to puppies like 'sweeties', perhaps used as a reward for good behaviour, for coming quickly when called, or for coming into kennel or run when told.

Beagles are such naturally healthy dogs that when well fed, kept clean and exercised, they are rarely ill. In the unusual circumstances when an invalid diet is prescribed by the vet, his instructions must be followed to the letter. If he orders a 'light diet' this can be taken to mean white fish, boiled or steamed, and never herrings, which are too oily and rich. Milk puddings, boiled custard, cornflour or arrowroot puddings, baked egg-custards, are all suitable. A convalescent hound doing well on such a regime may progress to carefully boned, well-boiled chicken and rabbit, and thence to best-quality, fresh-minced raw beef and to a normal diet. 'Carefully boned' means what it says. Just stirring the pot and picking out the more obvious bones is not enough. The food should be turned on to a board or large flat dish and hand-picked so that it is certain no bones remain. Time-absorbing and fiddling it may be, but the process is very necessary.

Most dogs dislike arrowroot, but can be persuaded to try it when it is mixed with a little sugar or glucose. Some sick animals will enjoy a spoonful of honey in water or milk. Honey is very digestible and sustaining.

This brings us to 'natural rearing', for no chapter on feeding hounds would be complete without it. The pioneer of this method was Miss Juliette de Bairacli Levy, and her revolutionary principles are highly regarded by many very successful breeders. Her methods are complex, and should be studied in detail. She has produced several books on the subject of her herbal diets and treatments, and these can be obtained from the offices of *Our Dogs* and *Dog World*. They are full of interest, and no doggy library is complete without them.

Although Miss Levy's views on the prevention and treatment of some diseases are not universally supported, her puppy-rearing diets are found to be excellent, and her curative diets and the use of herbs give remarkable results in other instances. The diets are not really suitable for large kennels—something she frankly admits, at the same time deploring the fact that large kennels exist—since they take time to prepare, but there is no doubt that puppies do well on them.

Whether or not they do better than on our own diet is debatable; ours is very simple and as time-saving as the preparation of dog food can ever be, and we think puppies grow up strong and sturdy, with lovely bone and robust good health, when fed by our rules.

CHAPTER VII

TRAINING

THE Beagle possesses many excellent qualities, all of which go a long way towards making it a most attractive house, family, and companion dog. While there have always been people who enjoyed Beagles as pets, it is comparatively recently that there has been a spectacular increase in the public's appreciation of the merits of what has long been regarded as primarily a hunting breed, suitable only for life in packs. The United States of America was quicker at adopting the Beagle as its 'number one breed' than anybody else, but the speed with which it has caught on over here in the past few years suggests that it may well become a fashionable 'top of the pops' breed in Britain.

Why, when Beagles are so far from being a newly introduced or recently manufactured breed, have they not achieved popularity before? There are several reasons why they have not become more widely known, and possibly one is that not all hunting hounds are as intelligent and good-natured as our 'merry Beagles'. Because other breeds have been dubbed stupid, wayward, and hard to train, there has been a tendency to regard Beagles as being in the same category, even though far-seeing individuals have kept them as companions and found them clever, clean, and fun to own.

Another reason is the fact that those who are principally interested in hunting have always feared that too much popular appeal might result in Beagles being bred in large numbers for their looks alone, without due regard to temperament and working qualities. They have, therefore, discouraged the keeping of Beagles as pets, spreading the idea that there is something infra dig. about them in this capacity, so that far from publicizing the little hound's merits as a pal for the family, the reverse policy has been adopted.

A Beagle is an ideal member of a family, for there is much about it that appeals to all ages, and chief among its most admirable characteristics is the fact that the breed certainly possesses brains. It is because it is a remarkably intelligent animal that it is at once both easy and hard to train! A contradiction? It sounds like it, but the truth is that the Beagle is smart enough to outwit anybody sufficiently dumb to let it do it. It is also strong-willed, and not easily intimidated. There are plenty of breeds with far less character which are more easily trained simply because they lack initiative. They are easily influenced, less inclined to think things out for themselves, and also easy to spoil if not handled in the way best suited for their rather colourless dispositions. Yet some people, who do not seem to possess the knack of really understanding how a canine mind works, might make a success of training such dogs but would be quite unable to teach a Beagle.

A young Beagle will become very attached to its human family, and is capable of showing great affection towards the people it loves. Other breeds have this same habit, but many carry it to excess, always yearning over somebody, jumping on their laps, screaming if shut in a room or car, never happy unless they are being fussed and petted. The Beagle, on the other hand, preserves its sturdy independence in any situation. It certainly enjoys a word of praise and a caress, and will invariably grow into one of the most faithful of friends, but it is never likely to lose its inquisitive, questing nature, and its liking for going about its own business occasionally. It may be something to do with its highly developed sense of smell, but its nose is constantly on the ground, and if it seems inattentive it is only because it is concentrating on some scent or other and is puzzling out what it means to it. Because of this strength of character the Beagle needs intelligent training and firm handling, when it will straightway recognize its owner as one not to be trifled with, and respect such a person.

If a Beagle is allowed to be disobedient, if its minor misdeeds are passed over, it will take advantage of this and do exactly what it wants, when it wants. At seven weeks old a Beagle puppy is quite irresistible. That pseudo, so misleading, look of soft innocence slays us all, and how can we be cross with that cute charmer as it shakes the edge of the hearth-rug, even when it tears our best bedroom slippers into shreds or puts us in the dog-house by eating a library book? Yet a few weeks later the rug is in tatters, there is a mass of stuffing hanging out of the settee, and the pup is condemned on all sides as a destructive animal. But the fault is all ours. We laughed

Ch. Derawuda Vixen

Ch. Twinrivers Garland

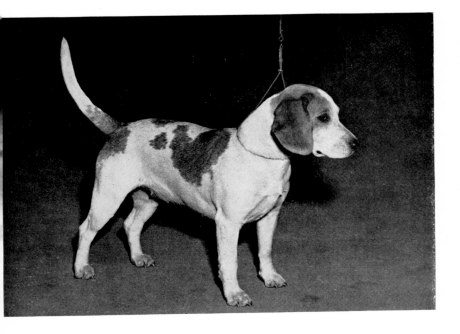

Am. Ch. Double-Jac Chirpette

Barvae Benroe Wrinkles

Diane Pearce

Aust. & Eng. Ch. Rozavel Starlight

Ch. Wendover Billy

Diane Pear

Ch. Rossut Foreman

The author, judge at San Mateo, California, awarding Best of Breed
to the under-13-inch, Am. Ch. Bravo of Sun Valley

Bennett Associa

at it when it was tiny, and as it grew bigger and the damage grew with it, we realized that we should have checked it at the start, and that it is going to be harder to correct it afterwards.

At the same time, it often jumped up at us when it ran to greet us, and we picked it up and hugged it. But when it is almost full grown its muddy paws make a mess of our clothes and we wish we had pushed it down when it was tiny and taught it that it must not cover us with dirt and dust.

Training should start early, the earlier the better in fact, and it must be firm and consistent. A house-dog is no pleasure to its owners unless it is spotlessly clean, and does as it is told. It should come when called, and learn to lie down in its allotted corner or on its own bed. Also not to worry round the table at mealtimes.

There should be no difficulty in having a Beagle that is trouble-free if it is taught what is required by someone who will devote patience and perseverance to this task, which should be a pleasure to hound and handler. A famous dog-trainer has said that there are no bad dogs—only lots of bad owners. This may be considered a slightly sweeping statement, since we believe that there is the occasional counterpart of the juvenile delinquent—and even the 'old lag'—within the canine race, but there is no doubt there is more than a grain of truth in it. A good many dogs described as difficult or naughty have been made so by mismanagement, bad training, or lack of discipline.

House-breaking is bound to be easier in the summer than in winter-time. One of the important principles is to put the puppy outdoors and to stay until he has relieved himself in the proper place. On a cold, windy night it takes great devotion to duty to stand around shivering, especially as it is probably too dark to see what is happening, anyway. It is all too easy to lose patience with the puppy, who probably does not understand why it is outside and merely wants to play; it doesn't feel cold, thinks it all great fun, and could not care less that one's teeth are chattering. Mild weather and long hours of daylight greatly simplify this part of the training, but if we have to undertake the task in winter we must make the best of it, realizing that the always rather trying period may be somewhat protracted owing to the disadvantages of the season.

A great many Beagle puppies prove exceptionally easy to teach to be clean, for all but a minority are naturally fastidious. We are constantly meeting owners who tell us that their hounds were reliable in an astonishingly short space of time, though naturally there are always some that take longer to learn.

In any case, very young puppies are babies. Nobody expects a human baby to use the right place—its 'potty'—at the right times until months of careful training have elapsed. The little puppy's inside works at frequent intervals, too, through the day and through the night.

The first thing, therefore, is to arrange a place where the puppy can sleep, and where it can be left during the day at any time when it is not convenient to watch it, choosing a small room such as a downstairs lavatory or wash-house, with a tiled or linoleum-covered floor. The floor can be covered with newspapers, easily collected and burned if soiled. If no such room is available, it would be best to fix up a pen in the corner of the garage or the garden shed, just for the night hours, and a vigilant watch must be kept on the puppy if it is to spend the day running about on precious carpets and rugs.

If the puppy is allowed the run of the house without any super-vision, accidents are going to be frequent. If an accident does happen, do not beat the dog. Take it by the scruff of the neck, drag it to the scene of the crime, point it out, and scold it angrily, giving it a slight shake. Then, with one slap on its backside, put it out in the garden for a few minutes. When it is observed to do its jobs outside always make a tremendous fuss of it, pat it, caress it and call it 'clever', 'good'. A small tin of clean sawdust and a shovel cope best with the big mistakes, and a clean cloth dipped in soda water will prevent puddles staining the floor coverings. Always put the puppy outside first thing in the morning and last thing at night. Also after each meal, and any time it wakes up from a sleep.

Talking of sleep, it may well be that the puppy will not like the idea of sleeping alone when it has just left its litter brothers and sisters. So long as it has doting humans playing with it it forgets them, but once it is shut away by itself it may miss their warmth and company, and then it will point its little nose to the ceiling and howl. Some puppies settle down philosophically right from the first day in a new home, and in any event a pup is unlikely to be miserable and unsettled for longer than the first night or two. It is not a bad idea to have a big marrow-bone ready for the new puppy, and if it is placed by the door of its room or shed it will find it there when it starts whining and fidgeting. The novelty of it will take its mind off its troubles and with any luck it may be tired out after it has finished gnawing it, and fall asleep.

Some people believe that a ticking clock, wrapped in a blanket and put in the puppy's bed, helps it to settle and to feel that it is not alone. Others give a very young whelp a stone hot-water bottle, well covered with blanket, which undoubtedly gives it some comfort approximating to the familiar, lost feeling of having other puppies snuggling close.

If a puppy persists in whining, it must be made to understand that this is not to be tolerated. It should be taken by the scruff of the neck, given a light smack, and put on its bed. It will get straight off it again, and must once more be corrected. This is where one's patience can get more than frayed, but it is such an important and crucial point in the puppy's education. Use the same scolding word or sound each time, and persevere until the little Beagle gives in; once it obeys, the first battle is won. Never indulge in all punishment and no praise, however. It is impossible to overdo the latter. When the Beagle does exactly as it is told, always pet and praise it, and if possible reward it with a tasty titbit. Constant punishment and nagging will make a sour-tempered animal, which becomes discouraged and sullen because it believes it can never do right. Plenty of praise, when praise can possibly be given—and this means at times when something is only half done right. Only by these methods can the Beagle's clever brain absorb that certain things are permitted and others not. If a Beagle is habitually dirty something has gone wrong with its training. It may be that in its early weeks with its breeder it has not been kept in clean surroundings, or has not had access to places where it can relieve itself without soiling the bed or the kennel. Unfortunately hounds are not always as immaculately kept as one could wish, and this has some bearing on their habits. Generally, however, it is the new owner who has made some mistakes. For a busy person to be constantly alert to rush a puppy into the garden at the psychological moment is not easy; things happen, callers come to the door, the telephone rings, there are many distractions, and that is when accidents occur. It is never much use scolding a puppy long after the offence, it should ideally be apprehended whilst in the act or very soon after when the memory of what it has done is fresh in its mind.

The rule is never to let the puppy roam the house if one is too occupied to watch it. We cannot devote every minute of the day to its training, but when we have other things to attend to, we must shut it up where it can do no harm.

When the puppy is young, receiving several meals daily—and some of them milky feeds—it will be bound to need to pass water and faeces quite frequently within twenty-four hours. We must endeavour to let it outside every two or three hours, otherwise we must take the blame if the worst happens. But as the hound grows older, we can expect it to acquire some control over bladder and bowels, and by the time it is fully grown it should be able to go for hours without discomfort, should this be necessary.

From the time the puppy is about three months old it should start to learn to go nicely on a lead. We begin by putting a light leather collar round its neck for part of each day. The puppy will not like it very much, will sit down and scratch, roll on the ground, and try to shake it off. It will soon cease to notice it, especially if the collar is attached just before a mealtime, the thrill of a tasty dinner helping the pup to forget the disagreeable collar.

Next attach a light leash, carry the puppy down the garden, and holding the lead, let it follow back to the house. Just before a meal is a good time to choose for this. The little hound will probably trot along well, but it will be another story if it is asked to go in a different direction. It is important that the person undertaking early leash training is somebody whom the puppy loves and wants to follow anyway. A favourite titbit is invaluable, used as the proverbial 'carrot in front of the donkey', though carrot would not be greatly appreciated and donkey is certainly not the right name for an intelligent little Beagle.

If the puppy is very resentful, pulls backwards, tries to escape from the collar, and shouts its annoyance, a combination of firmness, encouragement, and reward must be tried. Walk on, hauling steadily, and stopping occasionally to induce the puppy to come forward to receive a scrap of meat or a biscuit. Plenty of patting and talking in an affectionate tone will help. The various inflexions of the human voice are rapidly understood by a dog, and although it is a rule when training that the same words must always be used for the same commands, it is possible that the tone of voice has a greater impact than what is actually said.

When teaching a young puppy to lead, five minutes twice daily is sufficient to spend on the one exercise. Too much tugging or nagging tires and confuses the puppy, and dulls its capacity to absorb its lessons.

The hound will learn to come when called if it knows that a caress and a titbit will be received from an outstretched hand. Never—but never—strike a dog for remaining out of reach. All it will remember is that pain and displeasure resulted when it eventually reached its trainer—and another time it will stay away longer, and may not be persuaded to return voluntarily at all.

Clearly, however, something has to be done with a persistently disobedient animal. In fact, prevention is not only better than cure, it is sometimes the means to the cure. The incorrigible miscreant should never be taken out loose at all. Until it can be depended upon to come when called it should be exercised on a long cord, summoned by name, and, if and when it ignores its call, given a sharp jerk on the end of the line, hauled in, and praised and rewarded as soon as it is within reach. The fine chain slip-collars are extremely good for this type of training, as a jerk feels uncomfortable and is a well-understood rebuke by remote control. The hound does not associate this punishment with its handler, since it happens while it is on the end of the length of rope. It only associates the pleasant petting it receives, when it has been hauled in to heel, with the trainer.

This is quite a time-absorbing method of instilling obedience but it is really effective, and it should be continued until the hound—still on the cord—wheels round at the sound of its name, and trots happily back to see what is wanted.

If a disobedient dog is allowed to run loose during this period of schooling, and if it discovers that once out of reach it cannot be compelled to do anything it does not want to do, then it is well on the way to becoming a very headstrong and tiresome animal, which, out of control, may make a thorough nuisance of itself.

A world-famous trainer of the pre-World War II era specialized in training police dogs for working trials, and also rehabilitating delinquent dogs of various breeds. He had his own method of dealing with those that ran away or which stayed, frolicking, out of reach when called. He always kept a catapult and some marbles in his pocket, also a very thick, heavy-link chain-collar. If the dog was sufficiently close he would crumple the chain in his hand and throw it at the miscreant; if out of range he would fire a marble. With either method he always managed to hit the dog in the same place —on the thigh or flank where it could not possibly cause any injury. His aim, with chain or catapult, was always accurate; he never missed, and he always timed his missile a moment after the dog had disobeyed a loud, sharp call. The effect was immediate.

The fact that retribution came from such a distance seemed to have a great effect, and usually, as chain or marble stung the spot, the dog, looking startled and worried, would wheel round and trot straight back to the invariably outstretched hand, which, if not to bless, was always there to pat and caress.

The only trouble with this method is that most of us are poor shots, but even so it is worth trying, even though the culprit has the last laugh if we aim and miss.

Hound puppies are mischievous little creatures, and like most dogs are inclined to be destructive when young. They should have a large bone occasionally, and one or two safe, chewable toys, but it is unfair to leave them alone surrounded with valuable furnishings, carpets, or other personal possessions. The puppy can learn to resist temptation if severely scolded when it starts to chew a forbidden article, but it will be some little time before it can be reliable in this respect.

Because of their universal good temper, Beagles are extremely popular in the nursery. Their cheerful demeanour fits them for the rough and tumble of life with a young family, and there are few more dependable breeds with children. At the same time, it should be appreciated that no puppy should be looked upon as a living toy. The best of children are sometimes thoughtless and rough, and need to be educated to show consideration to pets. While they are generally very well disposed towards them, they do not always realize that a puppy requires periods for rest; that, like them, it gets bored with games and can become irritated, as they would, if bullied into doing uncongenial things.

Very young children should not be left alone with dogs. An adult should be on hand to stop teasing or excessive mauling on the one part, and perhaps over-affectionate and overwhelming demonstrations on the other. One never hears of a Beagle snapping at a child, and, in fact, it would probably need to be goaded beyond endurance before it would do so. The customary report, when a Beagle has settled into a new home, is, 'It is so wonderful with the children.' This all the more reason why there should be no taking advantage of its sweet nature. Parents must remember to train the children to consider the Beagle's feelings, and apart from the humanitarian aspect it is a golden opportunity to foster a child's natural, inborn compassion for animals.

The family Beagle is sure to accompany its own people on motor-car excursions. Training a Beagle to behave well in a car is usually simple. Short runs are best to start with, especially if the puppy shows signs of suffering from car-sickness. The cure for this is to give the little fellow confidence. It will travel some distance before a feeling of nausea causes it to dribble and eventually makes it sick. If it gets used to short runs which end before the motion of the vehicle upsets it, it will stop thinking about the unpleasant sensation and soon settle down to enjoy the rides. Then it can motor long distances without being affected.

Chronic travel-sickness can be treated with any of the varied makes of medicines designed for sea-sick passengers. Some seem more effective than others, so if one brand fails try another. It seems best to give one tablet at night, and another the following day, half an hour before setting out on a journey. Desperate owners try other 'cures'. A chain, suspended from the axle of the car and just touching the road, newspapers or lawn-mower clippings for the dog to sit on. Some travel best if they are enclosed in a dark travel-ling box, or made to lie down on the floor, others seem less affected if allowed to sit near a partly opened window. Most car-sick dogs eventually grow out of the trying habit, provided they are taken for sufficient trips by road. In any case, many Beagles are good motor-ists, and they thoroughly enjoy a ride. They need no special training, other than to heed instructions to stay quietly on the back seat, and not to jump about and distract the driver.

If it is intended that the pet Beagle should do much motoring it is best to start the process of accustoming it to the car as soon as possible, if only because it makes it so much pleasanter to take about. The exhibition Beagle is a nuisance if it is habitually car-sick, since it will arrive at the show feeling distinctly under the weather and may not have recovered its high spirits before it is judged. It is the show hound, too, that requires to be specially trained for the ring, for unless it behaves well it is unlikely to win a prize.

A Beagle is seen to its best advantage when shown on the end of a loose lead, standing four-square. This means that it must not lean back on its front legs, nor must it stand with its hindquarters tucked underneath or over-stretched behind. The stern should be carried high, and the hound should appear alert and interested.

When required to move up and down the ring, it must not rush ahead, drag back, or pull sideways. It should trot beside the handler, jaunty, carefree, bright, with stern waving. The hound must submit to being examined by the judge, who may look at its teeth, feel its limbs, muscles, and head, and there must be no struggling or resisting.

If the hound has not the temperament to enable it to show well on a loose lead, it will have to be set up and steadied in position. The handler may need to hold it by the collar with the one hand and stroke the stern upwards with the other. Many hounds do not enjoy being shown, become bored in the ring, or dislike wearing collars and being led. These need very skilled and sympathetic handling, not to mention plenty of training and practice at home, before they will give of their best when parading before a judge.

It is a help to get friends and callers to act the part of the judge— ask them to handle the puppy, to lift the lips and inspect the teeth, and to pick up the feet and feel the pads. Practise, also, moving the hound on the leash. Get a friend to move it for you, so that you can decide on the best speed, for some hounds look smarter taken along at a very brisk pace, while others look much better going slowly. But never allow the hound to break into a gallop in the ring, nor to jump up or play.

Training the hound to stay quietly on its bench will have to be done at the show. It will tire itself out if allowed to get excited, not to mention the annoyance to other owners of better-behaved exhibits on adjacent benches, for there is nothing more trying than a dog which barks incessantly. Beagles are not ordinarily noisy at shows, and the section set aside for them is often most peaceful. Any tendency to 'speak' may be checked with a firm 'No! Be quiet!'

Training for obedience classes and working trials is quite a specialized art, especially nowadays when clever amateur trainers have brought so many dogs of so many breeds to the peak of perfection. Anyone with patience and determination, and a great love of dogs, can make a success of obedience training.

There are large numbers of training classes held all over the British Isles, where owners and their dogs can receive instruction together, and practise working in the company of others under conditions simulated to those prevailing at shows. The clubs help to promote classes at shows, these being immensely popular with spectators. There has been a great wave of enthusiasm for dog-training in the past twenty years, not only here but in various parts of the world. Especially in the U.S.A. the Beagle has shown that it is perfectly capable of holding its own with all the other breeds which do well in these competitions. As yet we have not seen a Beagle taking top honours in the working ring in this country, but we may do so one day.

Some people feel that a Beagle would be out of character per-forming obedience tests, and that its independence makes it unsuitable for this type of work. Yet we know that it can do it, and there is no doubt that an obedience-trained companion is a delight. The tests are not fancy tricks or circus stunts. They have all been designed to make the subject useful, easily controlled, and capable of instant and willing obedience; they instill in a dog the love to serve and please. Certainly Beagles can be obstinate, but they are clever and they can learn quickly when their attention is held, so it would not be surprising if we saw a Beagle gain a working-trials qualification or an Obedience Certificate one of these days.

Even if they have no ambitions for distinction in the obedience ring, anyone who has any difficulty in training a hound should attend a course of obedience classes. Hound and handler would be sure to iron out their misunderstandings.

Addresses of local dog-training societies can be gleaned from the columns of *Our Dogs* and *Dog World*, or can be found in a list in *The Kennel Club Stud Book*. The Kennel Club itself will help to put enquirers in touch with suitable clubs.

The training of Pack Beagles needs a book, not a chapter, to itself. Beginning when the puppies come in from their 'walks' with farmers or other hunt supporters, they start by being coupled to a well-behaved, experienced hound and, after learning their names, need to understand hunting terms and commands, and to answer to the sound of the horn. The whole process can be studied only by constant contact with the hounds and the huntsman.

Perhaps, in closing, we should digest the words take from a delightful little leaflet entitled *Meet the Beagle*, distributed by the Blossom Valley Beagle Club in California, U.S.A.

'The Beagle is the most intelligent of the hounds, and among the smartest. The habit of persistence in the hunt makes the Beagle stubborn. Even this is useful in training. He is not quick to adopt new patterns, but, once he has them, he is reluctant to give them up. So make sure what you want your Beagle to do, and he will do it for the rest of his life.'

That, clearly, is the key to the whole matter. The Beagle is a creature of habit. The habit(s) can be good or bad. Either way, the habits will tend to stick, so it is up to you and you alone.

Just remember, before you blame the hound if it does something that displeases you, the expert who tells us that there are no bad dogs—only bad owners.

CHAPTER VIII

THE STALLION HOUND

THE importance of the stallion hound cannot be over-estimated. Not only will he exert a profound influence on his home kennel, but it is possible that he may have considerable effect upon other kennels, and thus on the breed as a whole. His influence can be great or small, good, bad, or indifferent; and it will vary according to his degree of prepotency and to the amount he is used at stud. By prepotency we mean the sire's ability to reproduce his own qualities or the qualities of his—probably immediate—ancestors. When we talk about a male animal being 'prepotent' we are usually implying that he reproduces definite points or a definite type.

In the history of any breed of dogs there are almost certain to be, within such breeds, outstanding individuals, which have been notable producers. Some of these will have been excellent specimens, but there is likely to be a proportion of animals of even indifferent quality, or at least of apparently indifferent appearance, which in spite of shortcomings succeed in becoming legendary winner-producers. It is these apparent anomalies that help to make nonsense of rules of thumb such as patterns of genetical inheritance, Mendelian theories, and so on. If it were not for these deviations from the norm, the stock we breed would conform to the standard every time and we would all breed Champions in every litter. Because we know that two litter brothers, almost identical in appearance, can produce diametrically opposite results, we know that so much is empirical when we are breeding livestock.

Although the theory that 'like breeds like' is not universally acceptable, it is basically sound, and when what appears to be a mediocre hound makes itself a reputation as a winner-producer, it is an exception to the rule. Such sires are 'flukes', and while we do not dispute the fact that they may achieve distinction through one or more outstandingly good descendants, they do harm inasmuch as they raise false hopes among those wishful thinkers who use them as a yardstick. For every second-rate hound that tends to pass on good points rather than its own obvious faults there are hundreds which never throw any stock of merit.

What we have to consider is this. The intricate conglomeration of genes and chromosomes form a complicated background to the reproductive powers of a species. Two mated animals, nearly perfect in themselves, can easily produce a majority of offspring utterly devoid of the virtues of the parents, so it is clear that if we start by using faulty animals for breeding, our chances of getting anything better are poor indeed.

If we accept that a couple of poor-quality hounds are most unlikely to produce puppies better than themselves if we mate them together, and also that a pair of Champions, even though they have a better chance of breeding something good, may also have offspring with various faults, we must realize that it is a waste of time to use a stallion hound that is anything but top class.

We have studied in detail the desirable points of a quality Beagle in Chapter V, so it is to be hoped that we have a clear picture of our ideal in our minds. For our stallion hound must fit the breed standard in conformation, type, and soundness. He must be all Beagle in head, leathers, neck, and build. We seek in him proportionate bone and substance; also quality. The question 'What is quality?' is constantly asked within the world of dog-breeding, and while some attempt to define it, others cannot do so. But everyone agrees that quality is something we can recognize when we see it. Either it is present in an animal or it is not. And it in no way implies any slightness of build or lack of stamina through an over-abundance of elegance. Rather does it represent a balanced construction, free from exaggeration, without coarseness and, overall, an aristocratic appearance which places the animal head and shoulders above his fellows.

The hound worth breeding from must not only look good in stance, but he must move well. Our first thought may be that it is difficult to see how movement, good or bad, could be a transmittable factor, but because we know that movement is a result of conform-ation, we appreciate that it is something that may very well be passed on to a dog's progeny.

Naturally, a hound that is lame through an injury will never sire lame puppies. Nor, if it can be definitely proved that a light-boned hound was denied bone-forming nutrients during its formative years, need such an animal throw slightly built puppies. But a Beagle that is shelly and light, in spite of having been properly reared and nourished, will probably produce a considerable proportion of progeny with these disagreeable characteristics.

Finally, temperament is a prime consideration. Faulty temperament can be inherited or acquired, and in this category we include over-aggressiveness, nervousness, and that especially undesirable animal known as the 'shy-biter'. The Beagle breed is notably steady and even-tempered. It is exceedingly rare to get a dog or bitch that can be dubbed a fighter, and it is just as unlikely that one would come upon one that is savage or unreliable. This priceless characteristic should be rigidly maintained and greatly prized, for we live in a modern age when many other breeds come under fire because of alleged hysterical and uncertain dispositions. If we guard the inborn Beagle character, there is no reason at all why we should not keep it. Any tendency to fight other dogs (not including the perfectly natural animosity between stallion hounds when a bitch on heat is in the vicinity) or to bite the human race is shocking, and should never be tolerated in a Beagle.

We must admit that any animal, Beagle or otherwise, can be made nervous or savage by harsh treatment. Even kindly treated puppies can grow up shy if kept too much in enclosed surroundings and not introduced to modern hustle and bustle of crowds and traffic. Under circumstances of this type there may be some excuse for the dog that is nervous at its first few shows. But if we are honest with ourselves, I think we will admit that we are apt to be biased where our own dog is concerned. We tend to make excuses for it, to blame ourselves for its shortcomings, to persuade ourselves that it was some emotional upset such as a fright or an injection that caused it to become such a problem 'child'.

The stallion hound should be close to our ideal, and that means he must be handsome, and bold and gay. And even then we are not even half-way towards solving all our problems, for, ideally, the hound's immediate ancestors should have similar characteristics. They should be of good type, have even dispositions, and be free from glaring faults. For the beginner it looks as though a safari into no-man's-land is a necessity, for how is it possible to know all the animals in a two- or three-generation pedigree? Not easy, we know. But much can be learned from a study of a hound's career, its notable show successes, and in particular the wins of its progeny.

Every Christmas the weekly dog papers publish large illustrated supplements, in which many notable show dogs are depicted, brief pedigrees are given, and details of their get. Back numbers of these annuals can often be borrowed and sometimes purchased, since breeders regard them as treasures and mines of information to be kept indefinitely. A novice can learn a tremendous amount from these books.

Breeders of the stallion hound's immediate forebears are often to be found at shows, and if contacted between classes or after judging will usually spare the time to answer queries.

The *Kennel Club Stud Books* are another source of material, since pedigrees of notabilities in the show world are published annually, together with names and addresses of owners. Any Beagle which wins a first, second, or third prize in the Limit or Open class, also any Challenge Certificate or Reserve Challenge Certificate winners if entered in lower classes, will be included in the appropriate sections devoted to championship show awards.

Whatever the source, the more that can be found out about the stallion hound the better.

We have made particular reference to the first two generations because many believe that these six animals have the greatest effect on their descendants. This does not mean that our studies of the third, fourth, or fifth generations may not prove fruitful, because we know that there are often throw-backs, traceable to some dog or bitch a long way back in a pedigree. To illustrate this point, let us say that every name in the first three generations of a certain pedigree refers to a hound predominantly black and tan, with minimum white markings. In the fourth or fifth generation there is one lemon-pied, mainly white, hound. In spite of its being a minority, and in spite of its being so far back, this pied animal could easily cause the tri-coloured, tri-colour-bred, parents to throw some lemon-pied puppies in a litter. To do this, both parents need to have at least one lemon-pied in its pedigree, however far away, but as this rule applies to any breed point and by no means only to colour it goes to show that anything can crop up, and the life of the breeder is full of surprises.

But even among specialists in genetics there appears to be a difference of opinion as to the degree of importance we should attach to the more distant ancestors, and the amount of influence they are likely to have. Obviously their blood has become greatly diluted, and yet, though it may remain dormant through years of selective breeding, a link between two bloodlines may result in a demonstration that their prepotency is by no means inactive.

The study of genetics is fascinating, but complex, technical, and time-absorbing. It cannot be satisfactorily dealt with in a single chapter, for libraries of books have been written on the subject, and there are still gaps that are as yet unexplained. We recommend *Practical Dog Breeding and Genetics* by Eleanor Frankling, which provides a beginner with a clear outline of this vast subject.

How important is a knowledge of genetics? Is it true that many successful breeders ignore the scientific angle? Are we likely to succeed as pedigree dog-breeders if we do not understand it?

Difficult questions to answer, for probably a basic knowledge of genetics, however sketchy it may be, is of some help. How much a really close study will repay the time spent, one hesitates to say, for there is such a thing as being blinded by science, particularly where livestock breeding is concerned. Some breeders claim to have applied scientific methods with considerable success. Probably many more, who do not know a gene from a chromosome or a recessive from a dominant, have achieved very good results from a knowledge of the best points and the worst faults, and a flair for selecting breeding partners.

It is not without significance that one or two especially notable experts on genetics, who were themselves dog-breeders, were not outstandingly successful at applying their knowledge to their own stock, which was outstripped by that produced by others less erudite. For one thing, dogs are by no means the most suitable creatures upon which to follow the recognized principles, even if one understands them.

Mendelism is one of the oldest still-respected theories, and the most frequently quoted, but most of Mendel's experiments were conducted with plants and small animals with a rapid reproductive cycle. To apply Mendel's theories to dogs it is really necessary to keep whole litters to maturity—how many private individuals are in a position to do this?

Probably George D. Whitney, the American author of *This is the Beagle*, most neatly sums up the situation in his chapter dealing with heredity. He writes 'Mendel was a monk with plenty of time on his hands, and no wife to tell him he had too many dogs'.

The ability to apply any scientific principles to dog-breeding depends entirely upon a quite considerable knowledge of the individuals in the pedigrees concerned. However knowledgeable we may eventually become, few of us start off with such an asset, so we can only do our best with such scraps of information as we can collect as we go along.

Any beginner is advised to start a kennel with one or more top-class bitches, and not to spend money on purchasing a stud dog until well established. We know that choosing a puppy is a lottery, and by no means all of us have the luck to pick one that grows into an outstanding adult. We also realize that, to buy a fully grown hound of this calibre, we need to spend a large sum of money. The sensible course, then, is to take our good bitches and mate them to the best and most suitable stallion hounds at stud in other kennels. If all goes according to plan, this may mean that we can breed some good male puppies, and if we run on the best we may have a lovely stud dog of our own by the time they are fully grown.

If we find this idea does not work out quite as we hoped, and we decide that our puppies are not good enough to keep, then we sell them as pets and we plod on, hoping to do better with the next litter. Or, if we are still intent on owning a stud hound, we can lay aside the money recouped from our sales until we have enough to buy a good male. Even so, it has to be remembered that not even the best sire is suitable for every bitch. It is even possible to mate two litter sisters to the same stallion hound, and to get good results from one and disappointment from the other. It is because this is often the case that it is generally thought unwise for any beginner to buy a stud dog in the early stages. It is far better to use other people's hounds, paying for the services, and thus choosing what appear to be the most suitable mates for all the bitches in the kennel.

The beginner who uses a stud dog and pays a fee, as is customary, for this privilege, is inclined to envy the owner. Easy money, it is thought, but time and experience together show that this is not so. In fact, owners of stud dogs earn every penny they get, and in most breeds stud fees are far too low. The care and management of a stallion hound call for experience and skill, and trouble awaits the novice who sets out as a stud-dog owner without either. The dog must be well fed, on a diet that includes plenty of meat, and he must receive ample exercise so that he never becomes fat or lazy.

How many bitches can he serve, and how often may we accept his visitors? It is not easy to give a precise figure, because scarcely any dog receives a steady demand for its services. The requests hardly ever come at regular intervals, nor is it possible to space them out. The most fashionable sires generally get a rush of bitches all about the same time, followed by a quiet spell extending from a few days to a few weeks, according to demand. Therefore we cannot say that a hound can serve fifty-two bitches in a year (though he very likely can) because he will never get one per week. It is far more likely that four or five people will have bitches ready for him within the same single week, and none at all for the rest of the month. There is no special reason for this—it just happens to work out that way. Any stud-dog owner will tell you that this is true.

Common sense has to be used. A young, virile hound can serve a bitch a day for, say, three days, and after that he should have a few days' rest from his work. If the bitches were easy to serve it means he will have expended a minimum of energy in the process, but some are very difficult and cause the dog to become quite exhausted, so obviously he could not manage a number of the latter at about the same time, even though several willing bitches had taken little out of him.

A proven brood bitch, offered to the stallion hound at the best time within her oestrum, will certainly be quickly and easily mated, and the dog will rapidly achieve a 'tie' with her. A bitch that has not had a litter, always described as a 'maiden', can, on the other hand, be exceedingly capricious, snappy, and difficult, even if she is put to the dog at a time when she appears ready to receive his advances.

Many inexperienced people make the mistake of taking a bitch to a sire at the wrong time—either too late or too early. Some stud dogs are very perceptive and will take no interest in a bitch unless she is ready. A cursory sniff or two, an absent-minded lifting of the leg, and the hound walks away, bored and disgusted. Young stud dogs, full of enthusiasm, will persist in trying to serve a bitch from the first days of her heat to the last, and will wear themselves out in the process, unless removed and kept away from the bitch. A few experiences of this type can be harmful to a stallion hound, for such struggles sap his energy. If he has been allowed to work so hard he should not be used again for a few days.

Never leave a dog and bitch together at mating time, except under supervision. Ignore the 'know-alls' who maintain that they would get along all right in a wild state or if turned loose on the streets. Valuable stud dogs have been injured or incapacitated by unruly bitches. Somebody must be in attendance to hold the bitch and to stop her throwing herself about. The 'tie' can last from a very few minutes to as much as two hours, but probably the average period during which dog and bitch are locked together is about half an hour. How much the length of time has to do with the likelihood of conception is not completely understood, for bitches can and sometimes do produce puppies when the stud dog has made entry and has not 'tied' at all, but has slipped out again straight away. Veterinary experts think that sperm is ejaculated more than once during the 'tie', and if this is so it seems likely that a period of ten minutes or more offers a better chance of puppies than does a shorter time.

Before a 'tie' can be achieved, it may be necessary to assist the male. This is where the novice breeder is at a disadvantage, for considerable skill and 'know-how' is often required. If the bitch is quiet, sensible, and responsive, a restraining hand on her collar may be sufficient. If she is restless or inclined to snap—and the most placid and best-natured bitches are unpredictable when mating—it may need one person to hold her collar and another to put a supporting hand under her stomach and, with the other, help the dog. In extreme cases it may even be necessary to muzzle the bitch or to put a 'tape' on her. Taping consists of tying a wide bandage or a nylon stocking round the muzzle, crossing the ends under the chin and tying them firmly on the top of the neck. This is a last resort, when a bitch is clearly attempting to bite, in order to prevent her injuring the stud dog or the handlers.

If the bitch is much larger than the dog, or vice versa, it is difficult for them to effect a union unless the smaller one has a platform or cushion for its hind legs. Many breeders like to encourage their stud hounds to serve bitches on a large, firm table, as it is so much easier to render assistance when required and much less tiring if the animals need to be held for any length of time.

The moment the dog makes contact, the assistant should hold the bitch extra tightly, otherwise at the critical moment she may throw herself about and cause the dog to slip out. A few such incidents, and some ordinarily keen studs become discouraged and disinterested.

The other helper keeps one arm under the bitch's tummy and, with the other holding the male on top of the bitch's back, makes every effort to prevent his turning round for a minute or two lest he should come away before a satisfactory 'tie' is maintained.

After this pause the male can be gently turned round, his hind leg lifted carefully so that he and the bitch are standing back to back. At this stage it is usual for even the most fractious and difficult bitches to cease resisting and to relax, and the muzzle or tape can safely be removed. The hounds must still be held, however, and not allowed to pull one another around until they are free.

As they move apart, many breeders seize the bitch and raise her hindquarters high above her head, holding her in this attitude for a minute or two. The idea is that the sperm will tend to pass down the passage towards the ovaries. Whether or not this action does ensure conception is a matter for conjecture. Some scoff at the idea, others feel that it is so simple to do that it is worth trying if there is any chance of its helping to ensure that puppies result.

When a stud service is normal and straightforward there is no particular reason for repeating it. Owners of visiting bitches sometimes ask for more than one mating, especially if the bitch has failed to breed on other occasions or if there is some other urgency that makes it especially necessary that she should be in whelp. If the stud dog is not in very great demand it is customary to comply with such requests if it can be conveniently arranged, but clearly if the stallion is heavily booked it is impossible to give bitches two services within two or three days without overworking the male. Of course, if a bitch happens to 'miss', unless there are arrangements to the contrary, it is customary to give a free service at the next season.

After the service the dog should be taken out for a few moments and allowed to relieve himself. When he has lifted his leg he can be put back into his kennel, alone, and will appreciate a drink of water. The word 'alone' is important, because although several male Beagles may ordinarily live amicably together, the scent of the bitch will be strong on the dog and can be the cause of jealousy, leading to fights.

The beginner who places a hound at stud is strongly advised to accept accompanied bitches only, at least until more experienced. Only those well used to the wiles of strange bitches have much idea of the hazards and difficulties involved in keeping them in safe confinement. Models of good behaviour in their own homes, once they are in unfamiliar surroundings and spurred on by nature's primeval sex-urges, some become worse than troublesome. They may chew and tear at doors and windows, rip wire netting, dig under gates, scale fences, and howl day and night to make sleep impossible and neighbours' complaints inescapable.

Experienced kennel owners build special accommodation for their visiting bitches, as impregnable as it is possible to make it. Kennels are usually constructed from brick, or breeze, or concrete blocks. If wood, the door and lower parts of walls should be reinforced with metal. Runs should be roofed over with wire, and at least six feet high. Only the thickest-gauge chain-link wire netting is at all suitable; corrugated-iron walls, iron bars, or weldmesh are all safer. Concrete runs are best, since bitches can dig out of earth enclosures.

It would be maligning the breed to say that all the bitches are as difficult when kennelled away from home and when in season, for this tiresome behaviour is certainly not universal. While some bitches will howl and whine for the first night or two, the majority are philosophical and do not try to escape, especially when provided with plenty of food and a warm bed.

Because so many cause little trouble it is all the more important to be on guard for the ones that do. The stud dog's owner is expected to take the greatest possible care of bitches sent for service, and to let a visiting bitch escape is a heinous crime. Because such accidents happen all too easily, when inexperienced handlers are involved, and when really suitable accommodation is not available, it seems better to avoid taking risks. Refuse to accept bitches unless they are brought for service and taken away again afterwards.

It is customary for the bitch to visit the dog, and not the other way about. For one thing, some stud dogs are temperamental and put off by strange surroundings; they work better on their home ground. Owners of keen sires which are less exacting sometimes agree to take the dog to the bitch if it is mutually more convenient, but a sum to cover travelling expenses, in addition to the usual fee, is charged.

The actual fee a hound commands is dependent on his merits, his successes at shows, his progeny's wins, or the value of his pedigree to breeders. Beagle stud fees run around the £30 mark for good quality stallion hounds in England, although many less distinguished Beagles are available at lower fees. Sale prices and stud fees are very much higher in some other parts of the world.

It is generally good for a breed if stud fees and prices of puppies are kept at a high level, as this tends to check a tendency to the pernicious habit of turning bitches into puppy-factories in order to pour puppies into the pet market.

Sometimes some agreement about choice of litter is made in lieu of stud fee, though many breeders prefer to avoid arrangements of this kind.

Kennel owners who do not keep many bitches for breeding, anyone owning a stud dog and no bitches at all—such people may find it advantageous to take a puppy which might sell for more than the amount of the fee. But there may be no puppy at all, or the litter may not be well reared or good-looking, in which case it would have been far better to have had the fee.

The owner of the bitch often suggests a pick-of-litter deal, feeling that it is a better prospect than paying out a fee at mating time. When the time comes, however, it may mean that the best puppy in the litter—it could be the only good one, the much-desired dog or the longed-for bitch—is taken by the stud dog's owner, and it turns out to be not such a satisfactory idea as it promised. Puppy arrangements often lead to disagreements and ill-feeling. For instance, there may be one puppy only as a result of the service—so it is really much better to pay the fee and be done with it.

The new owner of a stallion hound will wonder how much revenue his expensive acquisition can be expected to earn, for expensive it is bound to be, whether reared from babyhood at home or bought in as an adult. A really good stud dog should contribute to the running expenses of the kennel lavishly in the first couple of years, and to a lesser extent as time goes on. The length of time during which a stud dog should be profitable depends upon its life-span, the wisdom with which its career has been guided, and the success or otherwise of its progeny. Most well-patronized sires enjoy a peak period, after which visitors become less numerous.

The reasons for this are quite clear. If the dog is a great success at stud it stands to reason he will throw a high proportion of puppies as good as, or even much better than, himself. This means that before very long he will have rivals in the shape of some excellent sons. These, in turn, are placed at stud, and they naturally draw off many of the bitches that might otherwise visit their sire. If, on the other hand, our stallion does not turn out a very outstanding sire, and if he does not get at least a few outstanding winners out of his first few bitches, then breeders will not want to use him any more and they will seek the services of other hounds.

So from this it would seem that, from the earning point of view, a stud dog's life is a short and a merry one. The owner can hardly win, unless he has a stud dog who produces beautiful daughters by the dozen, and no outstanding males to spoil his own stud career. Such cases are, of course, known, but they are not very usual. All that the wise stud-dog owner can do is to look to the future, and while the stallion hound is in his prime, carefully bring on another top-class youngster ready for the day when the older hound's star begins to wane.

The services of a stud dog will certainly be sought by his admirers, but it is a good idea to advertise him in the dog Press and in the annual supplements. Small, regular advertisements in dog papers often seem to bring better results than the occasional large and expensive displayed insertion.

The wise breeders make arrangements for mating a bitch well before she is due in season. Indeed, a few far-seeing breeders work out her future while she is still a puppy romping on the lawn. But there are always a few less provident folk who leave everything until the last moment, put off making final arrangements, and thus cause inconvenience all round. These are the people who wait until a bitch has been in season for days before they reach for the dog papers to see which stallion hounds are listed. If that is the week we failed to advertise our hound at stud, we may miss a stud fee. Hence the advice to put regular announcements where they are most likely to be seen.

Before we close this chapter we must consider the effect that showing has upon a stud dog's patronage. In general, unless he has been shown and done well, nobody is particularly likely to want to breed from him. The exception is an imported hound or one of rare and especially desirable breeding which, for some perfectly good reason, is not widely exhibited.

Owners of Champions find this question a knotty one. Should Champions be persistently shown, shown occasionally, or retired directly they gain the title? Opinions vary, and it is often difficult for the owners to decide what to do. The less successful exhibitors are not unnaturally piqued and discouraged if a reigning Champion appears, unconquerable, at one show after another. On the other hand, when one is lucky enough to own such a treasure—and for many of us this is a once-in-a-lifetime experience, remember—we naturally feel that we want the thrill of winning while we are able to enjoy showing our 'star'. We are but human, after all, and most of the critics would want to do the same if in our enviable position.

The predominant status of the breed should be one deciding factor. Often the retirement of a top show dog means that unworthy second-bests become Champions directly he is out of the way, and this in itself is the best of reasons for keeping a great dog in the limelight. This happens only when a breed has one or two outstanding specimens, and a general level of inferior dogs is being shown. More often, and especially in Beagles—which are universally very high-class at the present time—there are several worthy potential Champions being consistently pegged back by the ruthless and inconsiderate campaigning of a famous winner.

While it is depressing and frustrating to get a good dog beaten in such circumstances, one can hardly complain if the victor is really the better dog, and if it is also in perfect condition and looking its best when it goes up.

Unfortunately, it sometimes happens that a great dog still wins even when out of form, and then it is felt that the exhibit continues to win only on its prior reputation and because judges have got into the habit of putting it into first place. Rival owners have a very real grievance in such cases, and one hears murmured accusations of 'pot-hunting' which are at least understandable. So perhaps it is a question of good taste and a just appraisal of the status of the breed. If the owner feels that the Champion is keeping other worthy Champions back, if the dog is admittedly past its best, then wins are surely empty and the day is bound to come when courageous judges will depose the vanquisher. Better by far to retire him with his almost unbeatable reputation untarnished.

Showing him in different parts of the country may help him to get plenty of stud work, but only if he is looking good. He will probably get just as much patronage on retirement.

Entwined with this is the know-how of dog showmanship—when to show and when to stop at home. The one unwritten law is not to show a dog twice at a Championship show under a judge who has awarded it a Challenge Certificate. While a very few cases may be made out for doing this, exhibitors, in the main, feel it is just 'not done'. It is considered unsporting, since the Certificate adds little to its reputation, and nothing towards the title of Champion since only C.C.s won under different judges count towards this. It is not as though we in Britain were like a few other countries which have only a mere handful of shows in any one year. We have dozens of them—so surely we can give someone else a chance sometimes?

CHAPTER IX

THE BROOD BITCH

SOME of us find ourselves possessors of a brood bitch, others set out especially to buy one. If this statement seems a little cryptic, let us hasten to explain that there are many people who buy Beagle bitches as pets, without any thought of taking up breeding. Nothing is farther from their minds when they choose her as a family pal, but eventually they find themselves making arrangements to have a litter from her after all. And if the bitch is typical and well bred there is no reason why they should not do so.

A good many customers, some of them investing in a pedigree animal for the first time, are attracted by the idea of trying their hands at dog-breeding. They, and others like them, are spurred on by their well-meaning friends and relations. We know the 'spiel'. It is: 'Every bitch ought to have at least one litter. It is cruel not to let her have puppies. If she is not allowed to fulfil her natural functions it is sure to affect her health.'

There is about as much truth in all this as there is in the old saying that crusts make your hair curl!

It is, of course, a fact that when they become old some bitches suffer from disorders of the reproductive organs, but although many people believe that brood bitches are less affected, there is no evidence to support this; brood and maiden bitches not infrequently get troubles associated with the ovaries and the womb as they advance in age. Scores of bitches, both regular breeders and bitches that have never had puppies at all, remain perfectly healthy.

However, because there seems a prevalent belief that it is necessary to the bitch to allow her to breed, owners, commendably anxious to do the right thing for their pets, arrange for and burden themselves with litters of puppies which they do not want and would much prefer not to have at all. This laudable but totally unnecessary effort only results in puppies of mediocre quality being distributed to a public unable to discriminate between good and indifferent stock.

For, unfortunately, by no means all the bitches kept as pets are good enough for breeding.

While the demand for good-quality Beagles, even as pets, is always keen, as in other breeds the rubbish is hard to sell. So what naturally follows is the almost inescapable sequel: the puppies are advertised without result, grow bigger (and plainer), cost more and more to feed, crowd out the kitchen—since many such litters are born indoors and the owners do not have really suitable accommodation for them—and so become a real worry and expense. The very fact that the owner is quite unknown as a breeder is a handicap in itself, even if the puppies are typical and well reared, and while there is always a chance of selling this type of offspring in the end, the other sort will either be given away or find their way to the less reputable dealers.

It is, therefore, a great mistake to regard any pet-standard bitch as a prospective brood. If she is of pet quality and bought as a pet—let her spend her life in that capacity. She is unlikely to be in any way adversely affected by staying single.

Although we cannot deny that some bitches sold as companions are the throw-outs of the litter (and they are just as delightful as the Champions when it comes to those qualities that go to make up the lively family hound dog), there are also occasions when it is possible to get hold of really nice-quality females, especially from the larger litters or from those breeders who produce puppies on a fairly big scale.

Such breeders have one aim, which is to produce something better in every succeeding litter. It is most unlikely that a nest of half a dozen whelps will end up equally outstanding. The breeder will either retain the best with a view to showing it and breeding when it is old enough, or will sell the pick-puppies to other breeders and exhibitors. That leaves some more puppies, perhaps very promising but a little less outstanding, for disposal, and these may very well find themselves in pet homes.

A bitch of this calibre is another proposition altogether. She may be up to show standard, she may be not quite good enough for competition, but she is sure to be of good type and well bred. If her owner does not want the bother of rearing puppies from his bitch, well, that is up to him; it will not harm her. But if he feels inclined to try a litter with a nice bitch, put to a top-class dog, he has a fair chance of success.

If, therefore, one decides to buy a bitch as a pet with the fixed idea of eventually breeding from her, then this should be explained to the kennel owner at the time of purchase. The odd 'throw-out', with a few really bad faults, must go to somebody else who wants a playmate for the growing family and could never be bothered with litters. The prospective breeder, even if not prepared to go in for breeding in a big way, should have a good type of bitch. She should be typical, sound, of nice temperament, and of really good pedigree. A breeder can hardly be expected to sell a prospective Champion into a home where it is definitely destined to be primarily a pet, but if it is going to be bred from it must be of reasonable quality.

If the prospective pet owner is lucky enough to get hold of a good bitch, then it might be a pity not to take at least one litter from it. But the whole future of a popular breed can be jeopardized if the market is flooded with third-rate litters, and there is absolutely no justification for producing them. As we already know, most knowledgeable and experienced breeders get a proportion of pet-standard puppies in most litters, even in those litters which contain Champions. There are plenty of these about to satisfy the demand for pets. Consider this when buying a bitch for the family. If you feel there is any likelihood of an urge to have Beagle puppies romping on the hearth-rug (and chewing the fringe off it, too), then get a nice bitch, well bred, well reared, and well recommended by a well-known breeder.

This is advice to the pet owner who merely wants to have one, or two litters at most, as much to amuse the youngsters and keep the wife out of mischief as anything else. This rather casual approach is not for the serious would-be breeder, however much of a novice he or she may be. For anybody desirous of breeding Beagles, on a very small or much larger scale, must realize that success and failure are not just matters of luck, even though luck plays some part in the eventual result. The wise choice of the foundation bitch or bitches is vital to the venture. The better the bitch, the more likelihood there is of getting top-class puppies. This is a generalization that has been proved a safe one, even though we know that there have been Champions bred from fairly ordinary dams, and such Champions, too, as have never bred a puppy as outstanding as themselves.

The bitch we buy must be of impeccable pedigree, and before she is selected due attention should be paid to the background of the top show hounds of the time. Visits to shows where Beagles are on exhibition are so valuable. Comparing a number of hounds under ideal conditions is itself an education. Diligent study of catalogues shows us their parentage, and a study of strains, families, and blood-lines can follow. After a few days spent sitting by the ringsides at various shows, the beginner will notice that certain kennel prefixes or affixes—the kennel owners' 'trade-marks' attached to the names of their exhibits—crop up over and over again. In fact, names of certain sires and dams command attention and seem to be attached to the principal winners. As our 'eye' develops, we even begin to notice a certain similarity about the offspring of some of these successful families, and this similarity is most usually referred to as 'type'. A sire or dam which stamps its own qualities on its progeny, so that its get are immediately recognizable is of very great value to a breed. It is dominant, and anybody who obtains a brood bitch by or out of one of these treasures cannot go far wrong.

The obvious next step is to get into conversation with the owner, and to discover if there is any stock for sale from this coveted strain. Make an appointment to visit the chosen kennel, tell the breeder exactly what is required, and ask for help in selecting a good bitch with which to make a start. The best is seldom cheap—why should it be? And what is cheap is not invariably nasty—but very often not worth having, so pay as much as you can afford and get value for money. Never choose two indifferent bitches for the price of one good one—settle for the good one every time.

Naturally, the age of the bitch and the amount of the capital out-lay must be linked. For £100 it should be possible to buy a beautiful bitch puppy aged seven to ten weeks. A very promising bitch aged six months or over could cost a good deal more, but then it is more of a finished article.

Naturally enough, the baby puppy may develop a fault or faults as it grows up, but the half- or full-grown Beagle has done some of its developing. Its good and bad points are more or less there to be observed and assessed. The little puppy is a gamble, the older bitch is a more expensive investment, but you see what you are buying.

We have gone into the question of choosing a Beagle in Chapter V, and whilst we do not intend to dwell at great length on the subject again here, we make no apology for stressing some of the points raised since they are of such great importance to the newcomer to Beagle breeding. Mistakes are a waste of money and time. Study the chapter, and, according to the price that can be paid, and whether or not the start is to be made with a puppy or an adult, endeavour to get a sound, typical, well-bred bitch.

If we can lay out the money, there is much to be said for buying a prize-winner. If she has won in good company, then in addition to our own impressions, and the owner's recommendation, we are backed by the judges who thought her good enough to win. There is also the possibility that we might be able to get hold of a proved breeder, even a successful dam of winners. This last is a most sought-after paragon, but it is not always easy to persuade an owner to part with such a bitch. There are occasions, however, reluctant though the owner may be, when he finds it impossible to keep the best puppy from a young litter unless the dam is disposed of to avoid the kennel becoming overcrowded. This offers a rare chance to the beginner.

In seeking to equip ourselves with a really good bitch we must not forget that absolute perfection is never ours. Although we seek per-fection, we may nevertheless have to be content with something that falls short of our ideal. It has been said repeatedly that the perfect animal has never been bred. Many beautiful show specimens are difficult to fault, yet there is always something, some little feature, that could be a little more . . . a little less . . . a shade longer . . . a tiny bit shorter. . . .

It is at this point that we may reap the full benefit of our pre-liminary study of strains and families. It could be, for example, that we have in mind a bitch that is a little short of ear-leather, or rather lighter in eye colour than we think we like. Granted it would be more satisfactory if she did not have these faults, but if we found a bitch with big long ears and dark-brown eyes, she might have open feet, cloddy shoulders, a poor stern, or some other faults. From our study of the sires and dams and other well-known relations we should have noticed if our prospect's parents and grand-parents are better or worse as regards ears and eyes. If they have, in fact, ap-peared to be good in these respects, we can safely overlook them in our bitch, since we know that if we choose her mate carefully she is quite likely to produce a majority of puppies free from her own faults.

If the bitch under consideration has what appear to be common family failings, then we know that the faults may be harder to breed out, though, faced with this information and with a clear under-standing of the task ahead, we can still do it if we have a mind to go about it in the right way.

The right way would be to find a stallion hound especially noted for producing wide, lengthy ear-leathers and nice dark eyes, and although inbred faults sometimes take a generation or two to iron out, an achievement on these lines is an example of the tremendous fascination of breeding thoroughbred stock.

But one thing is sure. By this time we have reached a stage where we realize that the selection of a brood bitch has more to it than we thought when we lightheartedly decided to breed a few Beagles.

However, we must eventually take the plunge, so let us assume that we have made our choice. We take her home, feed her carefully and well, give her abundant exercise, and spend plenty of time training her to fit in with our routine.

In due course she will come into season. The first heat can be noticed any time between the ages of six and thirteen months, but it is probably most likely to happen when the puppy is about ten months old. Only the most precocious puppies come on heat at six months, it is generally later. If a bitch, destined for breeding, has not started her oestrum by the time she is eighteen months of age, she needs some treatment from a vet, who will probably advise an injection. Injections of stilboestrol are effective in bringing on a season, and the bitch will accept the dog as a result, but is seldom pregnant. The season is generally established in this way, however, and will resume its normal cycle, and at the following heat the bitch can be mated and generally proves in whelp.

The average bitch remains in season for about three weeks, in unusual cases for longer. The first signs are noticed when the exterior female organ—the vulva—becomes swollen. The bitch licks herself a great deal, and she may want to pass water more frequently than is usual. Within a day or two a bright-red discharge is seen, and this continues for a week or ten days. About this time the discharge becomes less apparent, and becomes a clear, pink mucus. It is when this happens—often at about the tenth to thirteenth day since the first show of blood was observed—that the majority of bitches are ready to mate. As this time draws near, the bitch will become increasingly restless and flirtatious. If she shares the company of another bitch she will make advances to her, and will twist her stern to one side to signify her anxiety to find a dog.

It should not be necessary to impress upon all who have charge of a bitch in season that extreme care must be taken from the first day of the heat period until the last, when she shows no exterior signs and snaps and growls at the males. The majority of bitches will not accept the dog until they have been in season at least a week, nor for a few days as the period draws to a close, but there are certainly exceptions to the rule. Many sad and sorry owners have discovered this—too late.

The desire to mate is a strong natural instinct, and a bitch will often go to almost any lengths to escape in order to seek a mate. Similarly, a male dog senses that a bitch is on heat even from a distance away, and with uncanny skill and maddening perseverance he will exhibit the utmost ingenuity and energy in endeavouring to satisfy his desires. He is capable of scaling walls or fences, ripping up and chewing doors, digging under wire netting or even solid partitions. It cannot be emphasized too strongly that every care must be exercised to keep a bitch safe from what are, at least to her owner if not to her, unwelcome attentions, until the time is ripe to take her to the stallion hound.

If a bitch is to be covered by a male in her home kennel everything is laid on, as it were, and no complicated arrangements are necessary except perhaps a careful avoidance of outside bookings for the dog around the time our own bitch seems likely to be ready.

When it is a question of taking or sending a bitch to somebody else's hound, more planning is involved. The hound's owner should be advised as soon as the bitch comes on heat—never at the last minute. This means that the sire can be reserved for her. If the bitch is to travel unaccompanied, have a light but strong box ready—and get it ready long before she is due in season. It is surprising how often this apparently obvious requirement is forgotten. At the last moment there are frantic attempts to borrow a box from a neighbouring dog-breeder or from the owner of the sire. Even if somebody has a box which they are willing to lend, it might have to be put on rail, and may well take days to arrive. If it is not possible to beg a box, then one must be made, but this also takes time. Therefore get a suitable box and risk no delays.

Various firms sell travelling boxes in a variety of sizes and different designs. Sometimes these are kept in stock, but often they are made to order and there may be some delay in obtaining one. As a matter of fact, a small or medium-sized Beagle fits into a large tea-chest very well indeed. These plywood boxes are obtainable from some grocers and from tea importers and specialists. A charge is made, but even at top price they are bargains. A door is easily made to fit at one end, the whole is painted and fitted with side handles to make it easy to carry, and the result is quite a smart container.

Be sure to see that a box has ample ventilation without being cold and draughty. Holes should be drilled near the top of the box and could be bored all round the sides; this is easily done with a brace and bit. The door can be made of strong wood—ply is less suitable and would need to be hung on a sturdy framework—and there should be a fair-sized grid or window. Weldmesh is ideal for this.

The crate must be large enough for the hound to travel in comfort. It should be able to stand up and turn round, also to lie stretched out full length. There is no great virtue in making a very big box, however, for it only means that the animal slides about inside if it is being carried or put on luggage trolleys in the course of the journey.

No particular mention will be made here regarding hampers. They are light, and therefore rail charges are kept to a minimum, but they are very draughty. They are also not entirely safe, since a hound can easily chew the wickerwork and might escape on a station platform.

Before sending a bitch on a train make careful enquiries as to the best time for her to be dispatched, having regard to possible changes *en route*. On long cross-country journeys it is nearly always best to send livestock overnight. The animal rests, misses no meals, and appears to get prompt attention on the way. Shorter trips, and those involving through trains only, are less complicated, and if an animal is sent on an early-morning train it usually gets through in reasonable time and without incident.

Dogs use the railways pretty consistently, and as a result there are now several firms and individuals specializing in escorting small animals across London. Their services are invaluable, because it is often when a dog has to change from one terminus to another that it remains forgotten in a parcels office for hours on end. Railway vans maintain a shuttle service from one goods yard to another but for various reasons may ply irregularly, and if a dog just misses one transport it may wait hours before it is taken and put on its next train. The useful people who will meet a dog in London can be contacted through advertisements in dog weeklies, or their addresses are usually obtainable from any breeder of long standing, most people making use of their services at some time or another.

When it is a question of sending an in-season bitch, it is best to arrange the day and train times several days before she is due to go, because all the 'escorts' are very busy and may not be able to help at short notice. Their charges are usually quite reasonable.

Advise the owner of the stud dog that the bitch will be ready on an approximate date, and send a telegram when she is finally dispatched. The person who meets her will not be pleased if she arrives unexpectedly and unheralded, perhaps followed by a letter announcing her arrival the day after she has turned up! Carelessness of this sort not only causes a good deal of inconvenience, but if nobody is expecting her it can mean that the poor bitch is left at the station far longer than she should be.

Put plenty of bedding in the box. Blankets and rugs may get wet and smelly, so clean straw or wood-wool are better. If these become soiled on the way they are easily replaced for the return journey. Attach a minimum of two clearly written labels on the box. One gummed on the top, another tied on with string, is a safe rule. See that each label includes the sender's name and address, also telephone number if available. Do not put meat or bones in the box; the air inside gets warm, food only becomes unwholesome, and the hound rarely eats on the journey anyway. The bitch should be well fed and watered, given a nice run, and will then settle down in the crate and need no further attention until she arrives at her destination. Avoid putting whimsy notes on the box. '*Kind porter, please give me a drink*' will melt any heart but may mean that a well-wisher opens the box on the station and allows the strange and uneasy bitch to rush out and escape.

Do not lock the box and send the key by post. Chances are the box and its contents will arrive well ahead of the key, when the lock will have to be forced or the door removed by its hinges. Far-fetched? Not a bit of it. It has actually happened on several occasions in our own kennel.

As soon as the bitch is mated, the owner of the sire will return her. It is usual to remit the stud fee in advance, and to pay the return carriage. Some railway stations will accept this return fare when the bitch is sent away, putting the stamps for the return journey on the lid. Other stations will not do this, in which case, as soon as the cost of the freight is known it should be added to the remittance.

If it is possible to take the bitch to the sire, then the whole process is simplified, but it becomes even more important to decide upon the right day for the mating, since if the bitch is taken too early she may have to be left and either collected later or sent back unaccom-

Am. Ch. Rozavel Ritter's Sweet Sue

Aust. & Am. Ch. J. Dons Salt of the Earth of Rozavel

Thomas Fall

Ch. Tavernmews Ranter and Ch. Tavernmews Bonnet

Rozavel Beagle puppies

Thomas Fall

Ch. Rozavel Elsy's Diamond Jerry

Rozavel Crystal Gift

Thomas Fall

Aust. Ch. Rosavel Circle the Earth

Ch. Beacott Buckthorn

panied. If she is taken too late—and many people like to put off these journeys until the week-end when it suits them better—then the stallion hound, the bitch, and two owners are in for a disappointment.

There is an idea that it is wise to allow a bitch to remain a day or two before and after service, and that the chances of her conceiving are jeopardized if she is taken home again directly the mating has been accomplished. There is no foundation for this, and many bitches, especially those inclined to fret, are better with their owners than they are spending days in a strange kennel. One thing is thought to be advisable, however, and that is to prevent the bitch from passing water for an hour or so after service.

Another idea, equally misleading, is that a bitch is 'safe' as soon as she has been mated. In fact, she will mate with another dog any time until her heat starts to wane, and she may remain willing and seductive for as much as a week afterwards. She needs to be just as carefully guarded towards the end of her heat as at the beginning. Any time from about the eighteenth day of season onwards, the bitch's external organ will shrink in size and become normal and dry. She will growl and snap if a dog approaches her, and when she bares her teeth at him repeatedly, and he, after a few exploratory sniffs, retires in disgust, the heat is over and she can be exercised with male dogs once more.

Conditions of service are what the stud-dog owner makes them, and there are no standard rules. The stud fee is paid for the act, and not for the result. If a bitch fails to conceive, it is customary to offer a free service at the next heat, but this is a courtesy and not something that can be regarded as a right. Stud-dog owners are always anxious for clients to get good value for the fee paid, and very few would refuse to mate a bitch again, provided the dog was still in their possession.

If a bitch misses twice, however, that is considered to be the end of the matter and the owner would expect to pay a further fee if it was felt that the bitch should be given another chance with the same dog.

The management of a stud dog and his visiting bitches is quite hard work, and a stud fee has usually been well earned when one service has been achieved, let alone by repeated visits from the same bitch.

It is accepted as a fact that a responsibility devolves upon the owner of the stallion to do all that could normally be considered necessary to ensure that his visiting bitches have every chance to prove in whelp. The dog himself should not be overdone and too many bitches should never be accepted for him at any one time. He should be well fed, on a diet containing plenty of meat, and kept in good, hard condition, spotlessly clean and free from parasites.

Nature takes a meddling hand in everything connected with breeding, however, and it is still possible for a bitch to 'miss' and have no puppies even though everything possible has been done to ensure success. Unfortunately it is often difficult to discover the reason, when this does happen. Sometimes there are obvious possibilities. The bitch may have been put to the sire a little too late, or rushed to him rather early, and, although a proper mating and a 'tie' were achieved, it could be that this slight miscalculation resulted in no puppies from the union.

Many indulgent, or lazy, owners let their bitches get too fat, and this is a common source of disappointment at breeding time.

Whatever the reason, nothing can be done until the next season comes round, but at least this can be anticipated and extra care taken to get the bitch into good, hard condition. A vet may suggest giving her some vitamin supplement, wheat-germ oil, iron tonic, or something similar. If a bitch should miss twice running, advice should be sought, and almost certainly, irrespective of any treatment given, she should be tried with a different male. There have been cases where a bitch has proved infertile with one stud and has immediately conceived from a mating with another, even if the first sire is well known as a dependable and prolific producer himself.

There are a good many mysteries connected with animals, both physical and mental, which we cannot fathom. We can only do our utmost, with what knowledge we possess, and hope for the best.

CHAPTER X

GESTATION, WHELPING, AND THE LITTER

Our bitch has been mated, and her season has finished. Now we face the long wait, that tantalizing period until the sixty-third day, when we expect our longed-for litter of Beagles.

For the first month or six weeks we do not give our bitch extra food; we step up her exercise and give her plenty of walks, and take her to open spaces where she can run free. All being well, we expect to notice a slight swelling about her waistline, any time after about the fifth week. This will first be apparent after she has eaten her dinner, when she will look even more rounded than usual. We may suspect that puppies are on the way even earlier, since the bitch may exhibit a change in her behaviour. If ordinarily very lively, she may by a little lazy and sluggish. Normally greedy, a pregnant dam often becomes fanciful and capricious over her food for a few days. Some bitches vomit white froth occasionally, and in the unlikely event of a Beagle being a poor doer, it is a certain sign that she is pregnant if she starts to eat ravenously. These indications may go unnoticed in a pack or a large kennel, but if the bitch lives in the house, and gets a great deal of individual attention, her owner knows her ways so well that the slightest deviation from the norm is suggestive that something is going to happen.

Novice breeders are too much inclined to over-feed the bitch in whelp. Their intentions are excellent, but it is a mistake to let her get too fat. The coming puppies do not strain her resources until the last stages, and it is quite soon enough then to start giving her extras.

The expectant mother should be fed well, just as she has, we hope, been fed throughout the weeks prior to her coming into season. The amount of meat and biscuits she requires depends upon her size and upon the amount of exercise she gets, also on the type of exercise. A bitch taken for walks on a lead does not burn up energy as does the country Beagle who follows her master or mistress when they are exercising their horses.

131

About the fourth week following her visit to the stallion hound, we start putting a heaped teaspoonful of bone flour on the main meal, plus a teaspoonful of Minadex. Not until the seventh week do we increase the ration, and then we gradually double the amount of meat. If the bitch is by now heavy in whelp and very hungry we increase the biscuits as well, but we are not too generous with these since we do not want her to put on a lot of weight.

At the beginning of the eighth week we put her on to two meals a day, adding a breakfast of milk and cereal and, sometimes, a raw egg.

As the bitch increases in size, so we use our common sense as regards her exercising periods. Violent running and galloping probably does her no harm in short bursts, especially if she rushes about of her own volition. No in-whelp bitch should be allowed to run behind horse or cycle, for instance, after she has passed the fourth week of her pregnancy.

Well before the whelping date a suitable place must be prepared, and the bitch should start sleeping in her new bed so that she is settled and happy when the puppies arrive. Any dry, draught-proof room, kennel, or building can be adapted, and if it is well away from other dogs and human passers-by so much the better. A bitch, and especially a maiden, can feel nervous and upset when giving birth, and all bitches seek solitude and quiet. The minority like to have the person they love best beside them when the puppies are born, and they dislike strangers about them at this time.

In spring or summer if the weather is normal a square, box-like bed, raised off the ground, should be cosy. In winter some kind of heating may be required if the room or kennel is not warm, and infra-red lamps suspended over the bed are popular, efficient, and safe when properly fitted. Some breeders prefer to heat the whelping place with tubular electric bars, also perfectly safe, but probably more expensive than the infra-red system both to install and to run.

There may be some readers who believe that artificial heating is unnecessary, and that puppies should be born and reared under more spartan conditions. It is true that hundreds of Beagles are born in bitterly cold weather and are dependent on their dam for warmth; many survive too, but quite a number die, some of which would have been saved with a little added comfort. New-born whelps, however sturdy, rapidly succumb if allowed to become chilled within the first few days after their arrival in such an unhospitable world. Keeping puppies warm for a week is not pampering, for after that the heat, whatever the form, can be gradually turned down or left off for increasing periods until at three-and-a-half or four weeks old the puppies have no artificial heating at all, just their mother and a snug bed.

If puppies are born in cold weather, and are not supplied with some sort of heat, the flat bench-type bed is not suitable. A large box, laid on its side with a board across the front at floor-level to stop puppies or bedding falling out, is better. A clean sack should be tacked over the open front so that it hangs like a curtain. The dam will push it aside when she wants to go in or out and it will enable her to get up a good fug in the box when she curls up with the litter.

If heating is provided every safety precaution *must* be taken. Year after year we hear of tragedies, valuable dogs being lost in kennel fires. Naturally these accidents occur most frequently in winter, and are commonly attributed to oil stoves or to faulty electric wiring.

Electrical appliances should always be installed by a qualified electrician. No 'do it yourself' where these things are concerned, and no help from a well-meaning amateur. Flex should never be loose in the hounds' buildings, but encased in a tough covering and attached to a wall. Infra-red lamps should be of the type known as the 'dull-emitter', and should be suspended at a height of 16 inches or more above the bed. Most makers supply instructions for using their lamps, and suggest a suitable height for use with puppies, pigs, chicks, and so on.

Oil stoves invariably carry some risk, however small, and however carefully they are sited. They can be upset, and most types can flare up, especially if a sudden draught hits them. A kennel containing a bitch and puppies was totally destroyed because the owner, with great care, placed the oil stove on a table in the corner of the hut. It was well off the ground, the bitch could not reach it to knock it over, but it was not realized how much heat came out of the top, and that it was dangerously close to the wooden roof.

A bitch senses that her time is near, and becomes restless. She will walk on to her bed and walk off again, go to the door, back to the bed, whining and gazing up enquiringly at her owner. Sometimes she will scratch the bedding into heaps. At such a time the straw or wood-wool should be removed, and a clean sack tacked down so that puppies cannot wriggle underneath and get squashed. Or news-papers may be given, but the tearing-up process that goes on makes the place very untidy, and once the messy process of the birth is under way paper gets very soggy.

The fidgeting and bed-making can continue for an hour or even for a day or a night, but in due course the bitch will lie down and pant. Then she will be seen to strain, grunt, and heave. More time goes by, but within an hour or two there should be a 'plop', and the first puppy will appear. Frantic licking, nibbling, and sucking noises indicate that the mother knows what to do next. She is tearing and chewing the afterbirth or placenta, severing the umbilical cord, and cleaning up the slimy little baby. The bitch will eat the afterbirth. At one time there was a belief that she should be prevented from doing so, but no harm ever results and it is surely going against nature to stop something which is clearly prompted by so strong a natural instinct.

The puppy will soon be squawking and 'swimming' about the box, nuzzling at its mother and looking for a teat. It tries and rejects them, but finally finds one to its liking, then sucks away lustily as the sweet warm milk comes down in response to the stimulation its efforts have given.

Soon there is further straining and heaving, and the next puppy is out in the world. The intervals between the births can vary from a few minutes to a few hours. Up to two or two-and-a-half hours between puppies is common and normal, but if a bitch strains for longer she may need some help to deliver a puppy, and she must have it before she is allowed to become exhausted.

The normal puppy is presented head first, the little front feet extended, for all the world as though the little creature is taking a high dive into the exciting new world that awaits it. Sometimes, however, a puppy comes down the vaginal passage the wrong way round, tail first. This is known as a 'breach' presentation. With luck a bitch may be able to give birth to such a puppy unaided, but it is harder for her than if it had arrived the correct way, and she may need some assistance. This should not be too long delayed, since the puppy may die if it remains wedged for long, and the puppies behind it might be lost as well.

Experienced breeders are generally quite capable of extracting a breach-born puppy, but the novice breeder would be well advised to let a vet show them what to do. A well-scrubbed finger is inserted in the vagina, and, if the puppy is presented, a foot or tail can generally be felt. Very gentle pressure can sometimes bring the legs sufficiently far down to enable them to be gripped between finger and thumb, using a scrap of clean towelling, for they are too slippery to hold otherwise. Pulling gently but firmly, with a downward motion, and easing the puppy first on one side then on another, the tension is timed to coincide with the mother's straining effort. As the puppy emerges, so it should be possible to grasp it round its body and thus to help it slide gently out. The whole process is a strenuous one for the puppy, and it is a tough way to arrive. Many breach whelps emerge blue in the face and almost lifeless. There is not a moment to waste. Seize a towel and rub the puppy hard, especially about the chest and back. Then try mouth-to-mouth breathing. To do this press the little jaws open and, using a finger, depress the curved pink tongue which is probably stuck to the roof of the mouth. Then blow hard down the puppy's throat. Bubbles may pop out of its nose, but keep on blowing. Then rub the little body again, and try artificial respiration. Press the sides of the chest together slowly and rhythmically. In . . . out, in . . . out, in . . . out. Keep trying one method after another and do not give up for a quarter of an hour. You may be rewarded by the puppy, apparently dead, suddenly giving a gasp, followed by a feeble squeak. The squeaks become louder and more vigorous, and the little legs start to wave. As the rubbing continues the clammy little body gets dry and grows warmer and the battle is won.

A puppy resuscitated by these means must be kept very warm. It is best not to let it go back to the mother until she has finished whelping, but to place it in a cardboard box by the stove, well wrapped in a piece of soft blanket. Later it can go back with the rest of the litter and be encouraged to suck.

Some puppies are slow about learning to feed, and can be helped in this way: Hold the puppy in the right hand, and with the left finger and thumb press a teat into the little mouth, supporting the puppy until it starts swallowing. It may turn its head and lose its grip, and if so it must be gently replaced until it hangs on. This all requires much patience, but may mean all the difference between a thriving puppy and one that gradually fades away and dies.

Once the puppies are all born the mother can be persuaded to go out for a run, staying away just long enough to make herself comfortable. She can be offered a bowl of milky gruel, and then settled down with her family. The following day she can be given her ordinary food, plus the extras she has been receiving throughout the last days of her pregnancy. If the litter is a large one—more than five or six whelps—the quantities of meat and milk must be gradually stepped up to enable the dam to feed them well without getting thin and debilitated herself.

Up to this point we have assumed that the puppies have all been born without undue difficulty, except, perhaps, for the momentary anxiety caused by the tail-first fellow which held up the proceedings but which eventually got itself born without too much trouble. There is no reason why a Beagle bitch should not whelp easily and naturally, but complications sometimes occur whatever the breed, and one must be prepared to deal with these even though all may go well.

If the bitch strains for more than three hours without having a puppy, the novice is advised to call the vet. Directly he is summoned a kettle of water should be put to boil, and one or two small enamel bowls, cotton wool, Dettol, carbolic soap, and a couple of clean towels kept handy. A big, scrupulously clean pan or wide, flat dish may be required if the vet decides to use forceps. He will bring his instruments with him but may want to boil them before they are used.

After examining the bitch he may decide to give her an injection of pituitary extract. This works with incredible rapidity, causing the womb to contract within a few minutes of the injection. The effect of the contractions is to expel the puppy or at least to urge it down the vaginal passage. The recommended dose for a Beagle is 1 c.c., and with ordinary luck this will result in a puppy being born without further trouble. Never leave the bitch unattended after a pituitrin injection. The puppy may be half ejected, and unless helped out will suffocate and die; this is likely to happen if it is especially large, the bitch being unable to expel it without aid. If the vet is present he will cope with it, but sometimes a busy practitioner is forced to give the injection and to hurry away to another case, leaving the owner to carry on, the vet calling in on his way back to see how matters are getting along.

In a very small percentage of cases the pituitrin may fail. Even if the puppy is presented in the passage, the vet may be reluctant to try to remove it with instruments, since it is so difficult not to injure the puppy, and great skill is required lest the bitch herself be torn and damaged. The only course left will be a Caesarian operation, and, assuming that this is decided upon before the bitch is worn out, the prospects of 100 per cent success are very good indeed.

Thirty years ago, before we had antibiotics and the wider understanding of the administration and use of anaesthetics, a Caesarian section was undertaken only as a last, desperate resort. Mortality of dam and puppies was, unfortunately, high. Modern breeders are much blessed, for nowadays the picture is very different. As a rule, it is perfectly straightforward. The bitch and her live puppies can be collected from the canine surgery a couple of hours or so after the operation, and although the bitch will require careful nursing for the next forty-eight hours, the prognosis is excellent. Mother and puppies must be kept very warm, and a couple of hot-water bottles and several blankets must be ready when they are to be taken home. Keep them indoors, because it will be a little while before the bitch is completely round after the anaesthetic, and she will want watching until she is quite conscious and has accepted her family.

As soon as possible the puppies must be put to their mother and got sucking, and they are almost sure to be shouting for food when they are fetched from the vet's surgery. The bitch is usually milking normally, but occasionally there is a delay of up to two days before the milk-flow begins. During that time the puppies must be fed by hand, kept very warm, and held on to the mother's teats several times a day in order to stimulate and encourage the secretion of milk.

It is not wise to leave the whelps with the bitch while she is wholly or semi-unconscious. She does not know what she is doing at such a time, and may throw herself about and lie on her puppies. A bitch used to puppies generally loves her new family from the moment she has possession of her senses again, but if a maiden bitch happens to undergo a Caesarian before she has ever produced a puppy naturally, it may be a different story. She recovers, dazed, from the anaesthetic, her tummy feeling a little bit sore, and she may possibly feel sick as well. All around her are peculiar little animals, noisy and wriggling all over her bed. They try to suck, and she recoils in disgust. What are they? She has no recollection of having had them, and if she could talk she would surely say: 'What revolting things—take them away! They are nothing to do with me!' She may not only refuse to let the 'objects' suck, but she may turn on them and snap or bite. Great care is required, in such a case, to get her to accept the tinies.

An assistant is needed, and it should be somebody well known to the bitch, who is undergoing considerable mental stress at this time. She needs to feel that she is surrounded by people she loves and trusts. One person must hold her down firmly, while the other helper adjusts one or two puppies on the teats. When they have fed to completion they can be removed and kept warm in a separate box. It is quite easy to tell when very young puppies have had a good feed—you can almost watch their tummies getting rounder and full.

After being forced to feed the puppies in this manner, even by compulsion, most bitches start to take an interest in them. Unless they are thoroughly bad mothers—and the bad mother is indeed a rarity within the Beagle breed—they will start to push the puppies about, and finally to wash and lick them. Once a bitch licks the puppies success is assured. Sympathetic, patient handling in a crisis of this description will usually bring good results.

We have gone to some pains to help the novice to be well equipped to cope with the situation if things go wrong, but we would not like to suggest that complications need be expected. Caesarian operations are not unusual in these modern times, and the very fact that the possibility of failure is so negligible is perhaps a reason why they are performed more frequently than was the case before World War II. They were probably required as often, but as success was so uncertain, veterinary surgeons usually resorted to instruments in an effort to avoid an operation which was regarded as a last resort to save the life of a bitch. Any breed can require a Caesarian, for a variety of reasons. A puppy may be misplaced, i.e. laid sideways instead of head or feet first. It can be extra large and thus get itself jammed on the way down. Sometimes one puppy, for some inexplicable reason, is dead, and this can become stuck and prevent the live whelps behind it from being born. A bitch due to give birth to a large litter can suffer from inertia—the distension causing her muscles to give up contracting—and if she cannot strain she cannot have her whelps without help.

Any of these things can happen even in a hound breed which normally whelps easily. Although there is no reason to look for trouble, one must be prepared to deal with it if it comes.

If a bitch has had a Caesarian the question of breeding from her again is bound to arise. The vet can be of help here, since he can explain the reason for the complications. For instance, if it was all caused by one dead or misplaced puppy this may just have been bad luck, and there would appear to be no reason at all why the bitch should not whelp easily and naturally another time. If the trouble was caused by something like a narrow pelvis, however, then there is a likelihood that the bitch is never going to produce her puppies normally.

A bitch can have more than one Caesarian operation. In fact, up to six such operations have been performed on some of the breeds notorious for their difficulties at whelping times. Most vets prefer not to do more than three on a bitch.

Beagles are ordinarily so straightforward to breed from that it is doubtful if it is worth while attempting to produce puppies from a bitch whose chances of whelping naturally are considered to be poor, and unless it is a very valuable bitch, and/or one whose bloodlines must be perpetuated, it would be best to consider her a pet and not a brood. This is not because a Caesarian section is in any way 'cruel'. Once a bitch is completely round from the anaesthetic she appears to suffer no ill effects, and is usually trotting about happily, enjoying her food, and taking care of her litter with an apparent freedom from discomfort. The stitches are removed by the vet at about the four-teenth day following the operation, and that is all there is to it. One thing can be categorically stated—a bitch that undergoes a 'Caesar' receives infinitely more consideration than one that has to suffer a forceps delivery, which must cause her great pain, distress, and apprehension.

If a Caesarian does not inconvenience the bitch it does, however, cause considerable wear and tear on the breeder, and more expense. The surgeon's fee for such an operation varies, but may cost as much as 20 guineas. If the 'Caesar' has been performed in good time, and there are live puppies as a result, it may not be quite so bad, but many an owner has had to meet a heavy bill and had no puppies at all, even though the bitch herself has come through with flying colours. But, as we have said, there are many reasons why an opera-tion could be required, and plenty of bitches whelp naturally on every subsequent occasion. Therefore it is usually wise to give a good bitch another chance. Then if she still fails to whelp naturally the question of retiring her should be seriously considered. When there are plenty of easy whelpers within the breed there does not seem much point in going to so much worry and expense over one that needs surgical help.

If the puppies are contented and feeding well, the dew-claws should be removed about the fourth day. Their needle-like toenails can also be trimmed at the same time, and they should receive atten-tion at intervals because if allowed to grow long and sharp they scratch the poor bitch and make her breasts raw.

The dew-claws are the extra toes on the inside of the front legs, a short distance above the toes. All dogs are born with front dew-claws; a few of them on the hind legs also. The latter must be taken off a Beagle, the front claws being optional, but all are better gone. They catch as a dog runs, tear, get sore and septic, and are a constant bother. Hounds, especially, are inclined to tear them on hard, ploughed ground or when running through woods, etc. They are easily cut with blunt curved scissors (sharp scissors cause excessive bleeding). Dig down deep before snipping them off, so that the roots are removed, otherwise they grow again. Dab with permanganate of potash crystals, which stops haemorrhage instantly. The tiny wounds heal rapidly, helped by the dam who keeps them clean by licking.

This is all that need be done to the Beagle puppy. He is a natural little creature, and carries his expressive stern just as nature made it—no fancy docking for him.

The puppies should increase in size and weight, and will thrive on the mother's milk. The number of whelps she can take care of depends upon her own size—five or six are quite enough for a 12-inch dam. A larger bitch needs to be exceptionally well fed to make a good job of rearing more than seven or eight, and even then early weaning is advisable. If a bitch has a very large litter, more, it is thought, than she can manage, some must either be put to sleep at birth or must be taken from her and adopted by a foster-mother or reared by hand.

As the puppies begin to toddle about the whelping box and to start exploring their kennel, so they begin to take an interest in their mother's dish. This is the time when they can start lapping milk and taking very small quantities of scraped raw meat. Scraped raw meat is prepared by taking a sizable chunk of fresh raw beef in the left hand and scraping it with a sharp carving-knife, starting at the end nearest you and moving the knife away from you.

Quantities are gradually increased until the puppies are being fed on the lines suggested in Chapter VI.

Between six and eight weeks of age the puppies should be dosed for worms. Most puppies suffer from these parasites to some degree, but if cleansed internally at six and eight weeks they should remain clear for a few months before they require further treatment. Modern vermifuges are very good. They do not upset the dogs, nor are they dangerous, and they do produce results. Most of them are given following a light meal—a far cry from the old days when the worm-cures necessitated a long fast which often had a debilitating effect on a puppy. In fact, one early dog book advised a mixture of powdered glass and turpentine as worm medicine! No wonder so many dogs died, probably more from the treatment than from the worms.

By this time the bitch will be getting rather tired of her maternal duties. She will gradually spend less time with the puppies, and by the time they are six weeks old she can stop away from them all day, returning to them at night for a further fortnight, when she can leave them for good. By this time they should be quite independent of 'Mum', and she can be bathed and given normal diet and exercise to get her back into show condition again as soon as possible.

Should she be mated again at her subsequent heat, or allowed to miss, and mated in twelve months' time? If she has been properly cared for throughout the process of producing and nurturing her litter she should not have suffered in health, and there is no reason why she should not be mated again in a few months, so long as she will be equally well fed and looked after. If she has had a complicated parturition, or a Caesarian, if she has reared a large litter, and if she leaves her puppies looking lean and run down, she should definitely have a year's rest before motherhood is again imposed on her.

Some breeders make a rule of mating a bitch twice running, and then missing her the third time, then twice running again, and in normal circumstances this probably works quite well. A few bitches incline to become very fat after having had a litter, and this should be checked by a reduction in diet and an increase in exercise. In extreme cases it may even be necessary to give really drastic slimming treatment, for, if neglected, the longer a bitch stays over-weight the harder it seems to be to reduce her to normal size.

When the puppies are eight weeks old some of them will doubtless have already been sold, but if any are retained the question of inoculations must be considered. At three months old they can have one injection which protects them against distemper, hard-pad, hepatitis, and leptospirosis. These terrible scourges are much less common at the present time not because they have in any way de-creased in severity, but because so many owners take advantage of the modern 'shots' and have their dogs immunized. If people slackened their efforts to get their dogs 'plus-injected' in puppyhood, these plagues would undoubtedly become endemic again, and nobody's pets would be safe.

It seems, therefore, that we have a moral responsibility to give our dogs this protection against the prevalent virus diseases. Instant immunity is not conferred upon the puppy as the needle penetrates the skin. Opinions vary as to the length of time required to build up a resistance. Some veterinary experts believe that a puppy has immunity two weeks after injection; others think a month is a safer estimate. Because of this a puppy should always be immunized at least a fortnight before it is taken out on the street, or into strange kennels, or anywhere where it is likely to be among other dogs.

Another point that is not unanimously agreed upon is whether or not the injections confer lifelong immunity. In many cases it seems certain that they do, in others the results have been less encouraging. It is best to discuss this point with the vet and to act on his advice. If necessary, have dogs re-inoculated regularly during their lifetimes.

We have mentioned Miss Juliette de Bairacli Levy's herbal treatments in Chapter VI, and she also has a plan which is designed to prevent distemper and hard-pad, or to cure. It is only fair to say that the experiences of other people with these methods do not invariably tally where the virus diseases are concerned, though almost everybody has had very good results with herbal medicines when other complaints have been thus treated.

Our own view is that inoculations give adequate protection, and in our own kennel we have never had any ill effects on the hundreds of dogs so treated. We do not hesitate to recommend them. It is a sad and very well-known fact that heavy losses occurred among pack hounds, as well as in kennels, before the egg-adapted vaccines were discovered. Even if the cost of the injections is not inconsiderable, at least it is as nothing to the veterinary surgeon's bills that can mount up if a hound frequently becomes ill, not to mention the fact that one often has the account to pay and a dead dog as well. And, of course, a broken heart.

Before closing this chapter we must offer some advice to the owner whose bitch has whelped live puppies but is unable to feed them. This is a worrying but very rare occurrence. It may happen because the dam dies during or shortly after whelping; or, if a bitch has had a Caesarian operation, her milk may not come down for a day or two, and until it does the puppies must be nourished somehow; or a bitch's milk may go wrong or dry up. Whatever the cause, if the dam cannot feed her whelps they must either be given to a foster-mother or reared by hand.

The foster-mother is by far the best of the alternatives, but it is not always easy to find a bitch that has whelped at about the same time as the mother of the puppies, or, if such a bitch is available, one that is not already fully encumbered with a large litter of her own.

Foster-mothers are occasionally advertised for sale or hire in the dog weeklies; possibly your vet may know if a suitable bitch is to be found within his practice. Other breeders, especially those who keep large kennels, will readily sympathize and co-operate if at all possible.

If a 'foster' is found, the following method of persuading her to take the 'orphans' is advised. Remove the foster-mother from her own whelps, and put the new babies in the bed among them, rubbing the two families together. Then let the bitch come back to her kennel, and as soon as she lies down in her nest offer her a drink of milk. She will slop some of the milk as she laps, and drops will fall on the puppies. Between gulps she will turn to lick the whelps dry, and in her haste she may not notice that some of them are inter-lopers. Once she has washed them and allowed them to suck, she had adopted them. If, however, the hair along her back rises, if she shrinks from the new puppies or growls at them, never leave her alone with them or she may harm them. Soothe her, divert her attention as they suck, at the same time holding her by her collar so that she cannot whip round on the litter, and with any luck she will accept them in time.

If the puppies have to be fed by hand it is likely to be a long, tiring process which will require great care and devotion, endless patience, and rigid adherence to the set programme. For the first few hours following their birth, the best supplement for the puppies is tepid boiled water containing a little glucose. This is best fed from a pipette, fountain-pen filler, eye-dropper, or one of the Bellcroy baby feeders, the latter being particularly useful if the puppies are normally strong and able to suck.

If the dam is available and not ill, but for some reason unable to give her puppies milk, they should still be put to her at regular intervals to encourage her milk to come down, and also in order that she should not become disinterested in the puppies until such time as, it is hoped, she can look after them herself.

If the bitch is able to lick and cuddle her puppies they are best left with her in her bed. If she is not available or is unwell they should be placed in a box with a hot-water bottle, taking care to cover the bottle—and its metal stopper—with thick blanket or towelling. Put the puppies in a cosy place by the stove or near the fire, or site them beneath an infra-red lamp. Keep them away from draughts, and out of reach of other animals.

Various formulas have been used successfully for rearing puppies by hand. One of these is Benger's Food, made according to the instructions on the tin. Full-cream dried milk, fresh cow's milk, fresh goat's milk, and canned condensed milk are all suitable, with certain additions and/or modifications. What has to be remembered is that the milk of the bitch is so much richer than the milk of the cow. Goat's milk is much closer to it, and when available is very good for dogs.

An extremely good mixture has been devised and used with considerable success by Mrs M. Rider, of the 'Rowley' prefix. With her method she has not only reared a Champion Alsatian from birth, but also a complete litter of seven tiny Chihuahuas. She has kindly given me permission to publish her formula, and she gives the following instructions, advice, and account of her own experiences:

'My only worry was finding a suitable feeder. A fountain-pen filler was, I found, easiest, but the end was hard to the mouth so I pulled a piece of bicycle valve-rubber over the mouthpiece. This served admirably and the puppies took to it happily after a few tries.

'Now for the actual food; it must be remembered that bitches' milk is much stronger than ordinary cow's milk, and should be mixed accordingly. I commenced with this mixture:

To $\frac{1}{4}$ pint of Grade-A Jersey milk I added 1 teaspoonful of cream, 1 teaspoonful of dried full-cream milk powder (well mixed), 1 teaspoonful of glucose, 1 drop of Radiostol, $\frac{1}{2}$ teaspoonful of Woodward's Gripe Water, half a crushed tablet of Howard's Sodium Citrate, all mixed and heated to a temperature of 38°C (100°F)—the normal blood-heat of the dam.

'This formula was fed at the rate of one fountain-pen fillerfull to each puppy every two hours, night and day, increasing the quantity as the puppies demanded. Usually at a week old they were taking two pen-fillers full at each feed, but to the inexperienced—make haste slowly. Feed very, very carefully, and let the puppy take its time and get the taste of the food, thus avoiding indigestion and wind. The puppies must, of course, be kept very warm all the time.

'Next comes the job of "topping and tailing". As you probably know, the mother normally cleans the puppies up as they feed, so a supply of cotton wool, a bowl of warm water, and a jar of Vaseline must be at hand. Firstly, with a piece of damp cotton wool, clean round the puppy's mouth, removing any food which may have spilled. Then gently smooth the puppy from tail towards the tummy to encourage and assist the puppy to pass water and excreta. Afterwards clean and dry, finishing off with a smear of Vaseline to prevent chafing.

'The two-hourly rota continues for about ten days, when the puppies will be taking more food, and the time between feeds can be extended to three hours, and so on, until they start to lap. As soon as this happens night feeds can be suspended and only day feeds continued, as necessary and until the little orphans feed well and are able to consume scraped raw beef. Food must, of course, be available for them to seek out during the night, once they can lap and hand feeding has been discontinued. At this stage cereals such as Farex can be added to the milk. I did not find raw egg a suitable diet for the very young, but I did add beaten egg to the milk to be consumed by the puppies when they were about four to six weeks old.'

The quantities stated above were for a small toy breed. Beagle puppies would take several pen-fillersful for a feed, and would need the quantity increased as they developed. Unless the Beagles were premature or delicate, the pen-filler might not be required after the first twenty-four hours, since normally strong puppies would suck lustily at a Bellcroy feeder or an ordinary baby's bottle with teat and valve.

The 'topping and tailing' need not be done if the dam is able to lick her puppies—but somebody has to do it, for it is as essential to the puppies as the feeding. They cannot pass water or motions without gentle massage, and will die if they are not assisted.

It can be seen from Mrs Rider's programme that the hand-rearing of puppies is time-absorbing, tiring, and a great tie. It is also very rewarding, however, though many people lack the patience and energy to carry the process through to a successful conclusion, involving as it does so many sleepless nights and disorganized days. But it is rewarding when a bonny litter of puppies are playing about, and you know that but for your devotion and care they would certainly have died.

There are just one or two other things to bear in mind. It cannot, for instance, be too strongly emphasized that any milk mixture fed to puppies must be absolutely fresh. A suitable quantity to cover a couple of feeds can be mixed and put in the refrigerator until needed, but ideally it should be made up fresh for each feed. The mixture must be carefully warmed. All utensils, feeders, bottles, should be sterilized, by boiling, between meals, and kept beneath an upturned basin or protected in some other way from germs and dust.

For the two-hourly interruptions through the night it is suggested that the task may be made less onerous by having a thermos flask, or one of the new gadgets designed to keep babies' bottles warm. Sufficient mixture can be prepared to last until morning; if too hot, it can be cooled easily enough, but in the middle of the night it is more than trying to have to pad round the house in dressing-gown and slippers, heating up milk on a stove.

If the rearing is a family responsibility it naturally makes the position much easier. If one person stays up until say 4 a.m., and then somebody else takes over while the other gets some sleep, the two can change shifts the next night and it becomes very much less exhausting. But sometimes no help is available, and then there is only one thing to be done: to nod off in an armchair beside the fire, confident that the puppies on their hot-water bottle will soon start to shout when a meal is due. Or set the alarm clock for regular two- or three-hourly intervals.

Hand-reared puppies are always full of character, and they never fail to have outstanding personalities. They have received so much contact with human hands, have had such devotion and attention bestowed on them from the start, and this all seems to stimulate their intelligence.

But of course it is not always necessary to take the puppies away from the mother for good. Sometimes her inability to feed them is only temporary, and soon she is able and willing to take back her babies and to rear them herself. Provided they have been kept warm and have been carefully fed the transition should not upset normal strong whelps, and they should go on well. For, after all, their own mother is better equipped to look after them than anybody else.

It is not often that things go so badly wrong at whelping time, but that is no reason for ignoring the fact that these situations can and do arrive—always unexpectedly—on occasions. When there are puppies to hand-rear the situation is urgent and critical; two or three hours' neglect and they will never recover their lost strength. For this reason it is as well to know what to do, for when prepared there is no reason why the puppies should not survive the crisis and grow up strong and healthy.

CHAPTER XI

EQUIPMENT AND HOUSING

PACKS of hounds are often accommodated in stables, loose-boxes, or coach houses adapted for the purpose, but sometimes in specially built kennels, usually constructed of brick or stone, and almost always with paved or concreted yards attached. Beagles kept primarily for show and breeding live happily under any of the conditions suitable for prize dogs of any breed of comparable size.

For many of us the choice of accommodation for our Beagles is limited. We may be lucky enough to have good buildings adjacent to our homes, already available and easily adapted for our requirements, or we may need to build kennels or to buy sectional wooden kennels, or huts that can be partitioned. Present-day prices of bricks and stone blocks have put these useful materials in the luxury class, and even their close imitations—the not-to-be-despised concrete and breeze blocks—are not exactly inexpensive.

From the aesthetic angle some materials are more attractive than others, but from the hound's point of view the material from which the house is built is not of great consequence, provided the finished building is draught-proof and damp-proof.

Wooden kennels need a certain amount of maintenance. The exterior calls for applications of creosote about every twelve months, and the interior will need a coat of white or cream distemper or water-paint about every six months. Wood, even if well seasoned, tends to warp, and this means that doors may jam in the wet weather and shrink when it is hot and dry. This also applies to other joints and the places where the walls meet the roof. Ready-made kennels usually bolt together, which is an advantage if one wants to move them at any time, though they seldom go up well a second or third time, and there are sure to be draughty gaps and sections that never fit very well again.

Most kennels made of wood also have wooden floors, since if

made to stand on cement it always seems impossible to prevent the rain seeping in and making the place damp. The two worst draw-backs to wooden kennels are that they are vulnerable to chewing, and that the floors, though warm, are difficult to keep really clean. The doors and all projecting boards or battens should be covered with sheet metal or sheet asbestos—we prefer the former. This prevents a bored or mischievous hound tearing the interior to pieces, and is particularly important if visiting bitches or other boarders are to be accommodated. Restless, ill at ease, anxious to break out and make for home, such animals can do a lot of damage in a remarkably short space of time.

If the floorboards, when new, can be treated with a couple of coats of marine varnish, this goes a long way towards keeping it sanitary, for urine does not soak into the wood and can be mopped up easily on the glossy surface. Marine varnish is expensive however, and needs renewing from time to time, the frequency depending upon the wear and tear it receives in the kennel. Many owners prefer to use fresh sawdust. This is a great help in keeping the floor clean. Waste matter can be removed with a handbrush and shovel, and carried, in a bucket kept for this purpose alone, to the incinerator or bonfire. The floor should be swept clean of sawdust every morn-ing, and fresh sawdust sprinkled. It should also be well scrubbed with hot water and soap, once or twice a week being often enough when adult dogs are housed, three times a week to keep puppies really clean and sweet-smelling.

One insuperable trouble is that the floorboards invariably develop small cracks, and the sawdust sifts between them and collects in a dank, smelly mass under the kennel. If the kennel is raised up on bricks or brick piles it may be possible to rake out the stuff from time to time, but there are disadvantages in having kennels raised too high, though they must always have plenty of air-space beneath them and must not be pitched so low that rats can gather and breed under the floors and be hard to dislodge and discourage.

Unless kept very clean, wooden floors can become saturated with urine and very smelly and disagreeable indeed. Fleas will breed in cracks in the wood, so the importance of keeping boards scrubbed and well aired cannot be over-emphasized.

Attention to hygiene is essential whatever the type of building, but it is doubly important when wooden kennels are involved. A high standard of cleanliness can be, and often is, achieved, as evinced by the popularity of wooden kennelling and the obvious good health of the dogs housed therein. But this standard is maintained only by plenty of hard work and vigilance on the part of the owners and their assistants, and by no shortage of that invaluable aid known as 'elbow grease'.

It would be wrong to suggest that the other types of houses do not have faults, None is perfect. Kennels built of bricks, of breeze or concrete blocks, are solid and permanent; they are also fireproof and chew-proof—the last-named being one of their greatest assets. True, the wooden doors need to be metal-lined, but the solid floors are comparatively easy to clean. They can often be swilled down with water and mild disinfectant, though in damp weather they are slow to dry out.

The most commonly voiced objection to this type of building is that they are cold, and it is true that this is often the case. Where floors are concerned, much research has been done in recent years to discover methods of making concrete warmer for animals to lie upon, in particular for cowsheds and piggeries. It is now possible, for example, to put concrete down on layers of air-bricks, which constitute a considerable improvement, and anybody planning a range of kennels with cement floors would do well to discuss the matter with one of the firms specializing in farm buildings.

If dogs are to be housed on concrete, wooden sleeping benches are a 'must'. The size naturally depends upon the number of animals that will be required to share the kennel, and, of course, the size of the occupants has some bearing on this, too.

It is surprising how many Beagles of the smaller type can curl up together in a bed three or four feet square. A bench of this size should be raised on legs a few inches high, and should be surrounded with a ridge at least 6 inches deep, to stop the bedding from falling out. While owners of many breeds of dogs find that it is only practicable to kennel one dog with one bitch, owners of Beagles discover what good mixers they are. It is rare to find a discordant personality within this even-tempered breed, and a number can live together in harmony. Naturally a roomy kennel is needed if several live together. After all, we must remember that these benevolent little hounds have had the community spirit bred into them—they have lived in packs for many generations, so it is scarcely surprising that they get on so well with one another. Because of this agreeable characteristic, a beginner planning accommodation for Beagles is likely to find it best to provide a few large kennels rather than a lot of small individual pens.

If farm or stable buildings are available, they can be converted to provide very convenient and easily worked homes for the hounds. Loose-boxes, if not too dark, are almost ready-made kennels. Stalls have sturdy partitions in between and need only fronts with doors, and these can be constructed of iron bars or of weldmesh, even of heavy-gauge chain-link wire.

We all have a 'kennel-in-the-air' (the dog enthusiast's version of the castle!) which we would provide for our pets if we won the football pools or even struck a lucky number with a premium bond. This dream cannot often be achieved if existing buildings have to be adapted, and we can only do the best we can with them.

The fortunate few who can start from scratch, building a range of kennelling to their own or some expert's design, are much to be envied, for however modest the scheme may be, a substantial capital sum will be involved.

There is much to commend kennels that are built side by side, with a corridor into which all the sections open out. This appeals to the attendant, who does much of the work under cover, and anybody who has worked in this type of building and also cared for dogs kept in separate kennels knows how convenient the former layout can be.

It is possible for each kennel within a range to have its separate run, but for Beagles one larger run to every two or three sections is adequate. Sometimes only two large yards are made available for the adults, one for the dogs and the other for the bitches. But ideally there should be one or two runs for puppies and at least one or two attached to isolation kennels, so that bitches in season, or any hound that appears unwell, can be segregated.

A special kitchen, exclusively for the hounds, is essential if many are kept. Naturally, where there are only two or three house pets, it is different, but the preparation of dog food in large quantities is invariably a messy business. The lady of the house is not likely to enjoy the canine *cordon bleu* in her own kitchenette, creating havoc involving stove, sink, and table, even if she makes the muddle herself and still less if it is done by somebody else.

The building set aside for use as a kennel kitchen need not be large. A floor space of 12 feet by 12 feet will do very well. First essential is a large, strong table. Big, old-fashioned kitchen tables have been displaced by the neat little plastic-topped numbers, and because enormous kitchens are no more, the tables they contained can often be picked up quite cheaply in junk shops or at sales. Get a sheet of aluminium cut exactly to fit the table-top, and screw it down tightly. This saves daily scrubbing, for it can be wiped over with a damp cloth. A board will be needed upon which to cut meat, however.

One or two sound corn-bins or clean dustbins with well-fitting, mouse-proof lids are required, to contain biscuits and hound meal, etc. If there is room for a cupboard it will keep the dishes and cutlery tidy, otherwise one or two shelves will do instead.

A refrigerator especially for the hounds' meat and milk sounds an extravagant luxury, but in fact it probably pays for itself in a short time, apart from the fact that fresh food is so much more pleasant to handle. Kennel meat-supplies are all too often irregular, particularly in the summer months. Quality is variable and meat is frequently tainted when delivered, and if exposed to warm air and flies develops a horrible smell within hours. In a refrigerator it will keep for days. At the time of writing, commercial-sized refrigerators do not carry purchase tax, and it is also possible to obtain these large-sized cabinets second-hand at fairly reasonable prices. The best of these are models discarded because the exterior is shabby or chipped, but mechanically sound. We bought such a refrigerator for £50 seven years ago, and it has proved an absolute boon. Naturally we have it serviced regularly by a local expert.

Some kennels, especially those with a fluctuating dog population, have invested in deep-freeze units. While there is a limit to the length of time food keeps fresh at ordinary refrigerator temperature, meat placed in a deep-freeze will keep indefinitely provided it is in perfect condition when stored. It is not likely to be retained for any length of time, of course, but it does mean that supplies for an emergency can be kept for a long period and there is never any risk of running out of food for the kennel inmates.

It is as well to remember that chilled or frozen food should always be thoroughly thawed out before being fed to dogs. Also that deep-frozen meat, or any other foodstuff for that matter, when once thawed should not be re-frozen, unless it has been well cooked in the meantime. Neglect of these principles can mean stomach upsets for the hounds.

A mincer is almost an essential in a busy kennel. Virtually no hand-operated mincers deal efficiently with the type of meat usually supplied to kennels, though they mince boiled paunch well. The large commercial-type electric mincers, as supplied to butchers, do a wonderful job. Unfortunately they are rather expensive, but if carefully handled and serviced once or twice a year they have a long life. If there are many young puppies to feed it is hardly an exaggeration to say that an electric mincer does the work of one kennelmaid.

Like refrigerators and deep-freeze cabinets, electric mincers can be bought second-hand, but care should be exercised to ensure that these machines are not up for sale because they are damaged or worn. They come on to the market in good condition if their owners have decided to exchange them for newer models, for instance, and can give years of service to the next buyer. Unless the price asked is so low as to make the appliance a worthwhile gamble, or unless the buyer has sufficient technical knowledge to make a proper examination before purchase, it is wise to get an expert to express an opinion as to the condition and probable value.

A method of cooking meat for the hounds will have to be decided upon. Even if it is planned to feed raw meat, it will be necessary to boil flesh to make a broth to be used in soaking biscuit meal or oatmeal or maize for 'pudding'. For the larger kennels, boilers of the type used to cook potatoes or swill in large quantities to feed to pigs are best. The ordinary boilers burn solid fuels or wood, and they certainly cook the food, but they need recurrent attention to re-fuel and rake ashes, and they are rather dusty and dirty. They give off a quantity of steam, so are best sited out of doors or under a lean-to shelter.

Similar boilers or steamers operated by electricity are efficient and comparatively labour-saving, but cost rather a lot to buy and are not particularly economical to run. Some kennelowners manage very well with an ordinary domestic boiler of the type used for household laundry. These can be heated by gas or electricity, and are more economical if filled with hot water from the tap rather than with cold that has to be warmed up to boiling point in the boiler itself. Some kind of wire-mesh grid is almost essential as a modification fitted at the bottom of the container, otherwise the meat sticks to the metal and burns.

Naturally, cooking for the smaller kennel is easily done in a large billy-can on a gas-ring. Bottled gas is obtainable everywhere and is used in many kennel kitchens. The cylinders are easily replaced, and the larger size lasts a breeder with about forty hounds a whole month. The cost is not high.

A good deep sink, with running water, is more than useful. Not only does it enable the dishes to be washed up speedily and on the spot, but if large enough it serves as a bath for the Beagles.

It is not always possible to arrange for a supply of constant hot water to the dogs' kitchen, especially if the room is located at a distance from the house. There are gas and electric water-heaters in many and varied shapes and sizes, some designed for domestic use and others for heating large quantities of water for dairies, etc.

Ideally, the floor of the kennel kitchen should be tiled or faced with smooth concrete. It is sure to get dirty and greasy, and any surface that can be easily swilled down with warm water and a broom is the best.

The cupboard or shelves will hold dishes, also items such as cans of cod-liver oil, tins of vitamin supplements or calcium, dried milk, and so on.

Otherwise, the less there is to clutter up the kitchen the better it is for the worker or workers. Space is at a premium when all the dishes are being doled out, and the best use of it must be made so that the feeding can be speedy and efficient.

It is a help if all the kennel buildings adjoin, and if they are encompassed in a ring fence, so much the better. For such a fence chain-link fencing is a popular choice, but only the heavy-gauge wire is really suitable. Angle-iron posts are sturdy and look neater than wooden stakes. Beagles can jump and climb, so runs and enclosures are useless if under 5 or 6 feet in height. The most escape-proof runs are those constructed of blocks—breeze or concrete—to a height of 3 or 4 feet, topped with chain-link or weldmesh fencing so that the height totals about 8 feet. If chain-link alone is used, this should be buried in the ground to a depth of 12 inches, and this means that 7-foot fencing will be required to provide a run 6 feet high.

Some dogs have a tiresome habit of trying to dig a way out beneath fences, others will chew the wire. A few more will try to jump over the top. Visiting dogs or bitches are generally the culprits, but one's own hounds are not above such things if a bitch in season is around, or if they resent being shut in and wish to follow the family about the place. Escape-proof yards, therefore, require high, strong fences, buried deep in the ground.

The best runs are planned to extend near a tree or trees, so that there is shade in the hot weather.

We have decided that the best place for a whelping kennel is a site well away from the other hounds. While this is not absolutely essential, there are times when a young bitch can be very upset if she hears other dogs barking or running about near by, and almost all brood bitches are better for being kept very quiet at a time when the puppies are arriving and for the subsequent week.

On the other hand, when possible we like to have a kennel for growing puppies, and we place this in a busy situation. It has a sizable run, and the puppies can look out at farm traffic, tradesmen's vans, callers, etc., and they get used to strange sights and sounds and are not shy when taken out for walks or to the shows. A spacious yard is essential so that the youngsters can get plenty of fresh air and exercise, and can romp and play in the sunshine.

Two such kennels are ideal, for there is an intermediate stage when the puppies are growing up, are no longer babies, but are hardly ready to move in with the adults in the main block. At the same time younger litters will be coming along, and will need similar accommodation.

Finally, a storehouse or shed will almost certainly be required. The sawdust has to be kept dry, and so does the bedding, whether it is straw or wood-wool. Travelling boxes need to be stored under cover, and there will be drums of disinfectant and buckets, and much more impedimenta.

The trouble is, when we keep animals, we never seem to have enough buildings. No sooner do we put up a new one than we fill it up and wish we had another like it!

CHAPTER XII

SELLING, EXPORTING, AND IMPORTING

PUPPIES are customarily offered for sale at from seven to nine weeks of age. If weaning has been completed early, it is possible to allow whelps to leave their birthplace at the sixth or seventh week, but if they are in any way backward it is well worth while keeping them a little longer, especially if the weather is at all bad at the time when they are about to change homes.

No puppy should go away until it is independent of its dam, and this means that the mother should have been leaving her babies gradually, first for a couple of hours at a time, later for the best part of the day, and finally at night as well. Then the puppies need a clear week, at least, on their own to be completely used to doing without 'Mum', before they have to start getting used to strange surroundings, new owners, and perhaps a change of time-table or food.

In any case, a puppy less than eight weeks old should be entrusted only to someone who has at least a little experience of such young animals. An extra fortnight at home is not such a very long time, but it can make a tremendous lot of difference to the sort of start in life the puppies are going to have.

The first ten weeks are formative and all-important, and any setback within the period can have serious repercussions, even affecting the little hound's further development; many experts believe that no amount of subsequent care can ever completely offset a sharp check in growth in the early stages.

Some breeders used to keep their puppies until they were nine weeks old, when it was possible to have them inoculated against the canine virus diseases.[1] A puppy is thought to have a natural immunity for the first few weeks of life, which means that injections given within this period are likely to be ineffective if infection is contracted later on. A good many buyers prefer to take puppies as young as

---

[1] Recently, veterinary opinion has undergone a sharp change and ten to twelve weeks of age is the recommended stage for the immunization.

possible, in order to enjoy every stage of their engaging 'child-hood', and always, when there are children in the family, to introduce them young in order that they can all grow up together. Similarly, a few people prefer to take a new dog to their own veterinary surgeon for inoculation with a particular choice of vaccine, so are likely to seek a dog that has not already been treated. Such buyers are really to be preferred, since the cost of the injections has to be added to the purchase price and this occasionally has a deterrent effect upon sales. Veterinary surgeon's charges for these injections vary slightly, according to the amount charged for the visit, but it is usually about £8. This sum should be added to the price charged for a puppy, otherwise the seller will be sadly out of pocket, if not already in the red after the many expenses incurred in rearing a litter.

Distemper, hard-pad, hepatitis and leptospirosis are the three diseases encompassed in what are generally referred to as the 'plus' inoculations, and all are dangerous illnesses with a distressingly high rate of mortality. Consequently most people, buyers and sellers alike, agree that every puppy should be given this immunity, and one might imagine that the offer of a dog already inoculated would be though so advantageous that the addition to the price would not be considered any disadvantage at all.

Curiously, the dog world is full of folk who won't pay, say, £60 for a fully inoculated puppy, but will go elsewhere and buy one for £55, take it to a vet and hand over £8 for its injections! Odd, isn't it? This idiosyncrasy supposedly has its roots in that other quirk of human nature—the urge to buy something costing £4.99 when we would reject the same article if it cost £5! Doubtless a psychiatrist could explain it to us but it still leaves the seller to deal with the problem, for if there is 'customer resistance' when the cost of the 'plus shots' are added to the sale price, it may be necessary to reduce the price of the dog during a period when sales are slack, and this makes the whole deal thoroughly uneconomic from the kennel owner's point of view.

Some well-known breeders say that they never have the puppies they offer for sale inoculated for this very reason. 'One never gets the cost back,' they say, 'apart from having to keep them until they are three months.'

This is all right, of course, until trouble crops up and that malignant spectre, the epidemic in the kennel, make its unwelcome appearance. This can happen in the best-managed establishment, for infection can be brought back from a show, by a visiting bitch, by puppies 'bought in' for re-sale or any other purpose, even by visitors who have the habit of calling at one kennel after another, especially when several breeders happen to reside in the same area. These strangers fondle the hounds, and perhaps have thoughtlessly done the same elsewhere where the dogs were not so healthy. Virus infections are easily passed from one dog to another in this manner, and can be carried on hands or the soles of the shoes.

So it really resolves itself into two things—either we gamble on losing money when we sell a dog that has been protected, always hoping that a sensible customer will agree to pay the cost of its injection, or we run the very real risk of keeping young dogs which are vulnerable to germs that, we all know, are quite easily introduced.

As puppies cannot be injected until they are twelve weeks old, clearly the best thing is to sell them at about eight weeks of age, when this is possible. Well-bred and well-reared Beagle puppies are in good demand, so it is often quite possible to dispose of them quickly and easily, when the responsibility of getting them 'plus-ed' is on the new owners—but they must always be urged to have their dogs immunized at the proper time. So much care, expense, and time is involved in the rearing of a litter of puppies that it is always a major tragedy if the young lives are cut short by accident or disease.

Let us now consider the best way of selling the puppies. If the dam has succeeded in making herself something of a reputation in the show ring, and if she has been mated with a worthy stallion hound, we can assume that a nice litter is the result. We can also assume that no expense has been spared in rearing the puppies well, in which case they should be saleable at sensible prices. It is sometimes best to grade a litter, asking, say, ten or fifteen pounds more for the best puppies than for these that show less promise. A completely un-known breeder, disposing of puppies from a well-bred, good type of bitch of no very great merit, may have to be content with prices round the minimum price level, even if the sire is of some consequence himself. We make no secret of the fact that breeding and rearing good-quality Beagles is not an inexpensive business if it is to be done properly. Bona-fide breeders are inclined to recoil if the word 'commercial' is used, and perhaps rightly, since it is often used in a derogatory sense where the indiscriminate breeding of dogs, purely for what they will fetch, is concerned. But there is nothing 'commercial' in trying to recoup the amount one has expended upon a litter of puppies, and indeed there is a lot to be said for keeping prices high, if only on the grounds that people care for, and prize, the things that cost them money.

There is, however, one important fact to be considered, which is that holding out for too high a price occasionally results in one's being stuck with the puppies long past the most salable age. Certainly too low a price is uneconomic, it harms the breed and spoils the market for other people, and very occasionally it is detrimental to the puppy for the opposite of the reason stated above—something acquired cheaply is not always valued by a certain type of person, and this means that the puppy might not find its way into the best kind of home.

The demand for puppies ebbs and flows, and there are times of year when they are generally more in demand than others, and they are not, as is commonly supposed, more easily sold in the summer months. We so often hear a breeder planning 'summer puppies', and of course the reasons given are perfectly sound. Longer days, less chilly weather, the prospect of more sunshine when the litter starts to toddle out of doors. But, ideal though all this may be, two things emerge. First, because so many people act on this premise, a great many puppies are bred at about the same time. Secondly, it is around the peak holiday periods that such litters are ready to go to new homes. It is seldom convenient to take a new puppy away on a holiday, which means that it has to be left with friends or put into a boarding kennel—and very few kennels of this type accept young puppies during the busiest boarding season. The result of this is that although people would like to take advantage of the spring and summer days, when the weather makes the process of house training easier, many of them reluctantly put off buying a dog until vacations are over. It is mainly this situation that gives us a sales graph that rises and falls.

Just before Christmas there is sometimes a little 'boom' in sales, for dogs are often bought as presents. For some rather obscure reason, January is often a month during which kennel business is brisk. And, largely due to the publicity given to Cruft's Dog Show through the Press and over the air and on television, the public becomes very pedigree-dog-conscious during February, both before the exhibition and afterwards.

The demand wanes a little about the beginning of March, but it is still quite steady throughout April and May, after which it tends to diminish, and only the luckier breeders get floods of enquiries until about October. It is true that plenty of people are home from their holiday resorts long before then, but often they have had an expensive trip and need a little time to save up money to buy a dog. October often seems a very busy month in a breeding kennel, but after that the winter sets in and people's thoughts incline away from dogs until 'Jingle Bells' heralds the Christmas spending spree.

Of course there are regular enquiries, on and off, all through the year, especially from other breeders or would-be breeders who are less affected by the things that happen to discourage the average 'pet' dog buyer, and who will purchase whenever they feel inclined to do so. But, looking back over the years, the pet sales do seem to group themselves as described above.

There are nothing like so many puppies born in the late autumn and the winter, and this in itself provides some reward for the extra trouble that may be involved in bringing them up in the dark, cold months, and sales are often satisfactory, if not very brisk, at times when the market is not flooded and there are fewer litters offered for sale.

Advertisements in *Dog World* and *Our Dogs*, the excellent papers devoted entirely to dogs, which are published every Friday, bring good results. Breeders who live in the greater London area or the suburbs sometimes find that they get a good response from insertions in the *Evening Standard* or *Evening News*. Others swear by *The Times* and the *Daily Telegraph*, placing advertisements in either the Personal column or the section set aside for dogs and other livestock. Other well-known periodicals run classified-advertisement columns, such as *Country Life*, *The Field*, and *Horse and Hound*. *Exchange and Mart* is a paper that seems to contact a public interested mainly in the less expensive pet puppies. Most country-dwellers are served by local newspapers, their degree of usefulness, as mediums through which dogs can be sold, depending on their circulations. Too much expenditure on advertising, although it may bring sales, can be too costly, and probably the dog weeklies, whose rates are lower than some of the other publications, are the best value. The breeder with puppies for sale is strongly advised to try a few advertisements in these books first, resorting to the general press if for any reason the puppies are not placed as rapidly as could be wished.

It is always worth while advising the owner of the sire, as well as the breeder from whom the dam was acquired, that there is a litter for disposal. Quite a number of well-known and established breeders, especially any who own fashionable studs, are unable to produce enough puppies to satisfy the constant demand for their stock, such individuals being only too pleased to buy in healthy puppies by their own hounds or to pass on surplus enquiries.

There are always a number of pet-shop proprietors and livestock dealers who advertise their willingness to purchase litters of the more popular breeds, but as a general rule they do not offer prices acceptable to serious breeders of carefully bred and lavishly reared puppies. Sales into such channels are frequently a last resort on the part of somebody who has unfortunately been 'stuck' with a litter, and who is simply unable to hang on to the puppies until individual, negotiated sales at good prices can eventually be effected.

The wording of advertisements needs careful thought, and results are often dependent on the general layout. A box number can be used, if for any special reason this is desirable, but if the seller's full name, address, and telephone number can be given it is almost certain that the response will be better. Arrange for the advertisement to be inserted on a date when you are sure to be at home, especially in the evening when most people decide to telephone enquiries. Some people may write, of course, and a few may decide to call, but it is normally the telephone that is busy after dogs have been offered for sale. If nobody is available to answer the calls, or if the person who does so has not got all the information and facts ready, very few callers bother to try again and sales may be lost.

If unexpected callers are likely to prove inconvenient it is as well to state in the wording that the puppies are to be seen 'by appointment only'. A definite price can be stated, or such words as 'reasonable prices' used. Never undertake to reserve a puppy unless a deposit has been paid. The amount of the deposit is a matter for mutual arrangement, but should be in the neighbourhood of ten per cent of the agreed purchase price, at least. There are plenty of breeders who have been sadly let down by callers who decide upon a dog, promise to collect and pay for it later, and who never turn up and are not heard of again. In the meantime the unfortunate seller has had the expense of feeding and caring for the puppy for an indefinite length of time, and has probably lost several chances of selling it elsewhere.

If a buyer selects a puppy and is unable to take it away then and there, it is usual to charge a nominal sum for its board until such time as it is collected. This, and the fact that the purchase price in total, or alternatively a deposit, must be paid, should be made absolutely clear at the time the transaction takes place. The charges people make vary but, in general, sums ranging from 65p per day, according to the age of the dog, would be fair. Such charges are in accordance with those made by boarding kennels.

Do not send dogs to strangers unless payment is made in advance, and if such payment is made by cheque, clear this when possible and get the name and address of the person who writes it. These are practical rules in any sort of business, though in fact most experienced breeders will say that by far the greater majority of people who buy pedigree dogs are perfectly honest and reliable in their dealings. It is only occasionally one hears of the other kind, and perhaps it is because regrettable experiences with them are unusual that it is as well to be on guard.

Disputes may arise if the question of carriage is not settled before a purchaser's dog is consigned to him by rail. It is customary for the buyer to pay these charges unless the dog has been specifically offered as 'Carriage paid' or 'Price, including carriage . . .' If the dog is dispatched in a returnable travelling box it is also usual for the purchaser to send it straight back from the station and to pay the cost. Buyers are sometimes exceedingly dilatory about returning these crates, delays causing inconvenience to the sender, who not infrequently awaits their return with great impatience if other dogs are waiting to be sent away. It may help to have printed or written on labels: *Kindly return empty box to —— station.*

When sending a dog by rail always put at least two labels on the box—preferably one tied on with string, the other gummed on the lid.

Supply a diet sheet with every puppy, and when possible send it to the customers a few days before a puppy is due to arrive. They can lay in all the items necessary for its well-being, and have everything ready. This is most advisable if the puppy is to be collected in the evening or at a week-end, when the shops may be closed.

One thing is common to all breeders: the new, the old, the famous, and the little known—a gnawing anxiety lest the puppy should not land up in a really good home. Up to a point one can try to ensure its future by talking to the possible owners, finding out if the home is town or country, etc. If the former it is as well to be sure that there is either a garden or a park close by, and that somebody in the family is going to be willing and able to devote time and energy to take the Beagle for walks. If the latter, is the garden fenced, and, if not, is there a dangerous road near by? Are there sheep in adjacent fields, and, if so, will every effort be made to get the puppy used to them and to train it to be obedient and safe to take about? It is possible to make these enquiries without appearing presumptuous or rude, and the right type of dog-lover appreciates the fact that you seek only the best for your animals.

If the enquiries elicit the fact that the home will be 'an upstairs flat' and that the family will be at work all day—do not sell them a puppy. While a flat is not the most ideal environment for a lively youngster, it can live in one happily if there is somebody prepared to give it sufficient exercise and make the outings frequent, for it is the owner rather than the place itself that will make or mar the hound's life. The most palatial house and garden is no fit home for a dog if the people who live in it are the type who will not put themselves out for the puppy, who will find caring for it a nuisance instead of a joy. One may say, 'But surely that type of person is not going to acquire a dog.' Yet they do. Goodness knows why, but indeed they do. Perhaps it is a desire to 'keep up with the top people', the desire to have an ornamental pet but to make no effort to take care of it. These persons should keep tropical fish—not dogs.

There are still a few people, with ideal accommodation and the best of intentions, who for various reasons are not really suited to keeping dogs, and this type of individual will never make a success of a hound. Some of these well-meaning folk are far too indulgent, just as there are others who are impatient and unkind. It is not easy to sum up people in a few minutes spent discussing a kennel full of puppies, but it is surprising how astute one becomes as one's experience with dogs increases. The more we can find out about them the more likely we are to be able to fit the right Beagle to the right household. If we fail to do this the result is sure to be a disappointed and exasperated owner, and an unhappy, and generally badly behaved, hound.

Occasionally sales are transacted at dog shows. There is a space on the regulation printed entry form where the person entering the dog can state if it is for sale, and its price. It will be noted, when reading the show rules, that the Show Committee sometimes requires a commission on any sales effected at their fixtures. In the event of a sale taking place on their premises, the show regulations are still binding and the new owner may not remove the dog until the time stated in schedule and catalogue.

A dog already entered for a show may still be exhibited there, even if it has been sold after entries have closed. It is only necessary to obtain a transfer form from the Kennel Club, 1–4 Clarges Street, Piccadilly, W1Y 8AB, and to send it back to them completed, with the current fee. Particular care should be taken, in the case of a dog already entered for a show, to fill up the paragraph relative to such transfers.

Selling dogs abroad is naturally a complicated business compared with the simplicity of transactions in one's own country. Even when the deal is clinched by telephone, cablegram, or airmail, some delays are inevitable. Dispatch to some of the Continental countries is the least complex and deliveries can often be arranged within a couple of days. Arranging to send dogs to some of the other parts of the world, however, takes very much longer, especially if the journey is to be by sea. The sailings may be infrequent, it will be discovered that only some of the ships accept dogs at all. and then only in limited numbers. Some countries require special blood tests and certificates, consular invoices, special stamps on documents, declarations that the animal has never been out of the country, that there are no cases of rabies in the land, and sworn statements before Commissioners for Oaths and Justices of the Peace. Most countries require a veterinary surgeon's certificate, sometimes in triplicate, that the dog is in good health and condition, and while there are a few instances when the Kennel Club's Export Pedigree Certificate is not demanded, it is essential in others. Happily, the beginner can easily obtain expert assistance, for otherwise the complications might deter any inexperienced breeder from selling dogs abroad.

There are several firms and individuals specializing in livestock export. Two or three handle nothing but dogs, and, as experts, can be depended upon to make all arrangements perfectly. Such people offer a high standard of personal attention, will make reservations with the air companies or shipping agents, provide suitable crates, supply the necessary food, utensils, grooming materials, etc., and laboriously collect the necessary documents or give the seller clear instructions how to obtain them themselves. The charges for this invaluable work are reasonable, and it is well worth while to ensure that there is no hitch at either end, and that everything is done for the dog's welfare.

The warning already given, to obtain payment before parting with a valuable dog, applies even more when selling to strangers overseas. In the event of such a buyer defaulting, once the dog has left these shores the chances of recovering payment are indeed slender. The charges for freight, veterinary surgeon's a/c, Kennel Club documents, etc., should also be estimated and charged in advance.

In general, air transport is always to be preferred to a sea voyage. Where a large hound is concerned it may add quite a lot to the cost if it is flown to its new home, but it is sure to arrive quickly and in good condition, a journey across the Atlantic, for instance, taking six or seven hours in an aeroplane but up to a week on the ocean.

Dogs exported to New Zealand or Australia have to travel by sea, and although the standard of care on board most of the ships is very good it is hard for an active animal to remain cooped up for several weeks. Happily, Beagles can usually be depended upon to eat well under any circumstances, otherwise a capricious feeder would be in rather poor shape by the time it docked at the other end. Officers and crew often get very much attached to their charges, and give them the maximum amount of attention and exercise possible under the circumstances. They often go to a lot of trouble to deliver them in good condition, but, even so, a journey of that duration is bound to be fraught with some risks.

It is particularly important, in sales involving this type of journey, to enlist the assistance of the animal export specialist, who will know precisely the type of travelling kennel required, and the most suitable measurements. The right type of food for the hound will be put on board and detailed instructions for feeding it given to the ship's butcher who will be in charge of the dogs. Bedding, collar, chain, towels, all sorts of things have to be remembered.

The trouble involved in planning a journey for the dog, the telephone calls, the extra weeks of board, all these items should be taken into consideration when the dog is offered for sale, and included in the quotation. Otherwise, frankly, there is no incentive to export dogs at all. The work and worry are not worth while unless the price is a fair one and all the extra expenses are added. Otherwise one is far better off selling the dog to somebody nearer home.

As we have seen, it is quite an involved business sending dogs out of the country, but it is absolutely nothing compared with the commotion that ensues when one is brought in! For many years Britain has had in force inflexible quarantine regulations which order that dogs brought from abroad must be detained, in kennels approved by the Ministry of Agriculture and Fisheries, for a period of six months. No exceptions are allowed, apart from special arrangements in connection with performing dogs brought in for musical halls and circuses. Such animals are quarantined, too, but on the premises where they perform. They may not be exercised outside, nor removed to alternative buildings except by special licence and under strict, officially appointed supervision. No reduction is ever made in the period of detention, and there are no loopholes, as many people believe, whereby dogs can be smuggled into the country through Eire or the Channel Islands.

An import licence has to be obtained from the Ministry of Agriculture, who supply a form to be completed with all manner of details, including the name and address of the kennels, selected from their official list, on whose premises the dog will spend its period of isolation. The dog will also be met at the airport or port by an agent appointed as an official carrier, who will conduct it to the quarantine station. The importer pays all the charges connected with this service, and a weekly boarding fee for the six months' kennelling.

The charges made by the carrier varies according to the mileage undertaken and the length of time kept waiting for the 'plane or ship, but is unlikely to come to less than £15.

The kennel fees are about the same as the charges fixed by ordinary boarding establishments, and may be 75p or more per day for medium-sized dogs. Therefore, at a rough estimate, the cost of importing and putting a Beagle through quarantine is likely to amount to several hundred pounds over and above the price paid for the dog, and there are always other extras such as veterinary surgeons' fees for any ailments or medicines supplied, tips to kennel staff, and so on.

The standards of accommodation, types of buildings, runs etc., vary, though the majority of the kennels on the Ministry's list maintain a good standard of care, but if a kennel is personally recommended by friends who have previously imported dogs successfully, one is naturally reassured and such a kennel is the best choice. The best quarantine kennels are always very full, and it is often necessary to book up well ahead of the import's scheduled arrival date.

Quite a number of kennels are run by resident veterinary surgeons who attend to the health of the inmates, but much depends upon the kennelmaids and kennelmen who have constant contact with the dogs. Such people are handicapped because they cannot take the dogs out for walks, as would be the case in ordinary boarding kennels, and the rules are so strict that it is normally not even possible to turn more than one dog loose in a run to romp and exercise. The dogs belonging to different people can only be put into runs, alone, for short periods each day. A new rule has come into force, however, whereby a person importing more than one dog at the same time may arrange to have them share a kennel and run, a far happier state of affairs which alleviates loneliness. Seldom are these runs or enclosures large enough for dogs to exercise properly, and indeed, even if they were, it is doubtful if one dog alone would ever do much more than wander about, or sit by the gate waiting to go back to the kennel again, since most solitary dogs behave in this manner. Naturally the staff are busy and they seldom have time to play with the dogs in the runs. Owners are permitted to visit the dogs on most week-days within certain times, however.

Beagles require careful feeding in quarantine, otherwise, with the forced inactivity and lack of freedom, they get very fat. If this tendency is checked, there seems little evidence that they suffer in any way through enforced detention. Fears on this point are often expressed by breeders overseas, and some are reluctant to send dogs to England because of the quarantine rules. Some hundreds of dogs —most of them pets but a proportion of them show dogs—are brought in every year and successfully emerge from quarantine none the worse for the term of 'imprisonment'.

Imported Beagles have, over the past few years, made a not inconsiderable improvement in the overall quality of the breed and provide a number of fresh bloodlines which appear to be exerting a most beneficial influence on the breed as a whole. Possibly we have sufficient material at our disposal now to continue the good work, but there may be others who would like to try importing further stock. It is for them that these hints have been set down in detail.

CHAPTER XIII

PREPARING FOR THE SHOW

EVERYTHING has a beginning, and each one of us is a novice at some stage or another. We occasionally hear a newcomer to the dog game saying, 'What chance can I possibly have against all the experienced exhibitors?' Yet all successful winners were once beginners themselves; many beginners seem to forget this.

There are few competitive fields wherein a novice expects to do well straight away, and yet this happens at dog shows. There are right and wrong ways of showing dogs, certainly, and experience is always the best teacher. We all make mistakes, but some of these could be avoided, and perhaps if we study this chapter we may by-pass a few pitfalls.

Mistake number one is to plunge straight into the ring without ever having been to a dog show at all. This *is* done, is usually a bewildering experience, and often a disappointing one as well. It is better by far to visit two or three shows, preferably at which there are the breed classes confined to Beagles, and to watch the whole procedure from the ringside. Do not dash in for half an hour or so. Turn up early, arrive with the dogs and their handlers, and note that the show routine actually begins well before the advertised judging time. It is useful to see such things as how to find a numbered bench, at a benched show, or an uncluttered corner at an unbenched event. A dog is secured to its bench by a special chain, which can be bought from the dog-requisite stalls often set up at shows. This chain has a swivel at either end, and rings conveniently spaced so that the dog can be attached at a length that will enable it to stand up or lie down, but not so long that it can fall over the edge when it could easily hang itself. The chain need not be heavy; those with light links are the most suitable for Beagles. Tying a hound to a bench by means of a leather leash is risky, as it will probably amuse itself by chewing the leather and thus could break free and get lost. The hound should wear a comfortable leather collar, preferably a flat one half an inch wide or one of rolled leather. Chain collars are not to be recommended for wear on the bench, as they are dangerous if they can be pulled tight and choke the dog, and equally so if they fit loosely and the dog can slip its head out.

The type of lead and collar used in the actual show ring itself varies. No one is more correct than another, and by a system of trial and error one usually finds that some hounds show best on one type, while others seem suited by a different kind altogether. It is a fact that some Beagles do not take at all kindly to chain collars, and will sulk if asked to wear them. Yet some hounds, especially the most exuberant which are restless in the ring, are more easily controlled by the slip-chains.

Various types of slip-leads are popular, and a narrow one should be chosen. Wide collars, whatever the material, are unbecoming and make a hound's neck appear shorter. Slip-leads are made from ordinary leather, whale hide, blind cord, and nylon; all are functional, some more attractively coloured than others.

It should be unnecessary to stress that show dogs never wear a harness, and a led Beagle would look idiotic except on a collar and lead. To many this warning may seem superfluous and even ludicrous, but as the writer has seen an Alsatian led into a show wearing harness of the type sometimes favoured for toy dogs, there can be a first time for anything!

A stroll round the aisles that divide the benches, or the space between rings, will reveal handlers or kennel assistants busily preparing their exhibits for the judging, even though few breeds require so little grooming as do Beagles. A great many dogs receive hours of trimming, clipping, brushing, oiling, chalking, and the like, before entering the ring. There is a high degree of skill called for in producing such dogs in their most spectacular condition, but any sensible person can take a Beagle to a show for the first time with every confidence that it will look as good as any of the exhibits shown by experienced exhibitors, at least in so far as its condition and general appearance are concerned; we are not, at the moment, referring to its finer points.

There is no particular art in grooming a Beagle. If this is done regularly for several weeks before the show the coat will be in fine form. It may be advisable to wash the hound two or three days before the event, using a good shampoo, drying it thoroughly, and being careful not to let it stand or lie about in the cold after immersion in warm water. If the hound does not seem to require bathing all over, it may be necessary to wash only the white portions of the body—chest, legs, and tip of stern. Vigorous brushing puts a polish on the coat, especially on black markings, and a final rub with a clean, dry chamois leather or a silk handkerchief imparts a lovely finish.

If, in spite of all this 'home work', the hound has got a little grubby on the journey, the white parts can be rubbed with a chalk block, of the kind sold especially for dogs, obtainable at a chemist's or from a stand at the show. The dog must be dry, and the chalk should be rubbed well into the coat, then brushed out. It is contrary to Kennel Club rules to allow powder to remain on the dog when it is judged; it may be used only for cleaning and should then be removed.

Trimming is entirely optional. Many hounds are shown exactly as nature made them, but some owners feel that they can improve the appearance of their Beagles by removing any long, untidy hairs on the underside of the stern, or by tidying up the neck and the breechings. Some judges do not care for much-trimmed hounds, and in any event it is unwise to attempt the job without expert advice. A novice who chopped the hound's coat about might spoil its appearance and have to wait a long time for the hair to grow again. If in doubt, leave well alone; mistakes of this kind are not easily put right.

The majority of dog shows do not have as many rings as they have breeds classified, so the various breeds take it in turns to parade before the judges. The order in which they will be required in the rings is sometimes printed at the beginning of the catalogue, but if no such particulars are given it is best to enquire at the secretary's office.

Watch the judging carefully. If you are out to learn it does not matter very much if the judge is good or indifferent (and it takes all sorts to make a world, and the 'dog world' is no different from any other). If you do not agree with the judge's placings, it will do you no harm to try to puzzle out the reasons, and at the next show you attend you may well see the same entrants being sorted out by a different expert, and can compare the awards. It is a wonderful way of developing an 'eye' for a breed.

At the same time note the different methods used by the other handlers and their efforts to get their dogs to show to the best advantage. Take heed of the routine whereby each hound is examined separately, its teeth inspected, and then sent up and down the ring to be judged for action and soundness. The judge may look at the exhibits on the ground, or may prefer to have each one placed on a table. This latter course is very much less tiring when a large entry has to be judged. There will be ring stewards in attendance who, having handed out numbered labels to each entrant, will marshal them in a circle or line. The hounds already examined by the judge will usually stand on one side of the ring, and the 'new' exhibits, not yet seen, on the other; it simplifies matters if they are not all mixed up together.

As soon as the last Beagle has been handled individually, the hounds will be led round the ring in follow-my-leader style. Handlers always walk anti-clockwise, and the hound is always led on the left side.

If the judge finds it difficult to decide between the best Beagles, they may be compared again or asked to walk the length of the ring either alone or in pairs. The judge may also ask to have an exhibit moved again if he or she wants to confirm an earlier impression that it is not perfect in either front or rear action, and this is frequently necessary when there are a great many being shown in the class.

Eventually the four or five winners are called out and asked to stand in line, placed in order, and the steward hands out the prize cards. The first prize card is red, the second blue, the third yellow, and reserve green. Sometimes a fifth card is awarded to an exhibit that is 'Very Highly Commended' and at a very few shows—notably Cruft's where enormous classes are the rule—white 'Highly Commended' and 'Commended' cards for the sixth and seventh in a strong class.

Some hounds entered in the early classes may also reappear in subsequent classes, perhaps with some newcomers which the judge has not yet had in front of him. The 'old' exhibits, having already been minutely examined, do not go all through it again, but stand at the ringside in correct order as placed in the previous line-up, while the judge devotes time to the 'new' dogs.

If the hound has won he may be required at the close of the judging to compete for some special award such as Best Puppy, or for Best of Sex or Best of Breed. The hound may also be entered in a

Variety class, as well as in the Beagle classes, and the all-breed competitions may be judged in the same or in a different ring; the stewards or the secretary can give information on this point. It is necessary to keep one's eyes open because it is quite easy to miss a class or classes at a busy show.

Stewards vary in the amount of work they do and the energy they apply to their tasks, and many are conscientious about rounding up the exhibits required for judging. Nevertheless, it is officially the responsibility of the exhibitor to bring the animal to the ring for judging at the right time, so one has only oneself to blame if through carelessness or inattention one has the misfortune to miss classes.

Shows close at a predetermined hour, although judging does not always end by the time stated, especially if the judge is particularly slow in making the awards or if the entry is unusually large. Exhibitors may remove dogs at the end of the show, or earlier if Early Removal orders have been issued to people living a great distance from the showground.

As we have seen, there is quite a lot to learn about showing dogs, and if we have heeded the advice given we will be glad, when we walk our pride and joy into the ring, that we spent a little time studying the procedure. It is just a question of 'know-how'; we need to know it all, but other people can show their dogs, and there is no reason at all why we should not 'have a go', with every prospect of success.

Before we make our début, however, we must go home and appraise our hound or hounds with as critical an eye as possible. It is not to be supposed that one or two visits to dog shows will turn us into knowledgeable judges overnight. But we will have taken particular notice of the Beagles placed high in their classes, and we have taken just as much interest in those standing at the ends of the line-ups. Naturally we will have found it a little confusing and have been unable to read the judges' minds, nor have understood exactly why they have made all their placings. But out of it all we begin to get an idea as to the type that gets to the head of a class and its opposite number at the wrong end. We may already have recognized certain points which, from the eventual result, seem to have especially pleased the judges, or the reverse. If this is the case, then we may congratulate ourselves for we are well on the way to acquiring something that is essential to our success—that is, an 'eye for a dog'. On the other hand, such enlightenment comes much more rapidly to some than to others, and let us not be too depressed if this stage all the Beagles look exactly alike to us except, perhaps, some of the more obvious differences such as those of colour or of size. It means only that we must diligently study hounds until such time as we are able to recognize the subtle differences between them, those small things that mean everything when it amounts to a dog being rated as 'great' or dismissed as 'ordinary'.

This 'eye' we covet so much—why is it so important to us? The answer is that without the ability to assess the good and not-so-good —and downright bad—characteristics of our stock, we are playing a game of blind-man's-buff instead of breeding pedigree stock intelligently.

All too few of us have bottomless bank accounts, so why should we squander precious pounds through entering a dog in a show where it stands no chance whatever? We need to know that he might well take all before him at a twenty-class Sanction show, yet leave the ring without a card at any of the larger events. If we love him he probably looks beautiful to us, but we have to look upon him with a cold, critical eye when we weigh up his chances. The fact that he does not, on reflection, seem to promise to be a Champion does not make us any less fond of him, but it suggests we should adopt caution when entering him for his first exhibitions. Both of us— two-legged and four-legged—need experience, and we may as well get it inexpensively by starting out at one or two small shows, rather than plunging straight into the Championship-show world.

We will buy the weekly dog newspapers, read the announcements regarding shows, and write in to ask for schedules of any that will be held on a convenient date and at a place we can reach without too much difficulty. If possible, we start by choosing a show which has put on classes for Beagles, though if there is no such suitable show we may have to enter in some Any Variety classes. There are sure to be a good many of these, and such classes will most likely consist of Puppy, Novice, Junior, Bred by Exhibitor, and suchlike classes. There may possibly be a class or classes for Any Variety Hound and/or Any Variety Sporting, and both these are suitable for Beagles. The class definitions are always published in the schedules, but if the beginner is in any difficulty in deciding whether or not a dog is eligible it is best to telephone the secretary, or to ask a doggy friend for advice on this point, before making the entries.

Entry fees are not refunded if a dog is entered in a wrong class by mistake, and if he is shown in it and wins, the Kennel Club will disqualify him and he will lose his awards which will be transferred to the dog that stood next to him. It is because of these strictly enforced Kennel Club rules and regulations that we have to read them up before we show. We check that our dog is registered, transferred to us if that is necessary, and entered only in the right class or classes. The Kennel Club will supply copies of its rules and show regulations, and send registration and transfer forms on request. As a general rule it is wise to enter a new dog in one or two classes to begin with, then, if it does well, we can be a little more ambitious next time. Complete the entry form in block letters, checking the particulars carefully, and send it to the secretary enclosing the entry fees as stated in the schedule.

Now we look our young hopeful over, noting whether he is on the fat side or whether a little lean. Ideally, we want him well covered, with no ribs showing and with a defined waist, but at the same time in hard, muscular condition, and in no way podgy or flabby. If he is already entered for a show we have not got too much time to put on weight or take it off, but we must do our best by increasing the amount of food, or by cutting it down, and by regulating the exercise according to the condition of our Beagle.

It would be entirely wrong to stop daily walks merely because the hound would look better with a bit more flesh on him, but so many dogs are allowed free range about the farm or the garden, and when running about the place all day, they take off a great deal of surplus fat. It is possible, in such cases, that shutting the Beagle up for a few hours each morning and afternoon, thus enforcing a rest, may make all the difference.

We must be conscientious about daily grooming, and we must spend a few minutes every day on ring training. This has been dealt with in detail in Chapter VII.

When the great day draws nigh we must start collecting together all the bits and pieces we will call our equipment. In a suitable canvas bag, holdall, haversack, or basket we put the bench chain and show lead, also an ordinary leather lead attached to a well-fitting collar for the hound to wear on the journey to the show. A clean bath-towel or a small blanket is needed to spread on the unhospitable surface of the bench, or on the floor near the ringside. Food for the hound—unless we are sure to arrive home in time to give him a meal somewhere about his usual dinner-hour—and an unbreakable plastic

or aluminium bowl for food or water. Brush, comb, polishing cloth
or leather. A small plastic bag containing a few scraps of boiled liver
as 'bait' to make him show, and, if we have taken canned food for
our hound, we must remember the tin-opener. Don't forget the titbits. All Beagles love their tummies and show better if rewarded
with tasty treats. Instead of liver, or if liver is not easily available,
little cubes of cheese are popular, as are pieces of cooked rabbit.
Many hounds go crazy over the tonic yeast tablets which are such
useful conditioners and so popular with dogs and owners alike, and
they regard these as 'sweets' and show just as well for them as they
do if tempted with meat. Even a sweet biscuit or two—ordinarily
taboo but produced on show days—will cause a Beagle to stand
nicely with its stern up and give it the alert expression which adds so
much to its appearance. There is only rarely such a phenomenon as
the non-greedy Beagle, but for those that exist—if they exist at all—
animation may be inspired by a hare's or rabbit's foot, or by a piece
of the 'frog' which the blacksmith cuts off the horses' hooves when
they are being shod.

Between the closing date for entries and the actual date of the
show the secretary will post admission passes to all the exhibitors.
Slip this into the show bag, together with the schedule. The latter
carries the address of the show, occasionally information as to the
bus and rail services that connect with it, and also details of any
Cups and Special prizes that may be on offer. The latter particulars
are sometimes repeated in the catalogue that will be obtainable at
the show, but these are not always duplicated so it is handy to have
the schedule to refer to, especially if one is lucky enough to be
eligible for one of these prizes.

We have thought only of our dog's well-being so far, but at this
stage we may be excused if we attend to our own, making up a
packet of sandwiches and filling a thermos flask. Nearly all the shows
have catering arrangements but these vary in quality and the buffet
is usually the most crowded place at any show. It may be more
convenient, in any event, to picnic near the bench, since our hound
may feel a little strange at his first show and settle down better if
we stay with him.

If we plan to travel by road, and if we have not had previous
opportunities of taking the hound in the car, it is probably advisable
to give him travel-sickness capsules. Never overdo these, and administer them strictly according to the instructions. With most

makes—and there are several, one or two made for dogs and some sold for humans but all quite effective—one last thing at night, and another half an hour before leaving for the show, is a suitable dose for a Beagle; but check with the vet or the chemist when you get the tablets.

Finally, allow ample time for the journey. Even some quite seasoned show dogs get harassed and bewildered if rushed straight into the judging ring following a belated arrival at a show. Inexperienced dogs, not to mention their equally inexperienced owners, should arrive at the show half an hour at least, and preferably one hour, before judging is timed to begin.

Even when one arrives at the hall or the show ground, it is quite surprising what a long time it takes to get settled—sometimes veterinary surgeons will inspect the entrants and a lot of exhibitors will converge at the same time and have to form a queue—then we have to find our numbered bench, look for a catalogue-seller, clean and groom the Beagle, and hunt for a water tap to give him a drink. Then we have to pin-point the ring, and still have a moment to ourselves for a wash and a cup of coffee or even something stronger to settle our 'first-night nerves'.

We earnestly hope, at the end of it all, to be rewarded with a prize, even if it is only a minor award on this auspicious occasion, our first show. If we are unlucky, then it is once more a case for reappraising our exhibit, and also ourselves. We may have to be honest and admit that, in spite of our careful preparations, the hound did not show himself particularly well, and it could also be that we ourselves did not show off his good points very cleverly. Possibly his condition put him at a disadvantage, and if we feel that his lack of success may have been due to these such easily remedied failings, rather than faults of conformation or movement in the hound himself, all that remains is to redouble our efforts when we get home and have the Beagle in spanking form when we try him out at another show.

If we are genuinely puzzled and cannot see why our entrant did not do as well as the others there is no harm at all in asking one of the other exhibitors if they can suggest a reason, though of course the person best equipped to set our minds at rest is the judge.

These days large entries are the rule, and most judges work to a strict time-table, and even so find it difficult to complete their classes before the close of the show. It is not advisable to engage the judge in conversation at any stage until all the judging is completed, when, if there is time, a judge will usually be willing to discuss an unplaced exhibit with its owner.

If a judge has put it down for a serious fault it is possible that, harsh as the advice may seem, it is best to give up the idea of campaigning it since it is likely to prove a waste of time and of money. If, on the other hand, the judge criticizes it for one or two small faults, these might correct themselves in time or at least different judges may not feel obliged to penalize them quite so drastically. In such cases one's chances depend very much on the competition, and in slightly less illustrious company a dog of this character may do quite well.

We often hear of 'Cinderella' stories—of the one-dog owner's first effort at exhibiting, with a Best in Show award or some other similar great win crowning the début, but these are rare occurrences. Real-life fairy-stories always are, but it does not make them any the less exciting.

Very naturally, most of the important wins do go to exhibitors who have some experience of showing behind them, and we must not be downcast if our Beagle does not rise to stardom overnight, even if he looks, to our doting eyes, twice as handsome as any of his rivals. Far from becoming discouraged, we should seek to discover just where he—or his owner—went wrong, correct our failings, and try again.

CHAPTER XIV

AILMENTS

BEAGLES are sturdy little animals, with a heritage of robust good health and plenty of stamina behind them. Therefore they are not subject to any of the fairly numerous dog diseases and ailments, and if a Beagle should become ill it usually makes a good recovery with normal care and treatment.

Unlike some other breeds which are notably prone to disorders of various kinds—one breed frequently suffers from eczema, another is bothered by cysts between the toes, while yet another is thought to be unusually prone to kidney troubles—the Beagle is healthy if kept clean, fed correctly, and well exercised.

With most beginners a great problem is 'When shall I call the vet?' Very naturally we do not want to run up bills unnecessarily, and many busy veterinary surgeons are not pleased if they are summoned for trivialities, especially at short notice or during the night hours.

At the same time they very much resent a case where a dog has been ill for some time before they are asked to attend to it, since many indispositions can be arrested in the early stages if prompt treatment is given, yet are difficult or impossible to cure when longstanding.

The best advice is: 'When in doubt, send for the vet', for it is far better to be safe than sorry. This is especially true of whelping, when delay in getting assistance when complications are manifest may well result in dead puppies and even a dead bitch.

Every dog-breeder will want to keep a kennel first-aid chest or medicine cupboard. Requirements may vary, but some useful items are:

Eye-dropper or fountain-pen filler.
Cotton wool.
2-inch bandages.

Curved surgical scissors.

Clinical thermometer (half-minute).

Peroxide of hydrogen.

Boracic powder.

Permanganate of potash crystals.

Friar's Balsam or tincture of steel.

Optrex Eye Lotion.

Golden Eye Ointment.

Penicillin ointment.

Terramycin ointment.

Antiseptic ointment, of the Zam-Buk type.

Vaseline petroleum jelly.

Dettol and T.C.P.

Worm medicines (puppy and adult strengths) and in small quantities only as some brands lose potency if stored for any length of time.

Syrup of Figs or rhubarb tablets.

Milk of Magnesia.

Garlic capsules.

Jar of Brand's Essence of Beef or Chicken.

Tin of Benger's Food.

Jar of honey.

Glucose.

Other items can be added as needs arise, but anybody keeping dogs on any scale at all will require some or all of the above. When such things are needed it is often in a hurry, and perhaps when shops are closed, and this is when the foresight of stocking-up is appreciated.

Different veterinary surgeons prescribe differently, and clearly one would need a chemist's shop to be prepared for every eventuality, but the above list provides the essentials for most emergencies.

The following lists the most common canine ailments, and the remedies that should be given.

Abrasions. Bathe the sore carefully, dry with sterile cotton wool, and apply an antiseptic ointment.

Acid Milk. This condition is often blamed when puppies fail to thrive or fade away, and while it can be the cause, there are many other factors that should be considered. If the milk of the bitch is over-acid, the puppies wail, cease sucking, and die. Get some blue litmus paper from the chemist. Gently squeeze a drop of milk from the dam's teat, and as it touches the paper it will turn bright pink if the milk is acid, or the stain will be mauvish if it is normal.

Dosing the bitch with Milk of Magnesia or bicarbonate of soda helps to right the condition, and for the next few days the puppies should be foster-mothered or bottle-fed. Test the milk daily, and if normal give her back her whelps. Small doses of Milk of Magnesia may be given to the puppies—one or two drops daily in a milk feed.

Anal Glands. Beagles seldom suffer from irregularities of these glands, which are situated on each side of the rectum. The glands can become congested, and if inflamed the hound suffers great discomfort and will be constantly licking the parts or dragging itself along the ground in a sitting position. The vet will show you how to empty the glands by gentle squeezing, and will supply penicillin in tubes, with instructions to apply it through the tiny nozzle which can be inserted right into the tender orifices.

Sufferers are usually old dogs, dogs that suffer from constipation, and those allowed to become and remain obese. In obstinate cases surgical operation is advisable and usually most successful.

Appetite, Morbid. Dogs of all breeds occasionally develop the repellent habit of eating filth and excreta. The cause is not completely known, though it is thought that it may stem from a vitamin or mineral deficiency. A tonic or supplement should be given, and if raw meat is not fed it should become a part of the diet, also chopped raw vegetables. Droppings in runs and enclosures should be promptly removed and incinerated. Sometimes owners claim to effect a cure by sprinkling a dropping with cayenne pepper.

Bad Breath. Beagles are clean, wholesome, normally sweet-smelling creatures, and halitosis is a sign of a digestive disorder or of dirty or decayed teeth. The diet should be checked, and if necessary the teeth must be scaled or the vet asked to remove any that are loose or unhealthy, and to check the condition of the gums which may also require treatment.

Balanitis. This is the name given to the slight yellowish discharge which is often observed on the prepuce of the male hound. It is regularly licked, and though it does not look pleasant it is not serious or harmful. If treatment is thought advisable the sheath can be syringed daily with a tepid solution of a bland type of antiseptic; one suitable for a gargle is safe.

Biliousness. Hounds occasionally vomit froth and bile, and usually this is nothing to worry about, especially if the vomit contains scraps of grass. Persistent vomiting is a serious symptom, however, and should not be ignored. The dog must be kept warm and out of draughts, water should be withheld, and nothing at all given by mouth until the vet has been consulted. He will probably suggest small spoonfuls of glucose in well-stirred, but not whipped, raw white of egg and water. He may allow soda-water or barley-water in small quantities. His treatment may also include a saline injection if he thinks the hound is seriously ill.

Bites. Beagles are not fighters and although they can get involved in an occasional argument, especially males when a bitch in season is around, there is seldom much damage done. Bites from larger dogs are perhaps more of a risk. A dog-bite is inclined to become septic, for the sharp canine teeth can make deep punctures. The wound should be kept open to drain, and should be fomented if it closes up, otherwise it might result in a nasty abscess. Penicillin ointment squeezed into the wound is usually prescribed.

Bladder Irregularities. Bladder disorders are quickly discernible. The dog or bitch urinates all the time, or tries to urinate and appears to be straining and producing either a few drops or none at all. It looks unhappy and uncomfortable and depressed and loses weight. Substitute barley-water for plain water, boiled white fish for meat and/or biscuit, and call the vet.

Bowels. A properly fed hound should pass firm, medium-brown or dark-brown motions. Sloppy motions, coloured yellow, grey, or tinged with blood are danger signs. Black motions do not necessarily mean trouble, and can follow a substantial meal of raw meat. Bitches, too, pass loose black faeces after whelping, and this is normal. It disappears after a day or two. Some dogs suffer from constipation, especially those living in towns. There is straining, discomfort, and distress. A dessertspoonful to a tablespoonful of olive oil or liquid paraffin usually provides prompt relief, but the diet should be checked. All-bran in the food is helpful, and plenty of fresh water to drink must be available all the time. Increased exercise is recommended. Milk of Magnesia is a gentle laxative, but purgatives such as castor oil only aggravate the condition.

Persistent diarrhoea should never be neglected, and if it does not clear up on the second day professional advice should be sought. Diarrhoea tinged with blood is serious, and a vet should see the patient without delay. A haemorrhage from the rectum is a sign of acute enteritis and needs urgent treatment or the hound can die in a matter of hours. Small, spiky bones can penetrate the bowel and should not be fed to dogs. Symptoms are straining, blood in the motions, and general depression and malaise. Do not delay—get the vet.

Bronchitis. Not very common, and if seen at all is generally found in the older hound. Rubbing the chest with Vapour Rub, giving an inhalant, and keeping the dog warm, comfortable, and happy all help, but the animal should be under veterinary supervision.

Choking. A distressing and dangerous emergency, it can be caused by the hound swallowing a fragment of bone, a stone, rubber ball, or some other foreign body with which it may have been playing. In the case of a young puppy it could also be a chunk of meat that has lodged in the gullet. Open the mouth and try, with the fingers, to push the obstruction down the throat. Hold the animal up with its head hanging down, and slap it on the back. If nothing works, rush it to a vet—'rush' is the word.

Chorea. This is a side-effect following one of the virus diseases of the distemper-hard-pad type. The hound develops a decided twitch or jerk. Sometimes it is the jaw, often a fore or hind leg. Any nervous symptom of this kind is worrying, since it can lead to worse things, such as convulsions, which may not respond to treatment at all. In mild cases sedatives may be tried, and fortunately a dog has a fair chance of outgrowing the twitching. If it is permanent, however, its effects on a show dog constitute a handicap in the ring.

Conjunctivitis. A discharge from the eyes may be a symptom of one of the serious canine infections, and a sufferer should be isolated when possible. This is always a wise precaution, even though the discharge may be due to some simple cause such as a draught, cold wind, dust, etc. Bathe the eyes with Optrex, dry with cotton wool and squeeze a little Golden Ointment into the corner of the affected eye or eyes. Other useful first-aid eye-baths are weak, strained, cold tea, or a solution made from a teaspoonful of boracic powder well dissolved in a half-pint of warm water.

Constipation. See Bowels, and Laxatives.

Convulsions. There are few more distressing sights than a dog in a fit. The animal looks wild-eyed and terrified, it twitches and falls to the ground, struggling and thrashing its legs, and writhing. It does not recognize anybody. Lift it gently—for a dog in a fit rarely attempts to bite—and put it on its bed until it recovers consciousness.

Never attempt to give water, brandy, or anything by mouth until the dog is completely round.

If it is a puppy, dose it for worms. If an older dog, dose for worms, and give a mild sedative such as bromide or phenobarbitone, both of which may be prescribed by the vet. If the dog has not been inoculated against distemper and hard-pad, take its temperature and isolate it. Keep a careful watch for other symptoms, since fits are sometimes associated with the virus diseases.

Coughs. Beagles rarely suffer from coughs, as such, certainly not in the way in which these affect the human race. If a hound coughs it is possibly a symptom of hepatitis. Isolate it, and send for the vet.

Cuts. See Abrasions.

Dandruff. Dogs, especially those with black hair and the type of smooth, flat coat which covers the Beagle, occasionally suffer from a scurfy condition which is unsightly, and an indication that all is not well with the hair. The best treatment is by regular weekly shampoos with one of the many much-advertised preparations sold for human heads, carefully avoiding the synthetic, soapless types that dry the skin. An overall rubbing with olive oil, followed by a bath, is often effective. Some fat, such as suet, added to the diet is also advisable. Try a heaped tablespoonful on the food each day.

Diarrhoea. See Bowels.

Dislocations. Not very common, but occasionally found in the Hunting Beagle. Professional treatment only advisable.

Distemper. The old-fashioned distemper is now uncommon and has been replaced by a no-less-virulent disease known as hard-pad. Both are very serious, and accompanied by a high mortality. Happily they can be prevented by inoculation with the reliable injections that can be given to puppies from the age of twelve weeks upwards. The injections do not upset the hound or make it ill, and they are believed to give almost one hundred per cent protection. Modern research suggests that 'booster' injections are required from time to time.

It is because a majority of dog owners take advantage of these priceless discoveries, made available in their present form only in the past few years, that both diseases have become uncommon. There is no cause for complacency, however, and public parks, busy streets, dog shows, and anywhere where a lot of dogs from various sources congregate, may lead to infection. The best advice is to safeguard all dogs by inoculation at an early age.

The symptoms of distemper and hard-pad are often similar. There is a loss of appetite, lassitude, diarrhoea, and occasionally vomiting. The eyes are dull and emit a yellowish- or greenish-coloured discharge. The dog looks miserable and the temperature is above normal. As the injections are therapeutic as well as prophylactic, the veterinary surgeon should be called as soon as possible, for the dog's best chance of recovery lies in early diagnosis and treatment.

The vet will give instructions as to the diet, and these should be followed with scrupulous care. The dog must be isolated, kept warm, and provided with newspapers upon which to pass water and excreta. Some house-trained Beagles, especially bitches, become very distressed if expected to attend to their toilets indoors, and will suffer discomfort rather than be dirty. In such cases the vet may allow the hound to be taken outside for brief spells to make itself comfortable, but it should wear a warm, fitted woollen jacket all the time if the weather is other than warm.

There are herbal treatments for distemper—complex diseases, which some people find successful.

Doses. Instructions should be read carefully, and a spoon or a measured medicine-glass used for liquids. Guesswork is unreliable.

Dysentery. A discharge of blood and faeces from the rectum. See also Bowels.

Ears. Beagles, in common with most of the pendant-eared breeds, occasionally suffer from canker, ear mites, etc. The hound shakes its head, rubs its ears on the ground, and sometimes scratches the sides of its head slowly, emitting grunts and groans as it does so. Clean the ears thoroughly, using an orange-wood stick well wrapped with cotton wool. This can be dipped in peroxide of hydrogen and gently inserted in the ear, but never pushed or used roughly. Twist it round and withdraw the soiled cotton wool, replace with fresh wool, and repeat till ear is free from brown discharge. Then, using dry cotton wool on the stick, carefully dry the ear, and dust in a little boracic powder. If this treatment does not bring about great improvement within three days, seek the advice of the vet.

Injuries to the ear-flaps are not uncommon, especially with the Pack Beagle, as the ears are naturally vulnerable to brambles or barbed wire, and are generally the first to suffer if a hound is involved in a fight. Bleeding can be stemmed by prompt application of permanganate of potash crystals, applied dry to the wound.

In hot summer weather, and at any time if flies bother the hounds, the ears can become pitted with small bumps, which become scabby and spoil the look of the animal. Temedex ointment, obtainable only on a veterinary surgeon's prescription, can be applied daily, and is effective. A dryness round the edges of the ears is occasionally noticed. This is nothing to worry about, but if the soft hair comes away it does not look very nice. Temedex will correct this, too.

Eczema. The first sign is a patch of wet hair on some part of the body, and on close inspection it will be seen that the skin looks shiny and red. The dog licks it incessantly and, later, it becomes a large bare patch, sore and sticky with yellow discharge.

External treatment starts with carefully cleaning the wound with cotton wool dipped in T.C.P. Dry flowers of sulphur can be dusted on to it thickly, and, if possible, the hound should be prevented from biting the place. This can be done only by fitting the animal with what is known as an Elizabethan collar. This is a wide collar, made of very stiff hide or from metal, which is constructed in the form of a large cone with the narrowest part of the circle arranged to strap or tie round the neck. The wider orifice fits somewhere around the skull, and the effect it has is to make it difficult for the dog to turn its head to gnaw at its body. These collars can be obtained from firms who specialize in veterinary supplies, or a good saddler should be able to make one from leather. Even small plastic buckets can be used.

Internal cleansing plays a part in curing eczema. The hound should fast for a couple of days on nothing but water, and the diet after that should consist of boiled fish, plus some chopped green vegetable; parsley or wild garlic (rampion) are splendid. A cooling medicine may be given, a human preparation—Clark's Blood Mixture—being particularly effective. The hound should have plenty of exercise. It should not be necessary to remind owners that parasites such as fleas and lice are a common cause of eczema, and the remedy is obvious—don't let the hound get them at all, or if it does get rid of them at once.

Emetics. If it is suspected that a dog may have picked up poison, an emetic is given to encourage vomiting and thus to rid the stomach of the obnoxious matter. A piece of plain household washing soda, given as a pill, will generally make the hound sick. So will common salt, a fairly strong solution given as a draught.

Fractures. Beagles have—or should have—strong bones, but accidents can always happen especially in these days when the roads are so dangerous. First aid follows the principles we have been taught to apply to a human victim. The limb should be splinted, and any suitable piece of wood or metal can be used, wrapped in rag, bandaged firmly but not so tightly that the circulation of the blood can be hindered, and the dog taken to the vet for X-ray, if thought advisable.

Gastritis. Frequent vomiting, thirst, and diarrhoea are the symptoms. The dog looks wretched and depressed, and frequently appears tucked up about its abdomen, with a decided 'waist'.

Keep it warm and quiet, offer pieces of ice to lick, and give nothing else by mouth except white of egg stirred into a few spoonfuls of cold water—and only a small dessertspoonful of this mixture at a time. Small doses of bismuth are indicated, but the animal can become rapidly debilitated and ill, so that it is usually best to ask a vet to look at it, and he will advise the gradual return to normal food, via milk in various forms, steamed fish, minced chicken or rabbit, and the like.

Gums. Bleeding gums are unhealthy for the hound, and unpleasant for the owner, especially if the animal lives in the house. The vet should examine the mouth, and will advise removing any badly decayed teeth. Swabbing the gums daily with an antiseptic mouthwash is the usual procedure. See also Bad Breath and Teeth.

Hard-Pad. See Distemper.

Hepatitis. A disease with variable symptoms. Temperature can be abnormally high or abnormally low. The dog is clearly unwell, looks worried and depressed, and may or may not vomit or pass diarrhoea. In advanced stages one or both eyes turn turquoise blue. Although diagnosis is sometimes difficult in the beginning, the development of a blue eye is an almost certain sign that the dog is suffering from hepatitis. Hepatitis is usually much less infectious than hard-pad or distemper. Even in a large kennel it often happens that only one, two, or three dogs are affected, the rest of the contacts remaining well. The dogs most likely to develop hepatitis are generally the young stock under eighteen months of age. Hepatitis is a killer, and in spite of careful treatment many dogs die from it every year. Those that recover sometimes do so completely, but others are left with permanent damage to kidneys or the liver. Prompt veterinary attention is essential. Hepatitis is easier to prevent than to cure, for reliable inoculations are now available, and can be given individually or combined with the distemper/hard-pad 'shots'.

Hernia. Many puppies have small umbilical hernias, which ordinarily are of little consequence and cause no trouble. They often disappear as the puppy grows older. A large hernia, or one located in the groin, may need surgical treatment. The operation under normal circumstances is not complicated and is generally very successful.

Hydrophobia. Also referred to as rabies. It is to prevent this terrible disease, easily communicated to man as well as to several other animals, that the quarantine laws of this country are in force. There have been widely-spaced outbreaks of rabies in Britain in the past fifty years or so, one caused by dogs smuggled into the country and others when dogs have developed rabies in quarantine or shortly after release. Death from rabies, for dog or man, is terrible and agonizing. Even the treatment for a person thought to have been in contact with a rabid animal is painful and lengthy. Rabies takes at least six months to develop.

Hysteria. Hysteria can occur in dogs of all ages. When it is endemic in a kennel it is often a sign of some acute digestive disturbance caused by unsuitable foodstuffs. For instance, dogs fed largely on white bread frequently have fits of hysteria. In uninoculated dogs hysteria is commonly a symptom of the nervous complications connected with distemper or hard-pad diseases. Hysterical attacks are also attributable to severe worm infestation. If one puppy in a litter has an isolated fit of hysteria it need not occasion much alarm, especially since the rest of the young stock are unaffected. It could be caused by the puppy gobbling its meal and suffering from indigestion. Dose such a puppy with Milk of Magnesia—a small dessert-spoonful for a Beagle—keep it quiet, and preferably shut in a dark, comfortable kennel for the rest of the day. Call the vet if the attacks continue.

Hysteria is quite unmistakable. The dog begins to bark on a shrill, high-pitched note, does not listen when called or told to be quiet, and then rushes round in circles. It looks wild-eyed, terrified, and may bite if cornered.

Impotence. Beagles are ordinarily strong, virile stud dogs. Impotence, when it exists, is usually caused by overwork at stud, or following a severe illness. There are various treatments which can be tried with the help of a vet, but unfortunately these are rarely very successful.

Jaundice. Usually leptospiral or caused by a chill. The hound is excessively thirsty, vomits a colourless fluid, and seems unable to retain the water it drinks so voraciously. The motions are greyish in colour. The whites of the eyes, and the skin, take on a yellow tinge. The dog must be considered to be extremely ill. It should be kept warm and made as comfortable as possible, and professional attention must be summoned at once if the patient is to recover. Prevention of leptospirosis is available through injections.

Contamination by rats is thought to be a likely source of infection, and also the urine of infected dogs and bitches, and if valuable hounds are likely to be in contact with either it is advisable to discuss the question of inoculations with the vet.

Kidneys. Various kidney disorders are not uncommon among dogs, especially as they grow old. Symptoms are scanty, dark-coloured, or strong-smelling urine, frequent unsuccessful attempts to urinate, and sometimes a temperature. The dog tends to arch its back, and looks very miserable. Sometimes blood is observed in the urine. There is excessive thirst. Drinking must be controlled, otherwiser the animal will keep vomiting, and small, fairly frequent bowls of barley-water may be offered. The diet is generally restricted to boiled white fish, with selected cereals as advised by the vet, who must always be consulted. Disorders of the kidneys are far too complex to be treated by the layman.

Laxatives. Healthy dogs should never require medicines to open the bowels. Diet should be checked. Gentle laxatives are Milk of Magnesia, olive oil, medicinal paraffin, Syrup of Figs. See also Bowels.

Mange. Sarcoptic Mange. An infection, parasitic, that spreads rapidly when large numbers of dogs are in contact, and in consequence it is not uncommon in pack kennels. A characteristic is violent irritation, the hound scratches almost incessantly, and pink scabs and pustules appear on various portions of the body. These are sometimes first noticed on the hocks, elbows, under arms, and round the eyes. Treatment is by application of an old-fashioned mixture of rape oil, flowers of sulphur, and kerosene; sometimes turpentine is added to the dressing, which should be well shaken and rubbed all over the dog—not just on the affected patches. After five days the dog should be well washed in Tetmosol solution, using also Tetmosol soap and household washing soda to remove all the grease. Meanwhile the kennel must be disinfected, the walls scorched all over with a blow-lamp, all cracks in the floor, ditto. Then walls and floor must be sluiced with hot soda-water with or without disinfectant. The bed must be similarly treated and any bedding burned. It may be necessary to repeat the oiling and bathing two or three times before the parasites are completely eliminated, and the drastic disinfecting must be done after each bath. A dog with mange must be well isolated, and attendants should wash hands and overalls after contact. It is easily transmitted and very difficult to eliminate if it becomes endemic in a large kennel.

Sometimes benzol benzoate emulsion is used in place of the dressing described above. This is toxic, and should not be applied all over on one day. It can be used on three consecutive days, dressing the head and forequarters first, the body and middle piece the next day, and the hindquarters and stern on the third day. After five days the bathing and disinfecting is the same. The use of Valpona strips in the kennel, and also Aerovap appliances are new weapons in the fight against parasites.

Follicular Mange. Differs from sarcoptic mange inasmuch as there is little or no irritation present, although it is also a parasitic affection. The hair falls out and the skin is rough, pustular, and blackish grey in colour. Unlike sarcoptic mange, which spreads rapidly over the entire body unless checked by prompt treatment, follicular mange spreads slowly and generally affects the dog in patches. It is also not considered to be easily transmitted and never spreads through a kennel as does the sarcoptic type. It is, however, far more obstinate and difficult to cure and veterinary attention is advisable when first signs are suspected.

Skin diseases are not always easy to diagnose, some forms of dermatitis and other affections caused by allergies much resembling mange. When there is doubt it is best to get a veterinary surgeon to take skin scrapings in an effort to discover the cause of the trouble, and in the meantime, to be on the safe side, the hound should be regarded as being a possible source of infection to its kennel companions and steps taken to isolate it.

Meningitis. This is an inflammation of the brain, and may occur in young puppies, or dogs of any age which have been suffering from distemper or hard-pad diseases. The dog has fits, during which it loses consciousness, sometimes froths at the mouth, and is incontinent. When it regains its senses it appears dazed, unsteady on its legs, and dizzy; it will cry and whine. The convulsions tend to become more frequent, more severe, and of longer duration, and when this happens the veterinary surgeon will usually advise putting the dog to sleep as it is suffering acutely and its chances of complete recovery are negligible. Similar symptoms can follow a blow on the head.

Nails. The Beagle has strong, thick nails, and set as they are on what should be a round, cat-like foot, they seldom need cutting. A flat foot, one with open, widely spread toes, or an elongated hare-foot, commonly has nails which grow very long and require regular trimming.

The nails which grow on the inside of the legs, an inch or so from the soles of the feet, are called dew-claws. These must be removed from the hind legs at birth, and should never be left on under any circumstances. The removal of the dew-claws on the front legs is optional but advisable. They catch on bushes, frosty ground, etc., and tear, causing nasty sores. The claws are easily removed when the whelps are a few days old, but if left until maturity must be taken out by a veterinary surgeon, using a local or general anaesthetic, should they prove troublesome. Proper nail-clippers are required if toenails need cutting. Care is taken not to cut too much of the nail away, for if the quick is damaged, bleeding results.

Obesity. Very common in Beagles, alas! Beagles are wonderful feeders, they have sharp appetites, and they enjoy their food. If this is not restricted in quantity or if they do not get sufficient brisk exercise they get very fat, especially in middle or old age. Obesity shortens life, and causes sterility in stud dogs and brood bitches. A fat hound should be intelligently dieted. One meal daily, consisting of raw meat only plus some chopped green vegetable, is the rule. No titbits, extras, saucers of milk, and the lids well rammed down on the dustbin and the garbage-pails, please, for the hungry Beagle will not be too discriminating.

Keep the bowels open. Fast the hound, on water only, one day per week. Increase the exercise, giving plenty of opportunities for the hound to run and play at its own inclination. Forced exercise—such as trotting on a lead beside a bicycle—is probably too violent if the hound is very fat, and if practised at all should be over short distances. It may be felt that all these rules are unkind, but it is not kind to allow an animal to become fat and unhealthy, and it is better to adopt what may seem severe measures to get it back into perfect condition.

Parturient Eclampsia. This is not very common, and occurs mainly in nervous or excitable bitches after whelping. It usually begins when the puppies are about two or three weeks old. The bitch's eyelids may twitch, she shivers and shakes and appears wobbly on her legs. She may have convulsions. A vet should be summoned immediately, and he will administer large doses of calcium. It may be necessary to remove the puppies and either put them with a foster-mother, if obtainable, or rear them by hand.

Prompt diagnosis and treatment will generally bring a satisfactory conclusion, but eclampsia should not be treated lightly for it can prove fatal. Unfortunately there is no real preventative. Calcium is not retained in the body, but passes out of the system in a few hours. Breeders sometimes seek to prevent eclampsia by giving large quantities of calcium throughout pregnancy, but this seldom has any effect in preventing attacks. A bitch that suffers from eclampsia will always be liable to get it again following subsequent whelpings.

Purgatives. See Laxatives, also Bowels.

Pymetria. This is a chronic inflammation of the womb, which can fill with pus. The bitch is very ill, runs a high temperature, may vomit, and there is usually a discharge from the uterus which is sometimes not obvious in the early stages if the bitch licks herself clean. The veterinary surgeon should be called; he may attempt to treat the condition, or advise an immediate hysterectomy operation.

Rabies. See Hydrophobia.

Rheumatism. Elderly dogs are often affected with this, and younger hounds if they have been allowed to lie on wet concrete or stone floors. The dog appears stiff in its movements, and cries out in pain when touched, or when it rises from a recumbent position. The bowels should be kept open, and an aspirin given whenever the pain seems acute. Warmth and freedom from damp are essential.

Rickets. Beagle puppies 'do' well under good conditions. They are sturdy at birth, and management is sadly at fault if they get rickets, for it is a condition caused primarily by malnutrition, and precipitated by lack of sunshine, lack of light, and by dark or damp living quarters. If rickets occur it is usually before the puppies are five months old. The puppies appear lame, the joints of the legs enlarge, and the legs become misshapen and weak. Apart from the common cause of poor feeding, rickets can be caused by worms, also from lack of liberty.

The remedies are nourishing food, plenty of meat and rich milk, cod-liver oil and malt with vitamin D supplement, and an iron tonic. Clean, dry bedding, gentle exercise in the fresh air and sunshine, preferably on gravel and not on cold concrete or in long grass.

Shock. Shock can be caused by a fall or an accident, by becoming involved in a serious dog fight, or by contact with a live electric wire. The hound may be semi-conscious, the breathing shallow and feeble, and the limbs cold. Place the dog in a box with plenty of blankets and a hot-water bottle or two, and hurry it to the vet.

Stings. Wasp and bee stings can cause great pain and discomfort, and if a hound is stung on the lips or tongue it can be most dangerous. Domestic pets often get stung by wasps, especially when the insects inhabit fallen apples or plums in the garden. Hunting Beagles get themselves mixed up with swarms of wild bees or disturbed wasps' nests occasionally. Stings should be removed with tweezers, and the spot rubbed with cut, raw onion, moist blue-bag, or T.C.P. or vinegar. If there is a great deal of swelling, especially about the head, and if the Beagle appears to be suffering great discomfort, the vet should be asked to administer an anti-histamine injection, which gives relief.

Teeth. Beagle puppies teethe easily and normally, and seldom suffer from teething fits or rashes. Hounds fed on wholesome food, and allowed occasional large bones and frequent hard biscuits, do not often need their teeth cleaned. When tartar does collect it should be scraped away with a proper tooth-scaler. This is quite easy to do, and any vet will demonstrate the method if required to do so. A brush with powdered pumice and precipitated chalk, mixed to a paste with a little peroxide, will finish the job nicely.

Temperature. The dog in health usually has a normal temperature of about 38.5°C (101.2°F). A small deviation one way or the other is no cause for anxiety, especially where puppies or nervous dogs are concerned. An incident such as an unaccustomed ride in a motor-car can send the temperature up a degree.

A sudden violent rise or drop in the temperature is always a danger sign, especially if it is accompanied by the smallest sign of malaise, and the cause should be sought.

A half-minute thermometer should have the end lubricated with a smear of Vaseline, and the bulb containing the mercury should be gently inserted well into the rectum. Before insertion the mercury should be shaken down below the numbers and it should be held inside the dog for rather more than half a minute. A second person should be present to hold the dog, otherwise it may struggle and break the thermometer. If the reading is over 39°C. (102.5°F.) or below 38°C. (100°F.), keep the hound warm and send for the vet.

Tonsillitis. The animal usually runs a temperature, the inside of the throat is red and inflamed, and the dog is listless and disinclined to eat. Tonsillitis is generally regarded as a contagious condition, and a vet should see the dog and advise treatment. It is best kept isolated from other dogs, which should, if contacts, be kept under observation.

Vomiting. See Biliousness.

Worms. Beagles suffer from worms as do other breeds. Most puppies harbour roundworms to a greater or lesser degree, and should be dosed at about six weeks of age and again a fortnight later. After this, with luck, they should keep clear for a considerable time and need not be treated again until signs of the parasites are noticed. Adult Beagles can also suffer from roundworms, but more often get tapeworms, and the latter are rather more difficult to eradicate. They can cause a lot of trouble, for hounds infested with worms do not thrive, remain lean, and have poor, lustreless coats. Both types of worms can cause convulsions.

There are plenty of excellent tablets and mixtures compounded to eliminate these pests; some can be bought over the counter from any chemist stocking animal medicines, others are obtainable only through a vet. One brand can be very effective on one dog, less so on another. If worms are known to be present, try one type of vermifuge, and if it does not give good results, wait a fortnight and try another make. Always follow directions exactly. Some vermifuges require the dog to be fasted before dosing, some advise a purge after the worm medicine has been given. Others suggest a sloppy meal just before or just after treatment. The effectiveness of these preparations depends upon their being administered according to the makers' instructions.

GLOSSARY OF TERMS

ALL ON! All members of the pack present.

ANUS. The posterior opening through which the contents of the bowels are eliminated.

APPLE HEAD. A rounded or very domed head.

APPOINTMENT. Place and time of Meet.

AT FAULT. When hounds have lost the scent.

BABBLER. A hound that gives tongue without reason.

BALANCED. No exaggeration anywhere, every part of the Beagle in proportion to the other.

BARREL RIBS. Rib cage excessively rounded so as to prevent the forelegs and elbows being correctly placed.

BLAZE. A white line extending from skull to muzzle.

BOSSY. A term commonly used to describe heavy or over-padded shoulders.

BREAK UP. When the pack eats the dead hare.

BREECHING. The profusely coated 'trousers' on the hind legs.

BRISKET. The chest, between the forelegs and beneath the withers.

BRUSH. The stern or tail, with particular reference to the longer hairs on the underside of same.

BUTTERFLY NOSE. A black or liver-coloured nose speckled with pink.

CANINE TOOTH. The long fangs, one each side of the jaw.

CARRY THE HORN. Undertake the part of huntsman.

CAST. Recovering a lost scent.

CAT FOOT. Round, thick, tightly closed foot, resembling that of the cat.

CHECK. When hounds have lost the scent.

CHISELLING. The angles dividing skull and foreface.

CHOP. Hounds are said to 'Chop a Hare' when they kill her without having chased her.

CLOSE-COUPLED. Short in back and loin.

CLOSE SEASON. The time of year when hares are not hunted.

COBBY. Close-coupled, thick-set, compact.

CORKY. Lively, active, full of spirit, a gay showman.

COUPLING. A word sometimes used to describe the act of mating.

COUPLINGS. The section of the body that joins with the hindquarters.

COWHOCKS. Hocks that turn inwards, weak hocks.

CROSSBREED. The result of a mating between two dogs of different pure breeds.

CROUP. The extremity of the backline, and point at which stern is set on.

CRYPTORCHID. A male animal in which neither of the two testicles is externally visible or functional.

DENTITION. The arrangement of the teeth.

DEW-CLAWS. Extra 'toes', complete with claws, set well above the feet on the inside of fore or hind legs. Hind dew-claws are usually removed at birth, front dew-claws optionally, but better removed.

DEWLAP. The soft, pendulous skin under the chin and neck.

DISH FACE. A concave muzzle.

DISTEMPER TEETH. Teeth pitted, decayed, discoloured brown as a result of disease.

DOE. The female hare.

DOG. Any member of the species *canine familaris*.

DOUBLE. When a hare runs back on her tracks.

DOUBLE COAT. A smooth upper coat with a closer, woollier mat of hairs growing near the skin.

DOUBLE THE HORN. A succession of short, sharp blasts on a hunting horn.

DRAFT. Discarded hounds or hounds sold from packs are 'drafted'.

DRAG. The line of scent leading to a hare in her form. The line of scent artificially laid as a preparation for a 'drag hunt'.

DRAW. Search for a hare.

DRY. Neat, tight skin formation. No loose, or surplus, pendant skin about mouth or throat.

DUDLEY NOSE. A light-coloured brown or flesh-coloured nose.

DWELL. Hounds that do not drive forward, dwell.

EWE NECK. A thin, excessively arched, proportionately over-long, neck.

FANG. A large canine tooth.

FEATHER. The gently waving stern on a hound is said to 'feather'.

FIDDLE FRONT. A crooked front, with legs out at elbow and sloping towards each other at the pastern joints, bent forearms, front feet turning outwards.

FLEWS. The pendulous lips.

FLYER. An outstanding specimen of any breed.

FOIL. A smell that cancels out the scent of the hare.

FOREARM. The long bone of the front leg.

FOREFACE. The muzzle.

FORM. The nest of the hare, any small depression in which she takes cover.

FRONT. The chest and forelegs as seen from directly in front of a hound.

GAY STERN, GAY TAIL. A stern carried higher over the back than desired, or very curly.

GAZE-HOUND. A hound that hunts by sight as distinct from a hound that hunts by scent.

GIVE TONGUE. The noise of hounds, referred to as 'barking' in other breeds of dogs.

GO TO CRY. When hounds run to other hounds which are giving tongue.

GO TO GROUND. Hares occasionally seek shelter in drains or burrows, and are said to 'go to ground'.

GOOSE RUMP. A sloping-away of the croup very sharply.

HACKNEY ACTION. The exaggerated lifting of the legs in the manner of the hackney horse, which is not considered to provide an enduring gait and movement.

HARE FOOT. A long, oval-shaped, narrow foot.

HEIGHT. The height of hounds is measured from a point between the shoulder-blades at the highest point of the slope where the neck joins the back, referred to as the withers.

HIT OFF THE LINE. Expression used when hounds recover a line after a check.

HOCK. The lower joint of the hind leg.

HOLD OVER. Command to hounds to keep to the side of the road.

HOLD UP. Command to hounds to stop.

HOUND-MARKED. Distribution of colour on white, often assumed to imply black and tan on white, in the manner associated with the markings of Foxhounds, Harriers, or Beagles.

HUICK HOLLOA. To draw attention to a view holloa.

HUICK TO MELODY (or whatever the name of the hound that, by its cry, appears to have found the scent). To encourage the pack to follow this hound.

IN BLOOD. Hounds are said to be in blood when they have killed on their last few days out hunting.

JACK. A male hare.

JELLY DOGS. A slang term used for Beagles, derived, no doubt, from the custom of eating red-currant jelly with jugged hare.

KNUCKLE OVER. Forelegs which bulge frontwards at the pastern joint are said to 'knuckle over'.

LEATHERS. Pendant ears.

LEVERET. A young hare.

LIFT. When hounds are forced to leave a line they are hunting and encouraged to hunt another line the huntsman is said to 'lift' the pack.

LIPPY. Lips longer, fuller, or more pendulous than desired.

LOADED. Shoulders are said to be 'loaded' when they are proportionately heavy in comparison to the rest of the hound, over-padded with muscle and/or flesh.

LOINS. The part of the body between the hip-bone and the ribs.

LUMBERING. A lumbering gait means that a hound sways or rolls from side to side, instead of trotting neatly and smartly.

MASK. The head of a hare.

MEUSE. The hare's track through a hedgerow.

MOLAR TOOTH. One of the smaller, grinding teeth towards the back of the jaw.

MONGREL. A dog of mixed ancestry, containing the blood of several purebred dogs of different breeds, or made up of dogs of mixed parentage themselves.

MONORCHID. A male animal with only one testicle in the scrotum. Monorchidism is a disqualification under Kennel Club rules and such animals are not eligible for exhibition.

MOVING OFF. When hounds leave the Meet to draw for a hare they 'move off'.

MUTE. When a hound follows a scent without giving tongue it follows 'mute'.

MUZZLE. The foreface.

OCCIPUT. The peak of the skull between the ears.

OLFACTORY. Pertaining to sense of smell.

OPEN. Hounds 'open' directly they begin to give tongue.

OUT AT ELBOW. Elbows turned away from the chest, uneven in appearance, loose.

OUT AT SHOULDER. Shoulder-blades loosely attached to the body, jutting out. Usually combined with loose elbows, and often with excessive width between the front legs.

OVERSHOT. A short lower jaw, or teeth arranged so that upper set project forward over lower teeth.

OWN. Hounds 'own a scent' when they speak to it.

PACK. A number of hounds from any one kennel, used for hunting.

PAD. The sole of the hound's foot. The foot of the hare.

PADDLING. A faulty gait, whereby the front legs are thrown outwards in a loose, unco-ordinated manner.

PASTERN. The small section of the front leg that joins the foot to the forearm.

PERIOD OF GESTATION. The length of time taken by a bitch to produce a litter—sixty-three days.

PIED. In Beagles, a white hound generously marked with one colour, or shadings of one colour.

PIG JAW. An overshot jaw.

PIPE-STOPPER STERN. A thin tail with insufficient substance to it.

PREMOLAR TOOTH. The small teeth placed between the large canines and the molars or large back teeth. Premolars are sometimes absent, commonly so in certain breeds, such absence being considered a fault.

PUPPY. A dog not exceeding twelve months of age.

PUT UP. Hounds put up a hare when they startle her from her form.

QUARTERS. Hind legs.

QUEST. When hounds are casting around for a hare.

RACK. See Meuse.

RATE. To rate is to scold.

RICKETS. A disease of the bones caused by malnutrition, lack of vitamins, dark or damp kennelling, lack of sunlight and fresh air.

RING TAIL. A stern curled over the back, touching the back.

RIOT. Hounds 'riot' if they hunt anything other than their proper quarry; for instance, rabbits or cats.

ROACH BACK. An arched spine.

ROLLING GAIT. See Lumbering.

SCISSOR BITE. Teeth which fit closely, the upper set sliding just in front of the lower set.

SCUT. The tail of the hare.

SECOND THIGH. The hind leg between the stifle and hock-joint.

SHELLY. Lightly built, lacking bone and substance.

SICKLE HOCKS. Hocks bent, the upper joints inclining outwards.

SKIRTER. A hound that cuts corners, by-passes angles, and does not follow faithfully the path of the hare.

SLAB SIDES. Very flat sides with insufficient spring of rib.

SNIPY. Narrow, slight, pointed muzzle.

SPLAY FOOT. A foot with loose, badly fitting toes with space between them.

SQUIRREL STERN OR TAIL. A stern extending forward almost flat upon the back.

STERN. The term used for the tail on hounds.

STIFLE. The joint immediately above the hock.

STOP. The section between the eyes and dividing forehead and muzzle.

STRAIGHT HOCKS. Lack of angulation (generally causing poor propulsion and short, choppy movement). Faulty proportion of hock-bone.

STRAIGHT SHOULDERS. Shoulder-blades too upright, resulting in restricted forward reach of front legs when moving.

SQUAT. A hare 'squats' when she stays sitting in one spot.

THROATY. Possessing too much loose skin beneath the chin.

THROW THEIR TONGUES. Hounds 'throw their tongues' when other dogs would be said to yelp, or bark.

THROW UP. Hounds lose the scent.

TIMBER. The term 'plenty of timber' is sometimes used by judges to describe ample, heavy bones.

TRI-COLOUR. Three-coloured.

UNDERHUNG, UNDERSHOT. Prominent lower teeth. The lower jaw extending beyond the upper jaw.

UPPER ARM. The section between the elbow and the point of the shoulder-bone.

VIEW HOLLOA. Holloa is always pronounced 'holler'. A shout from a member of the field, official or otherwise, indicating that a hare has been sighted.

WARE. Ware is always pronounced 'warr'. A scolding and warning to hounds to cease hunting things other than their intended quarry.

WEAVING. Plaiting the front legs in action.

WEEDINESS. Lack of bone, substance, stamina.

WHIP. A hunt servant who 'whips in' the hounds to keep the pack together and under control.

WRINKLE. Folds of loose skin on the skull or surrounding the eyes

LIST OF CHAMPIONS UNDER KENNEL CLUB RULES—1926–78

Beagle	Sex	Owner	Breeder	Born	Sire	Dam
1926 The Belton Scornful	B	Mrs T. Beaumont	Mr P. Roberts	18.7.20	The Stoke Place Schoolboy	Montgomeryshire Madcap
1927 Bilton Pedlar	D	Mrs H. G. Beaumont	Mrs H. G. Beaumont	9.6.23	Bilton Plunderer	The Belton Scornful Ch.
1931 Dauntless of Reynalton	D	Mrs N. E. Elms	Miss D. White	29.9.28	Marquis	Dutiful
Melody of Reynalton	B	Mrs N. E. Elms	Hon. Vivian North	Sept. 27	Chancellor	Fabulous
1934 Ranter of Reynalton	D	Mrs N. E. Elms	Miss D. White	13.7.29	Miser of Reynalton	Melody of Reynalton Ch.
1935 Crymmych Gipsy Queen	B	Mr E. G. Sergeant	Mr O. Jones	5.4.29	Ranter of Taf	Brenda of Vaeltrigan
Mischief	D	Miss W. M. D. Wills	Miss W. M. D. Wills	7.2.34	Boysie	Runlee Ragtime
1936 Pirate	D	Viscount Chelmsford	Mrs I. Lush	15.9.33	Reynalton Rackway	Modesty
Crocus	B	Mrs E. D. Stockley	Mr Davies	22.5.32	Limbourne Gambler	Wolverston Cautious
Bauble of Reynalton	B	Miss V. M. Forester	Mrs N. E. Elms	8.8.30	Dauntless of Reynalton Ch.	Tuneful of Reynalton
Runlee Ragtime	B	Miss W. M. D. Wills	Mrs Hawes	14.4.31	Brutus	Rosemary

Beagle	Sex	Owner	Breeder	Born	Sire	Dam
1938 Bellman of Reynalton	D	Viscount Chelmsford	Mrs N. E. Elms	2.4.35	Jollyboy of Reynalton	Music of Reynalton
1949 Acregreen Wellbred	D	Dr S. Young	Mrs M. K. Spowart	29.4.49	Grady O'Grady	Woodwren Ch.
Limbourne Violet	B	Mrs B. L. Bostock	Mrs E. D. Stockley	15.3.45	Eton Villager	Limbourne Riot
1950 Solomon of Stanhurst	D	Miss N. Wilmshurst	Mr J. S. Steward	16.10.45	Wolverston Ranger	Melody
Limbourne Playful	B	Mr B. Arnett and Mr C. Hardwick	Mrs M. C. Davies	12.12.46	Pilgrim	Limbourne Violet Ch.
1951 Acregreen Whimsey	B	Mr W. R. Anderson	Mrs M. K. Spowart	29.4.49	Grady O'Grady	Woodwren Ch.
1952 Acregreen Whynot	D	Mrs M. K. Spowart	Mrs M. K. Spowart	29.4.49	Grady O'Grady	Woodwren Ch.
Limbourne Plunder	D	Lt Col W. J. Bostock	Mrs E. D. Stockley	12.12.46	Pilgrim	Limbourne Violet Ch.
Rectory Patsy	B	Mrs A. P. Powell	S/Ldr P. E. Barnes	12.3.47	North Bucks Chaser	North Bucks Bashful
1953 Radley Triumph of Appeline	D	D. H. Appleton	The Radley College Beagles	1946	Springfield Traitor	Eton Wisdom
Woodwren	B	Mrs M. K. Spowart	Mr J. S. Steward	21.8.47	Eton College Woodman	Lively
1954 Appeline Matchless	D	Mr D. H. Appleton	Mr D. H. Appleton	8.1.53	Radley Triumph of Appeline Ch.	Catterick Sandal
Wilful	B	Miss P. Clayton	Mrs C. J. Davies	30.10.50	Limbourne Valiant	Jaunty
1955 Appeline Barsheen Ringwood	D	Mr D. H. Appleton	Mrs Y. Oldman	24.11.53	Radley Triumph of Appeline Ch.	Appeline Revelry

Beagle	Sex	Owner	Breeder	Born	Sire	Dam
1955—contd.						
Tavernmews Bashful	B	Mrs P. Parker	Miss J. Whitton	17.2.52	8th Hussar's Dolphin	East Nene Bridesmaid
Wellshot New College and Magdalen Gesture	B	Mr E. Sayer	New College and Magdalen Beagles	1950	New College and Magdalen Rebel	Eton College Gossame
1956						
Appeline Glider	D	Mr D. H. Appleton	Mr D. H. Appleton	30.6.52	Radley Triumph of Appeline Ch.	Appeline Cautious
Barvae Statute	D	Mr F. W. Watson	Mrs G. M. Clayton	21.7.54	Barvae Beckful	Spotlight
Wytchend Linkella	B	Mrs D. Crowther Davies	Major and Mrs Ellis Hughes	5.10.54	Solomon of Stanhurst Ch.	Lindsey Makeway
Wytchend Melody	B	Mrs D. Crowther Davies	Major and Mrs Ellis Hughes	28.9.53	Radley Triumph of Appeline Ch.	Lindsey Makeway
1957						
Appeline Rocket	D	Mr D. H. Appleton	Mrs K. M. Watt	29.5.56	Appeline Barsheen Ringwood Ch.	Feyfey
Barvae Paigan	D	Mrs G. M. Clayton	Mr J. Bowker	7.5.54	Stairaird Pagan	Castleton Fantail
Appeline Gaylass	B	Miss R. M. Brucker		Date of birth and details		of pedigree unknown
Cannybuff Barvae Playful	B	Mrs E. Crowther Davies	Mrs G. M. Clayton	20.9.55	Barvae Paigan Ch.	Barvae Bellmaid
Wellshot Wistful	B	Mr E. Sayer	Mr S. Young	19.6.54	Acregreen Wellbred Ch.	Wellshot New College and Magdalen Gesture Ch.
1958						
Cannybuff Clipper	D	Mrs E. Crowther Davies	Mrs E. Crowther Davies	18.6.56	Barvae Paigan Ch.	Wytchend Melody Ch.
Elmhurst Playmate	D	Mr and Mrs W. H. Herrick	Mr and Mrs W. H. Herrick	1.5.56	Barvae Paigan Ch.	Elmhurst Wistful
Barvae Willing	B	Mrs G. M. Clayton	Miss P. Clayton	2.9.55	Barvae Brimstone	Wilful Ch.
Derawuda Vixen	B	Mr F. W. Watson	Mr F. W. Watson	14.2.56	Barvae Statute Ch.	Barvae Ringdove
Tavernmews Bonnet	B	Miss J. Whitton and Miss F. E. Siddle	Miss J. Whitton	24.12.56	Barvae Paigan Ch.	Tavernmews Bridget

Beagle	Sex	Owner	Breeder	Born	Sire	Dam
1959						
Barvae Vesper	B	Mrs G. M. Clayton	Mrs G. M. Clayton	8.4.57	Limbourne Valiant	Barvae Wagtail
Deaconfield Rebecca	B	Mrs D. Macro	Mrs D. Macro	29.1.58	Barvae Statute Ch.	Stanhurst Rachel
1960						
Tavernmews Barrister	D	Mr R. H. Goddard	Misses J. Whitton and F. Siddle	23.4.59	Tavernmews Ranter Ch.	Tavernmews Bonnet Ch.
Tavernmews Ranter	D	Misses J. Whitton and F. E. Siddle	Miss J. Wilmshurst	12.1.58	Stanhurst Poacher	Stanhurst Rebecca
Barvae Tangle	B	Mrs G. M. Clayton	Mrs G. M. Clayton	25.4.57	Barvae Tatler	Barvae Progress
1961						
Appeline Bishopford Whipper	D	Mr and Mrs D. H. Appleton	Mrs M. E. Bull	30.10.59	Appeline Dancer of Camerlyn	Appeline Rosewood of Bramblings
Appeline Valet	D	Mrs and Mrs D. H. Appleton	Mr and Mrs D. H. Appleton	7.9.59	Appeline Rocket Ch.	Appeline Dreymin Danseuse
Barvae Acrobat	D	Mr D. W. Nightingale	Mrs G. M. Clayton	11.1.60	Barvae Benroe Wrinkles	Barvae Varner
Barvae Aider	B	Mrs G. M. Clayton	Mrs G. M. Clayton	15.1.60	Barvae Benroe Wrinkles	Barvae Progress
Barvae Garland	B	Mrs G. M. Clayton	Mr L. V. Green	27.6.59	Barvae Ponder	Barvae Vanity of the Lodge
Barvae Tamar	B	Mrs M. Spavin	Mrs G. M. Clayton	6.12.57	Barvae Paigan Ch.	Barvae Tartan
Joyful of Hialeah	B	Mr G. O'Hara	Mr G. O'Hara	19.5.59	Barvae Trooper	Barvae Skylark
Tavernmews Rainbow	B	Mr and Mrs H. Essam	Misses J. Whitton and F. Siddle	23.4.59	Tavernmews Ranter Ch.	Tavernmews Bonnet Ch.
Twinrivers Garland	B	Miss R. M. Brucker	Miss R. M. Brucker	15.4.57	Kirtlington Chief	Appeline Gaylass Ch.
Wendover Billy	D	Mr and Mrs L. C. James	Mr and Mrs L. C. James	31.8.59	Letton Rozavel Dwight	Reyas Clarion
Woodbeach Wisdom	B	Mr and Mrs R. E. Davies	Mr G. Leeson	31.5.59	Elmhurst Playmate Ch.	Barvae Tinsel
1962						
Twinrivers Bellman	D	Miss R. Brucker	Miss R. Brucker	5.5.60	Tavernmews Barrister Ch.	Twinrivers Garland Ch.

Beagle	Sex	Owner	Breeder	Born	Sire	Dam
1962—contd.						
Appeline Top Ace	D	Mr and Mrs D. H. Appleton	J. J. Geedes	15.9.59	Gay Fellow of Geddesburg	Fancy Free of Geddesbirgh
Appeline Ravish	B	Mrs C. Appleton	—	—	Further particulars unknown	
Rozavel Earring	B	Mrs T. Gray	Mrs T. Gray	26.3.61	Rozavel Little Dime	Rozavel Bangle
Barvae Wynder	B	Mrs G. Clayton	Mrs G. Clayton	15.1.60	Barvae Benroe Wrinkles	Barvae Willing Ch.
Wendover Viva	B	Mr and Mrs L. C. James	Mr and Mrs L. C. James	31.2.61	Letton Rozavel Dwight	Reyas Clarion
Appeline Cannon	D	Mrs C. Appleton	Mr & Mrs D. H. Appleton	16.7.61	Appeline Rocket Ch.	Appeline Ribbon
1963						
Appeline Rambler	D	Mrs C. Appleton	Mr & Mrs W. S. Morris	16.10.60	Appeline Valet Ch.	Appeline Unity of Nelmes
Barvae Varlo	D	Mrs G. M. Clayton	Mrs G. M. Clayton	11.4.61	Barvae Benroe Wrinkles	Barvae Vesper Ch.
Dialynne Huntsman	D	Mrs M. M. Spavin	Mrs M. M. Spavin	2.3.61	Barvae Benroe Wrinkles	Derawuda Vanity
Wendover Space	D	D. Gwyn Williams	Mr & Mrs L. C. James	15.12.60	Letton Americano	Wendover Sallyann
Deaconfield Ripple	B	Mrs D. Macro	Mrs D. Macro	11.11.60	Barvae Pagan Ch.	Deaconfield Rebecca Ch.
Derawuda Willing	B	F. W. Watson	F. W. Watson	4.5.61	Appeline Dancer of Camerlyn	Derawuda Vixen
Elsa of Centrevale	B	Mr & Mrs A. Steward	Mrs M. Steward	9.11.59	Barvae Pagan Ch.	Hardad Amethyst
Pinewood Crumpet	B	Mr & Mrs L. F. Priestley	Mrs M. Slapp	3.11.60	Alunscar Bondsman	Cannybuff Comical
Rossut Treetops Hasty Footsteps	B	Mrs C. G. Sutton	Mrs de Casembroot	16.12.60	Rozavel Texas Star	Treetops Holdfast
Rozavel Texan Starlet	B	Mrs T. Gray	Mrs P. Castle	14.6.60	Rozavel Texas Star	Rozavel Bashful
1964						
Appeline Replica	D	Mrs C. Appleton	Mrs M. Sedgley	13.1.62	Appeline Top Ace Ch.	Sedgford Dimple

Beagle	Sex	Owner	Breeder	Born	Sire	Dam
1964—contd.						
Beston Bugler	D	Mrs B. A. Martin	Mr H. C. Martin	6.7.61	Stormerbanks Music Master	Beston Wonderful
Cannybuff Curry	D	Mrs E. Crowther Davies	Mrs E. Crowther Davies	16.10.61	Barvae Benroe Wrinkles	Cannybuff Barvae Playful Ch.
Larkholme Andima Classic Major	D	Mrs A. S. Mawson	Mr & Mrs Gradwell	8.1.63	Appeline Cannon Ch.	Larkholme Andima Juliana
Manico Chancellor	D	Mrs M. Nuttall	Mrs M. Nuttall	1.9.61	Ravernmews Ranter Ch.	Cannybuff Can Can
Rossut Triumphant	D	Mrs C. G. Sutton	Mrs C. G. Sutton	2.5.62	Rossut Joker	Rossut Fashion
Rossut Vagabond	D	Mrs C. G. Sutton	Mrs C. G. Sutton	18.5.62	Rossut Joker	Rossut Trustful
Rozavel Elsy's Diamond Jerry	D	Mrs T. Gray	Mr & Mrs Elsey	13.5.61	Scholls Ferry Jeremy	Elsey's Black Diamond
Barvae Rimple	B	Mrs H. Harron	Mrs G. M. Clayton	5.7.60	Barvae Benroe Wrinkles	Barvae Rival
Barvae Shuna	B	Mrs G. M. Clayton	Mrs G. M. Clayton	13.1.62	Barvae Paigan Ch.	Barvae Wynder Ch.
Cannybuff Cider	B	Mrs E. Crowther Davies	Mrs E. Crowther Davies	22.8.61	Barvae Benroe Wrinkles	Cannybuff Cobweb
Derawuda Bashful	B	F. W. Watson	F. W. Watson	24.10.62	Appeline Top Ace Ch.	Derawuda Willing Ch.
Forradon Chance	B	Mrs P. Harris & L. Pagliero	Mrs P. Harris & L. Pagliero	7.7.62	Appeline Top Ace Ch.	Forradon Bothered
Rosebrooke Rebel	B	Mrs R. A. MacDonald	Mrs R. A. MacDonald	24.2.62	Letton Americano	Appeline Raindrop
1965						
Barvae Pilot	D	Mrs G. M. Clayton	Mrs G. M. Clayton	12.4.62	Barvae Benroe Wrinkles	Barvae Progress
Dialynne Ponder	D	Mrs M. M. Spavin	Mrs M. M. Spavin	3.2.63	Dialynne Huntsman Ch.	Willsue Dream
Gaytail Brigand	D	H. Marsden	Mr & Mrs E. Middleton	18.12.62	Tavernmews Butler	Gaytail Wunda
Letton Americano	D	Mrs J. Beck				
Barvae Rosebud	B	Mrs G. M. Clayton	Mrs G. M. Clayton	16.4.62	Barvae Vernon	Barvae Posy
Beston Slipper	B	Mr & Mrs Devereux	H. Martin	13.5.62	Beston Bugler	Barvae Stocking
Forradon Appeline Beeswing	B	Mrs P. Harris & L. Pagliero	Mrs C. Appleton	4.7.63	Appeline Replica Ch.	Beston Woodchop
Forradon Chantress	B	Mrs P. Harris & L. Pagliero	Mrs D. Freeman	18.9.64	Forradon Cardinal	Reaside Chinnor Fickle

Beagle	Sex	Owner	Breeder			
1965—contd.						
Rossut Deaconfield Ravish	B	Mrs C. G. Sutton	Mrs D. Macro	6.2.62	Barvae Paigan Ch.	Deaconfield Rebecca Ch.
1966						
Easthazel Candor	D	D. W. McKay	Mrs R. M. Mowbray	14.9.62	Barvae Benroe Wrinkles	Easthazel Butterscotch
Wendover Bertram	D	Mr & Mrs L. C. James	Mr & Mrs L. C. James	10.9.64	Letton Americano Ch.	Wendover Vica Ch.
Barvae Poola	B	Mrs G. N. Clayton	Mrs G. M. Clayton	29.5.63	Barvae Vernon	Barvae Progress
Cornevon Passive	B	Mrs A. M. & Miss P. J. Gibson	F. Carter	30.12.63	Crestamere Buzzyby	Cornevon Blossoms Bud
Diane of Centrevale	B	Mr & Mrs A. Steward	Mr & Mrs A. Steward	25.5.64	Appeline Juggler	Haroad Amethyst
Pinewood Wyrebrig	B	Mr & Mrs L. F. Priestley	Mrs Slapp	14.12.64	Tonawanda Sibiche	Cannybuff Comical
Roseeta of Glenbervie	B	A. B. Nicolson	A. B. Nicolson	17.2.64	Chaman Legend of Glenbervie	Wendover Sall
Rossut Colinbear Phantom	B	Mrs C. G. Sutton	Lady Moynihan	4.11.62	Rossut Plunder	Treetops Envy of Stubblesdown
Twinrivers Brevity	B	Miss R. Brucker	Miss R. Brucker	5.5.60	Tavernmews Barrister Ch.	Twinrivers Garland Ch.
1967						
Deaconfield Renown	D	Mrs D. Macro	Mrs D. Macro	25.1.63	Dialynne Huntsman Ch.	Deaconfield Ripple Ch.
Easthazel Miniman	D	D. W. McKay	Mrs Mowbray	6.1.64	Rossut Plunder	Easthazel Candytuft
Raimex Tally	D	Mrs D. Brown	Mrs D. Brown	16.8.65	Barvae Pilot Ch.	Raimex Tiffin
Rossut Juggler	D	Mrs C. G. Sutton	Mrs C. G. Sutton	9.5.63	Rossut Joker	Rossut Playful
Rozavel Madison	D	Mrs T. Gray	Mrs T. Gray	25.7.65	Rozavel Elsy's Diamond Jerry Ch.	Rozavel Alabama
Brookgilt Dingle	B	C. Lee	C. Shaw	24.10.65	Barvae Varlo Ch.	Sally of Brookgilt
Dialynne Opal	B	Mrs M. M. Spavin	Mrs M. M. Spavin	12.9.62	Dialynne Huntsman Ch.	Barvae Tamar Ch.
Dialynne Shadow	B	Mrs M. Spavin	Mrs Mallaby	27.3.65	Dialynne Huntsman Ch.	Moorcliff Sonnet

Beagle	Sex	Owner	Breeder	Born	Sire	Dam
1967—contd.						
Rossut Nutmeg	B	Mrs C. G. Sutton	Mrs Ormsby	13.9.65	Rossut Vagabond Ch.	Kempton Melody
1968						
Barvae Stamford	D	Mrs G. M. Clayton	Mrs G. M. Clayton	3.4.66	Barvae Varlo Ch.	Barvae Shuna Ch.
Deaconfield Rampage	D	Mrs D. Macro	P. Sargeant	30.5.65	Larkholme Andima Classic Major Ch.	Deaconfield Regan
Forrardon Foxtrot	D	Mrs P. Harris & L. Pagliero	Mrs P. Harris & L. Pagliero	12.9.65	Dialynne Ponder Ch.	Forrardon Appeline Beeswing Ch.
Houndsmark Manful	D	Mrs M. I. Field	Mrs M. I. Field	17.7.65	Deaconsfield Ransom	Houndsmark Melody
Crestamere Orchid	B	Mrs W. Mahoney	Mrs W. Mahoney	25.11.65	Crestamere Index	Crestamere Charming of Stubblesdown
Dialynne Posy	B	Mrs H. Harron	Mrs M. M. Spavin	3.2.63	Dialynne Huntsman Ch.	Willsue Dream
Forrardon Frolic	B	Mrs P. Harris & L. Pagliero	Mrs P. Harris & L. Pagliero	12.9.65	Dialynne Ponder Ch.	Forrardon Appeline Beeswing Ch.
Rossut Gaiety	B	Mrs C. G. Sutton	Mrs C. G. Sutton	25.11.66	Rossut Joker	Rossut Trustful
Southcourt Melody	B	Mrs G. Young	Mrs G. Young	9.8.66	Southcourt Tarquin	Southcourt Mandy
Strathdene Faithful	B	Mrs J. Limond	Mrs J. Limond	5.10.65	Tonawanda Sibiche	Strathdene Dainty
Tavernmews Rebecca	B	Miss J. Whitton & L. B. Cook	Miss J. Whitton & L. B. Cook	5.4.66	Tavernmews Rossut Ranter	Tavernmews Lansview Rachel
1969						
Southcourt Wembury Merryboy	D	Mrs G. Young	Mrs Hastie	28.4.67	Southcourt Tarquin	Wembury Tinkerbell Chantress
Dialynne Nettle	B	Mrs M. Sparin & Mr B. Moorhouse	Mrs M. Sparin	27.12.67	Ch. Dialynne Ponder	Ch. Dialynne Shadow
Dorfield Wendover Twiggy	B	Mrs K. G. Lupton	Miss J. Russell	1.1.67	Wendover Jaunty	Wendover Ambo
Cornevon Sandpiper	D	Mrs A. M. & Miss P. J. Gibson	Owners	16.1.66	Ch. Letton Americano	Cornevon Bashful
Penwarne Jonavere Apple Blossom	B	Mrs V. E. Dale	Miss S. Tarry	1.5.67	Ch. Deaconfield Rampage	Stanhurst Blackberry
Rossut Cinder	B	Mrs C. G. Sutton	Owner	9.11.67	Rossut Juggler	Zany Cindy

Beagle	Sex	Owner	Breeder	Born	Sire	Dam
1969—contd.						
Rossut Redgate Trueman	D	Mrs C. G. Sutton	Mr J. Hall	29.10.67	Ch. Rossut Triumphant	Redgate Dashing Rascal
Onform Rozavel Blackcherry	B	Mrs T. Laskowski	Miss M. A. Cole	25.9.66	Ch. Rozavel Madison	Freeborne Bracken
Redgate Marquis	D	Mr J. Hall	Owner	27.4.67	Ch. Deaconfield Rampage	Redgate Crestamere Edna
Foxgay Calypso	D	Mr J. Cordon	Owner	11.4.67	Ch. Gaytail Brigand	Foxgay Tytherington Pippa
1970						
Cornevon Pirouette	B	Mrs A. M. & Miss P. Gibson	Owners	16.11.68	Ch. Forrardon Foxtrot	Ch. Cornevon Pensive
Forrardon Kinsman	D	Mrs P. Harris & Mr L. Pagliero	Owners	1.9.67	Ch. Deaconfield Rampage	Ch. Forrardon Chantress
Leetor Loughjoy Emperor	D	Mr & Mrs S. G. Thomas	Mrs J. Batty	7.12.67	Proud Boy of Newtons Drive	Loughjoy Brandy
Rossut Bobbin	B	Mrs C. G. Sutton	Owner	22.12.68	Ch. Rossut Gaffer	Ch. Rossut Colinbar Phantom
Southcourt Wembury Fiddler	D	Mr P. Newman	Mrs E. D. Hastie	29.8.68	Southcourt Tarquin	Wembury Tinkerbell Chantress
Sylvahue Woodbarn Jemma	B	Mr & Mrs H. Foster	Mrs B. Fletcher	5.8.68	Ch. Barvae Pilot	Cherflet Woodbarn Holly
Tavernmews Trademark	D	Miss J. Whitton & Mr L. B. Cook	Owners	20.2.68	Ch. Rossut Triumphant	Ch. Tavernmews Rebecca
Webline Holly	B	Mr & Mrs D. H. Webster & Mrs D. George	Owners	4.8.67	Stanhurst Placid	Webline Countess
Beacott Cornevon Minuet	B	Mr P. J. Tutchener	Mrs & Miss P. J. Gibson	17.8.67	Ch. Raimex Tally	Cornevon Pensive Ch.
Pinewood Chimer	B	Mr & Mrs L. F. Priestly	Owners	22.12.68	Pinewood Custard	Pinewood Calico

Beagle	Sex	Owner	Breeder	Born	Sire	Dam
1971						
Grattondown Melba	B	Mr & Mrs D. Lester	Owners	16.2.69	Ch. Southcourt Wembury Merryboy	Grattondown Pickle
Dialynne Storm	D	Mrs M. Spavin & Mr B. Moorhouse	Mrs G. Richardson	28.2.69	Ch. Dialynne Ponder	Dialynne Promise
Webline Katy	B	Mr & Mrs D. J. Webster & Mrs D. George	Owners	18.3.69	Ch. Deaconfield Rampage	Webline Countess
Dialynne Gamble	D	Mrs M. Spavin & Mr. B. Moorhouse	Owners	5.9.70	Am. Ch. Appeline Validay Happy Feller	Ch. Dialynne Nettle
Rossut Fantom	B	Mrs V. F. Bradley	Mrs C. G. Sutton	20.1.73	Ch. Rossut Foreman	Rossut Trundle
1972						
Rossut Daffodil	B	Mrs C. G. Sutton	Owner	22.9.70	Rossut Gaffer	Dialynne Debbie
Deaconfield Random	D	Mr D. Macro	Mrs J. M. Ossowaka	20.4.69	Ch. Deaconfield Rampage	Joyway Willowbrae Trinket
Korwin Candida	B	Dr P. Dondina	Mrs C. Watson	7.1.69	Korwin Searcher	Rossut Ruffle
Raimex Wager	B	Mrs D. Brown	Owner	18.9.67	Southcourt Tarquin	Raimex Twinkle
Ditchmere Crestamere Norma	B	Mrs T. Hosking	Mrs W. Mahoney	8.9.70	Ch. Appeline Cannon	Crestamere Opal
Forrardon Rumba	B	Mrs P. Harris	Owner	31.5.70	Ch. Forrardon Foxtrot	Ch. Forrardon Chantress
Cornevon Garland	B	Mrs & Miss Gibson	Owners	22.5.70	Ch. Cornevon Sandpiper	Cornevon Pensive
Dufosee Bonnie Girl	B	Mrs V. Bradley	Owner	6.11.70	Baimor I'm a Rebel	Belinda of Gwanas
Broharron's Thistle	B	Mr & Mrs R. Harron	Owners	13.12.69	Broharron's Cornevon Finian	Ch. Dialynne Posy
Perrystar Vanity	B	Miss M. Meek & Mrs F. Fox	Owners	5.12.72	Ch. Houndsmark Manful	Perrystar Forraden Linnet
Bayard Olga	B	Mrs J. Weston	Owner	26.8.72	Bayard Garnet	Irresistable of Backmuir
Bayard Pisces	D	Mrs J. Weston	Owner	27.3.70	Yovec Beaufort	Irresistable of Backmuir
Southcourt Hatchet	D	Mr & Mrs F. Bothwell	Mrs Young	25.1.69	Ch. Southcourt Wembury Merryboy	Southcourt Harmony
Raimex Tinder	D	Mrs D. Brown	Mr & Mrs Deans	5.5.69	Ch. Raimex Tally	Raimex Walnut

Beagle	Sex	Owner	Breeder	Born	Sire	Dam
1973						
Korwin Monitor	D	Mrs E. Bothwell	Mrs C. Watson	29.3.71	Korwin Tattler	Rossult Raffle
Invermay Miniver	B	Mr W. C. D. Gilmour	Owner	19.1.71	Cornevon Ministrel	Korwin Serenity
Rossut Foreman	D	Mrs C. G. Sutton	Owner	27.5.71	Rossut Gaffer	Rossut Colinbar Phantom Ch.
Beston Harmony	B	Mr W. F. G. Hayes	Miss H. Martin	11.3.71	Southcourt Hatchet	Beston Dolphin
Dialynne Strathdene Fettle	D	Mr J. Peden	Mrs J. Limond	10.12.69	Dialynne Ponder Ch.	Strathdene Faithful Ch.
Houndswood Havoc	D	Dr D. Heywood	Owner	10.11.69	Deaconsfield Rampage Ch.	Rozavel Crystal Gazer
Crestamere Kerry Dancer	B	Mrs W. Mahoney	Owner	20.12.70	Deaconsfield Rampage Ch.	Crestamere Orchid Ch.
Dialynne Mystic	B	Mrs M. Foster	Mrs M. Spavin & Mr B. Moorhouse	23.4.71	Dialynne Strathdene Fettle	Solmars Tanfastic
Deanery Dream-Girl	B	Mrs J. M. Parker	Owner	12.2.72	Dialynne Gamble Ch.	Newton Everest
Solomist of Dialynne	D	Mrs M. Spavin & Mr B. Moorhouse	Mrs J. Brown	4.12.72	Dialynne Gamble Ch.	Sally Sunshine of Lingrise
1974						
Baimor I'm a Rebel	D	Miss M. R. Tolver	Owner	17.8.69	Colegren's Little Rebel of Clovergates Am. Ch.	Baimor Serenade
Raimex Tinder	D	Mrs D. Brown	Mr & Mrs J. Deans	5.5.69	Raimex Tally	Raimex Walnut
Southcourt Hatchet	D	Mr & Mrs F. Bothwell	Mrs G. Young	29.1.69	Southcourt Ch. Wembury Merryboy	Southcourt Harmony
Dufosee Clyde	D	Mrs V. F. Bradley	Owner	11.11.72	Dialynne Gamble Ch.	Dufosee Bonnie Girl Ch.
Crestamere Promise of Haliloo	B	Mrs W. Mahoney	Owner	23.4.71	Redgate Marquis Ch.	Crestamere Oona
1975						
Barterhound Southcourt Hamilton	D	Mrs B. B. Roderick	Owner	25.1.69	Southcourt Wembury Merry Boy	Southcourt Harmony

Beagle	Sex	Owner	Breeder	Born	Sire	Dam
Crestamere Soloman of Owlden	D	Miss J. Buchan	Mrs Mahoney	14.6.72	Rossut Gaffer	Crestamere Orchid
Dialynne Eldon	D	Mrs M. Spavin & Mr B. Moorhouse	Owners	16.4.72	Dialynne Gamble Ch.	Vancia Ballad
Fardene High Hopes	D	Mr A. J. Miles	Owner	9.11.72	Johjean Sunnymeade Bobby of Clovergates Am. Ch.	Fardene Evening Star
Forrardon Warrior	D	Mr L. Pagliero	Mrs P. Harris	20.6.73	Dialynne Gamble Ch.	Forrardon Rumba Ch.
Kernebridge Young Jolyon	D	Mrs P. A. Carmichael	Owner	22.8.72	Lanesend Tallarook	Rossut Chit Chat of Kernebridge
Kittoch Gallant	D	Mrs A. Kirkland	Owner	20.9.72	Dialynne Gamble Ch.	Ailand Lively
Saravere Hardy of Dialynne	D	Mr J. W. Emerson	Mrs L. J. M. Nicholson	23.9.74	Dialynne Eldon	Saravere Harmony
Cherflet Debutante	B	Mrs J. Y. Fletcher	Owner	17.4.71	Barvae Pilot Ch.	Cherflet Woodbarn Holly
Clovergates Liberty Belle	B	Mrs A. Pickthall	Owner	30.10.72	Johjean Sunnymeade Bobby of Clovergates Am. Ch.	Colegren Bill of Clovergates
Dancer of Korwin	B	Mrs C. Watson	Mr J. Stewart	17.2.70	Noslien Beau Brummel	Korwin Bramble
Dialynne Donna	B	Mrs P. Moncur	Mrs M. Spavin & Mr. B. Moorhouse	24.3.73	Appeline Rotany	Dialynne Primrose
Harque to Bella	B	Mrs A. Argyle	Owner	9.5.73	Dialynne Gamble Ch.	Harque Tavernmews Tuneful
Perrystar Vanity	B	Miss M. Meek & Mrs A. Fox	Owners	5.12.72	Houndsmark Manful Ch.	Perrystar Forrardon Linnet
Rozavel Starlight	B	Mrs T. Gray	Owner	14.4.73	Matchmaker of Rozavel	Rozavel Crystal Gift
Seamist of Pancrest	B	Mr & Mrs E. E. Turner	Mrs M. & Mr P. Banahan	20.6.73	Pancrest Saracen	Loughjoy Empress
Semple Candida	B	Mrs A. D. Gray	Owner	21.9.73	Korwin Rioter	Korwin Glitter
1976						
Cornevon Cornbob	D	Mrs A. M. Gibson & Mrs P. J. Parker	Owners	30.3.74	Deaconfield Rampage Ch.	Cornevon Pirouette Ch.

Beagle	Sex	Owner	Breeder	Born	Sire	Dam
Dufosee Harris Tweed	D	Mrs V. Bradley	Owner	21.8.74	Dialynne Gamble Ch.	Dufosee Bonnie Girl Ch.
Wembury Archie	D	Mrs E. D. Hastie	Owner	21.11.71	Annasline Pagemill Playboy	Wembury Tinkerbell Chantress
Beacott Belle	B	Mr P. J. Tutchener	Owner	27.2.72	Southcourt Hatchet	Beacott Cornevon Minuet
Brenglen Beauty of Bayard	B	Mrs J. Weston	Mr R. Buntin	12.7.74	Southcourt Smudge	Dorinor Folly
Broharron's Harlequin	B	Mrs H. Harron	Mr & Mrs R. Harron	20.11.73	Dialynne Gamble Ch.	Broharron's Clover
Chalmain Fancy	B	Mrs M. Borman	Owner	25.3.74	Johjean Sunnymeade Bobby of Clovergates	Chalmain Calypso
Crestamere Snowdrop	B	Mrs W. Mahoney	Owner	17,9.72	Rossut Paragon	Crestamere Harmony
Crestamere Twilight of Rossut	B	Miss Sutton	Mrs W. Mahoney	8.1.72	Rossut Paragon	Crestamere Katie
Dialynne Tamar of Charterwood	B	Miss J. L. Taylor	Mrs M. Spavin & Mrs B. Moorhouse	4.4.74	Dialynne Gamble Ch.	Vancia Bashful
Lanesend Tallarook	B	Miss A. M. Phillips	Owner	1.5.69	Southcourt Tarquin	Lanesend Raimex Holly
Norcis Hannah	B	Mrs E. Bothwell	Owner	7.3.74	Korwin Monitor Ch.	Korwin Rachel
Symbol of Dialynne	B	Mr J. W. Emerson	Mrs J. Brown	8.7.73	Dialynne Gamble Ch.	Sally Sunshine of Lingrise
1977						
Beacott Buckthorn	D	Mr P. J. Tutchener	Owner	12.11.75	Southcourt Wembury Merryboy Ch.	Beacott Cornevon Minuet Ch.
Kernebridge Trooper	D	Mrs P. A. Carmichael	Owner	13.1.74	Raimex Tinder	Rossut Chit Chat of Kernebridge
Pinewood Crib of Webline	D	Mr & Mrs D. J. Webster & Mrs D. George	Mr & Mrs L. F. Priestley	12.1.72	Southcourt Wembury Merry Boy Ch.	Pinewood Chimer Ch.
Crestamere Truth	B	Mrs W. Mahoney	Owner	30.7.75	Crestamere Soloman of Owlden Ch.	Crestamere Promise of Haliloo Ch.

Beagle	Sex	Owner	Breeder	Born	Sire	Dam
Dialynne Astra	B	Mrs M. Spavin & Mr B. Moorhouse	Mrs M. Spavin	3.1.73	Dialynne Gamble Ch.	Dialynne Petal
Rossut Sunset	B	Miss P. A. Sutton	Mrs C. G. Sutton	1.4.74	Rossut Foreman Ch.	Crestamere Twilight of Rossut
1978						
Barterhound Hammerlyn	D	Mrs B. B. Roderick	Owner	30.1.76	Barterhound Southcourt Hamilton Ch.	Barterhound Bramble
Jesson Fencer	D	Mrs B. H. Eades	Owner	28.12.75	Houndswood Havoc Ch.	Jesson Forrardon Rhapsody
Jesson Fantasy	B	Mrs B. H. Eades	Owner	28.12.75	Houndswood Havoc Ch.	Jesson Forrardon Rhapsody
Korwin Lottie	B	Mrs C. Watson	Owner	1.9.76	Korwin Rioter	Korwin Affable
Norcis Helene of Crestamere	B	Mrs W. Mahoney	Mrs E. Bothwell	7.3.74	Korwin Monitor Ch.	Korwin Rachel
Pinewood Castor	B	M. G. Chalmer	Mr & Mrs L. F. Priestley	13.2.77	Dialynne Gamble Ch.	Pinewood Chimer
Trewint Speculation of Dialynne	B	Mrs M. Spaivn	Mrs M. M. Stevenson	1.2.75	Dialynne Gamble Ch.	Trewint Pageant

THE KENNEL CLUB
BREED REGISTRATIONS

Date	Total	Date	Total	Date	Total
1951	101	1960	1519	1969	3979
1952	124	1961	2047	1970	3445
1953	138	1962	2518	1971	3209
1954	154	1963	2966	1972	3033
1955	200	1964	3214	1973	2871
1956	337	1965	3427	1974	2686
1957	381	1966	3401	1975	1895
1958	635	1967	3734		
1959	1092	1968	3841		

Note In April 1976 the Kennel Club changed its registration system, thus preventing the continuation of this method of listing annual totals.

BREED CLUBS
AND THEIR SECRETARIES

The Beagle Association.
The Beagle Club.
The Beagle Club of Northern Ireland.
Devon and Cornwall Beagle Society.
Four Counties Beagle Club.
The Northern & Midland Counties Beagle Club.
The Scottish Beagle Club.
The Welsh Beagle Club.
West Mercia Beagle Club.

The names and addresses of secretaries can be obtained on application to the Kennel Club, 1–4 Clarges Street, London, W1Y 8AB.

BEAGLE PACKS

officially recognised by the Association of Masters of Harriers and Beagles,
as listed 1976

Airedale
Aldershot
Ampleforth
Beacon
Bell-Irving
Bolebroke
Brighton and Storrington
Britannia
Catterick
Cheshire
Chilmark
Christ Church and Farley Hill
Claro
Colchester Garrison
Colne Valley
Crowcombe
Derbyshire and Nottinghamshire
Dummer
Ecclesfield
Eton College
Glyn Celyn
Holcombe Rogus
Holme Valley
Hunsley Beacon
Ilminster
Isle of Wight
Marlborough College
Meon Valley
Mid Essex
Mid Glamorgan
Monmouthshire
Newcastle and District
New Forest
North Bucks
North Dartmoor
Oakley Foot
Old Berkeley

Palmer Milburn
The Park
Per Ardua (R.A.F.)
Pevensey Marsh
Pimpernel (Royal Signals)
Radley College
Royal Agricultural College
Royal Rock
Sandhurst
School of Infantry
Shropshire
South Herts
Sproughton Foot
Staffordshire
Stoke Hill
Stowe
Stowford
Surrey and North Sussex
Trinity Foot
Warwickshire
Weardale
Wick and District
Woodfield
Wyre College
Wyre Forest

TRADITIONAL HOUND NAMES

DOGS

ABLE	Bonnyface	Clamorous	Dapper
Actor	Bouncer	Clangour	Dapster
Adamant	Bowler	Clasher	Darter
Adjutant	Bragger	Climbank	Dasher
Agent	Bravo	Clinker	Dashwood
Aider	Brawler	Combat	Daunter
Aimwell	Brazen	Combatant	Dexterous
Amorous	Brilliant	Comforter	Disputant
Antic	Brusher	Comrade	Downright
Anxious	Brutal	Comus	Dragon
Arbiter	Burster	Conflict	Dreadnought
Archer	Bustler	Conqueror	Driver
Ardent		Conquest	Duster
Ardor		Constant	
Arrogant	CAITIFF	Contest	
Artful	Caliban	Coroner	EAGER
Artist	Capitol	Cottager	Effort
Atlas	Captain	Counsellor	Elegant
Atom	Captor	Countryman	Eminent
Auditor	Carol	Courteous	Envious
Augur	Carver	Coxcomb	Envoy
Awful	Caster	Craftsman	Ernest
	Castwell	Crasher	Errant
	Catcher	Critic	Excellent
BACHELOR	Catchpole	Critical	
Baffler	Caviller	Crowner	
Banger	Cerberus	Cruiser	FACTIOUS
Barbarous	Challenger	Crusty	Factor
Bellman	Champion	Cryer	Fatal
Bender	Charon	Curfew	Fearnought
Blaster	Chaser	Currier	Ferryman
Bluecap	Chaunter		Fervent
Blueman	Chieftain		Finder
Bluster	Chimer	DAMPER	Firebrand
Boaster	Chirper	Danger	Flagrant
Boisterous	Claimant	Dangerous	Flasher

DOGS

Fleece'm	Harbinger	Linguist	NESTOR
Flinger	Hardiman	Listener	Nettler
Flippant	Hardy	Lounger	Newsman
Flourisher	Harlequin	Lucifer	Nimrod
Flyer	Havoc	Lunger	Noble
Foamer	Hazard	Lurker	Nonsuch
Foiler	Headstrong	Lusty	Novel
Foreman	Hearty		
Foremost	Hector		
Foresight	Heedful		PAEAN
Forester	Hercules	MANAGER	Pageant
Forward	Hero	Manful	Paragon
Fugleman	Highflyer	Marksman	Paramount
Fulminant	Hopeful	Marplot	Partner
Furrier	Hotspur	Marschal	Partyman
	Humbler	Martial	Pealer
		Marvellous	Penetrant
GAINER		Matchem	Perfect
Gallant	IMPETUS	Maxim	Perilous
Galliard		Maximus	Pertinent
Galloper		Meanwell	Petulant
Gamboy		Medler	Phoebus
Gamester	JERKER	Menacer	Piercer
Garrulous	Jingler	Mendall	Pilgrim
Gazer	Jockey	Mender	Pillager
General	Jolly	Mentor	Pilot
Genius	Jollyboy	Mercury	Pincher
Giant	Jostler	Merlin	Piper
Gimcrack	Jovial	Merryboy	Playful
Glancer	Jubal	Merryman	Plodder
Glider	Judgement	Messmate	Plunder
Glorious	Jumper	Mighty	Politic
Goblin		Militant	Potent
Governor		Minikin	Prater
Grapler	LABOURER	Miscreant	Prattler
Grasper	Larum	Mittimus	Premier
Griper	Lasher	Monarch	President
Growler	Laster	Monitor	Presto
Grumbler	Launcher	Motley	Prevalent
Guardian	Leader	Mounter	Primate
Guider	Leveller	Mover	Principal
Guiler	Liberal	Mungo	Prodigal
	Libertine	Musical	Prompter
	Lictor	Mutinous	Prophet
HANNIBAL	Lifter	Mutterer	Prosper
Harasser	Lightfoot	Myrmidon	Prosperous

DOGS

Prowler	Rural	Squeaker	Touchstone
Pryer	Rusher	Statesman	Tracer
	Rustic	Steady	Tragic
		Stickler	Trampler
RACER		Stinger	Transit
Rager	SALIENT	Stormer	Transport
Rallywood	Sampler	Stranger	Traveller
Rambler	Sampson	Stripling	Trial
Rampant	Sanction	Striver	Trier
Rancour	Sapient	Strivewell	Trimbush
Random	Saucebox	Stroker	Trimmer
Ranger	Saunter	Stroller	Triumph
Ransack	Scalper	Struggler	Trojan
Rantaway	Scamper	Sturdy	Trouncer
Ranter	Schemer	Subtile	Truant
Rapper	Scourer	Succour	Trudger
Ratler	Scrambler	Suppler	Trueboy
Ravager	Screamer	Surly	Trueman
Ravenous	Screecher	Swaggerer	Trusty
Ravisher	Scuffler	Sylvan	Trywell
Reacher	Searcher		Tuner
Reasoner	Settler		Turbulent
Rector	Sharper		Twanger
Regent	Shifter	TACKLER	Twig'em
Render	Signal	Talisman	Tyrant
Resonant	Singer	Tamer	
Restive	Singwell	Tangent	
Reveller	Skirmish	Tartar	VAGABOND
Rifler	Smoker	Tattler	Vagrant
Rigid	Social	Taunter	Valiant
Rigour	Solomon	Teaser	Valid
Ringwood	Solon	Terror	Valorous
Rioter	Songster	Thrasher	Valour
Risky	Sonorous	Threatner	Vaulter
Rockwood	Soundwell	Thumper	Vaunter
Romper	Spanker	Thunderer	Venture
Rouser	Special	Thwacker	Venturer
Router	Specimen	Thwarter	Venturous
Rover	Speedwell	Tickler	Vermin
Rudesby	Spinner	Tomboy	Vexer
Ruffian	Splendour	Topmost	Victor
Ruffler	Splenetic	Topper	Vigilant
Rumbler	Spoiler	Torment	Vigorous
Rummager	Spokesman	Torrent	Vigour
Rumour	Sportsman	Torturer	Villager
Runner	Squabbler	Tosser	Viper

DOGS

Volant	Warhoop	Whynot	Worker
Voucher	Warning	Wildair	Workman
	Warrior	Wildman	Worthy
	Wayward	Wilful	Wrangler
WANDERER	Wellbred	Wisdom	Wrestler
Warbler	Whipster	Woodman	

BITCHES

ACCURATE	CAPABLE	Delicate	Firetail
Active	Captious	Desperate	Flighty
Actress	Careful	Destiny	Flourish
Affable	Careless	Dian	Flurry
Agile	Carnage	Diligent	Forcible
Airy	Caution	Docile	Fretful
Amity	Cautious	Document	Friendly
Angry	Charmer	Doubtful	Frisky
Animate	Chauntress	Doubtless	Frolic
Artifice	Cheerful	Dreadless	Frolicsome
Audible	Cherriper	Dulcet	Funnylass
	Chorus		Furious
	Circe		Fury
	Clarinet	EASY	
BANEFUL	Clio	Echo	
Bashful	Comeley	Ecstasy	GAIETY
Bauble	Comfort	Endless	Gaily
Beauteous	Comical	Energy	Gainful
Beauty	Concord	Enmity	Galley
Beldam	Courtesy		Gambol
Bellmaid	Crafty		Gamesome
Blameless	Crazy		Gamestress
Blithesome	Credible	FAIRMAID	Gaylass
Blowzy	Credulous	Fairplay	Giddy
Bluebell	Croney	Faithful	Gladness
Bluemaid	Cruel	Famous	Gladsome
Bonny	Curious	Fanciful	Governess
Bonnybell		Fashion	Graceful
Bonnylass		Favourite	Graceless
Boundlass		Fearless	Gracious
Bravery	DAINTY	Festive	Grateful
Brevity	Daphne	Fickle	Gravity
Brimstone	Darling	Fidget	Guilesome
Busy	Dashaway	Fiery	Guiltless
Buxom	Dauntless	Fireaway	Guilty

BITCHES

Handsome
Harmony
Hasty
Hazardous
Heedless
Helen
Heroine
Honesty
Hostile

Industry

Jealousy
Jollity
Joyful
Joyous

Laudable
Lavish
Lawless
Levity
Liberty
Lightning
Lightsome
Likely
Lissom
Litigate
Lively
Lofty
Lovely
Luckylass

Madcap
Madrigal
Magic
Matchless
Melody
Merriment
Merrylass
Mindful
Minion

Miriam
Mischief
Modish
Monody
Music

Narrative
Neatness
Needful
Nicety
Nimble
Noisy
Notable
Notice
Notion
Novelty
Novice

Passion
Pastime
Patience
Phoenix
Phrensy
Placid
Playful
Playsome
Pleasant
Pliant
Positive
Precious
Prettylass
Previous
Priestess
Probity
Prudence

Racket
Rally
Rampish
Rantipole
Rapid
Rapine
Rapture

Rarity
Rashness
Rattle
Ravish
Reptile
Resolute
Restless
Rhapsody
Riddance
Riot
Rival
Roguish
Ruin
Rummage
Ruthless

Sanguine
Sappho
Science
Scrupulous
Shrewdness
Skilful
Songstress
Specious
Speedy
Spiteful
Spitfire
Sportful
Sportive
Sportly
Sprightly
Stately
Stoutness
Strenuous
Strumpet
Surety
Sybil
Symphony

Tattle
Telltale
Tempest
Termagant
Terminate

Terrible
Testy
Thankful
Thoughtful
Tidings
Toilsome
Tractable
Tragedy
Trespass
Trifle
Trivial
Trollop
Troublesome
Truelass
Truemaid
Tunable
Tuneful

Vanquish
Vehemence
Vehement
Vengeance
Vengeful
Venomous
Venturesome
Venus
Verify
Verity
Victory
Victrix
Vigilance
Violent
Viperous
Virulent
Vitiate
Vivid
Vixen
Vocal
Volatile
Voluble

Waggery
Waggish
Wagtail
Wanton

BITCHES

Warfare	Watchful	Whirligig	Wonderful
Warlike	Welcome	Wildfire	Worry
Waspish	Welldone	Willing	Wrathful
Wasteful	Whimsy	Wishful	Wreakful

BOOKS CONSULTED

The Beagle. E. Fitch Daglish. (Foyle's Handbooks. London, W.C.2. 1961)

This is the Beagle. George D. Whitney, D.V.M. (The Practical Science Publishing Co., Orange, Conn., U.S.A. 1955)

The Complete Beagle. William Denlinger. (Denlinger's, Richmond, Virginia, U.S.A. 1955)

Beagling. J. Ivester Lloyd. (Herbert Jenkins, London. 1954)

Pet Beagle. A. D. Holcombe. (All-Pets Books, Inc., Fond du Lac, Wisconsin, U.S.A. 1958)

The Dog in Health and Disease. Stonehenge. 3rd Edition (Longmans, Green and Co., London, 1879)

Our Friend the Dog. Dr Gordon Stables, R.N. (Dean and Son, London, 1890)

Beagles and Beagling. J. Otho Paget. (Hutchinson and Son, London, 1923)

Hutchinsons Popular and Illustrated Dog Encyclopaedia. N.D.

Cassell's New Book of the Dog. Robert Leighton. (The Waverley Book Co. Ltd. London. N.D.)

Modern Dogs. Rawdon B. Lee. (Horace Cox, London, 1897)

The Illustrated Book of the Dog. Vero Shaw, B.A. (Cassell and Co. Ltd, London, 1890)

The Kennel Encyclopaedia. F. T. Barton. Virtue and Co. Ltd. London. N.D.

The Book of the Dog. Edited by Brian Vesey-Fitzgerald. (Nicholson and Watson. London. 1948)

Show Dogs. Theo Marples. 4th Edition. (Our Dogs. Manchester. 1946)

The Art of Beagling. J. Otho Paget. (H. F. and G. Witherby. London. 1931)

Letters to a Young Beagler. H. C. Pyper. (J. A. Allen and Co. London. 1954)

The Sport Sketch Book. (J. W. Carleton. 1842)

INDEX

ABRASIONS, 178
Acid milk, 178
Advertising puppies, 159–60
Ailments, 177 ff.
Air transport, 164
Albert, Prince, 22, 23
Aldershot pack, 34
Allott's pack, 34
American field trials, 63
American Kennel Club, standard for beagle, 68–9
Ampleforth pack, 34
Anal glands, 179
Anderson, W. R., 53
Animal export specialists, 163, 164
Appearance of beagle, 69
Appleton, Douglas, 53, 55, 56
Arrowroot, 93
Association of Masters of Harriers and Beagles, 46, 49, 70

BACK of beagle, 68
Balanitis, 179
Barsheen prefix, 53
Beagle Club, 47, 51, 57, 58
Beagle packs, 20, 21, 22, 23, 24, 25, 27 ff., 32 ff.
Beagles
  ailments, 177 ff.
  American Kennel Club standards, 68–9
  as family dog, 95–8
  at whelping, 133–4
  breed standard, 58–9
  brood bitch, 120 ff.
  buying, 77–8
  children and, 102–3
  choosing, 70 ff.
  classification of, 67
  effects of terrain on hunting, 27 ff.
  feeding and management, 84 ff.

grooming, 168–9, 173
housing, 147 ff.
hunting, 27 ff.
imports from U.S.A., 55–6
in the show ring, 104
invalid diet for, 93
Kennel Club standard, 66–7
motoring and, 103
'natural rearing', 93–4
origins of, 16 ff.
pack, 49
preparing for showing, 167 ff.
show, 27, 48 ff.
size classification, 57, 58
stallion hound, 107 ff.
starting a pack, 70–73
training, 95–106
Beagles and Beagling, 32
Beagling, 36–46
Beaumont, H. G., 52
Beck, Mrs, 54, 55
Beckford, Peter, 21
Benger's food, 144
Berners, Dame Juliana, 17
Biliousness, 179–80
Bilton prefix, 52
Biscuit, 90
Bites, 180
Bladder trouble, 180
Blossom Valley Beagle Club, U.S.A. 105
Body, 66, 68, 78
Boke of St Albans, The, 17
Bowels, 180
Box, travelling, 126–8
Breach presentation at birth, 134
Breath, bad, 179
Breeding, 112–18
British Dogs, 24
British Goat Society, 92
Bronchitis, 181
Bronwydd pack, 32, 33

Letton kennels, 54
Levy, Juliette de Bairacli, 93, 94, 142
Life of Charles II, 20
Linlithgow, Marquis of, 32, 52
Lloyd, Sir Marteine, 32
Lloyd, Sir Thomas, 23
Loin, 68
Lord, F. B., 27, 30, 60, 62

MACKERNESS, Joe, 42
Macro, Mrs, 54
Makeway, Lindsey, 53
Mange, 187–8
Markings, 74
Mary, Queen of Scots, 19
Mating, 113–15
Mayhew, Mrs R., 61
Mayster of Game, 17
Meat, 87, 88, 89–90
Medicine cupboard, 177–8
Meet the Beagle, 105
Mendelism, 111
Meningitis, 188
Milk, 90
  condensed, 92
  dried, 92
  goat's, 92, 144
Miller, George, 35
Minadex, 93
Mincer, 151–2
Modern Dogs, 26, 28
Morbid appetite, 179
Motoring, beagles and, 103
Mottles, 74
Movement, 81
Muzzle, 68

NAILS, 189
National Beagle Club, U.S.A., 63
Neck, 66, 68, 79, 80
New Forest beagles, 35
Nickalls, Cecil, 35
North Worcestershire pack, 33, 47
Nose, 80
Nutt, G. H., 30, 61

OBEDIENCE training, 104–5
Obesity, 189
Of Englishe Dogges, 19
O'Halloran, Mrs C. R., 52

Oil stoves, 133
Oldman, Mrs Y., 53
Oughton-Giles, Mrs, 60, 61
Our Dogs, 60, 94, 105, 159
Oxford pack, 35

PACK
  starting a, 70–3
  training a, 105–6
Paget, Otto, 32, 33, 34, 35
Pantyblaidd prefix, 51
Parker, Mrs, 53
Parrish's Chemical Food, 93
Parturient eclampsia, 189–90
Paunches, 89
Pearce, Rev. T. ('Idstone'), 24
Peterborough hound show, 49
Pickthall, Mrs A, 56
Pocket beagle, 59
  standard, 68
Pope, A., 20
Practical Dog Breeding and Genetics, 111
Price, Mrs, 35
Puppies
  at birth, 134–5, 137
  buying bitch, 123
  choosing, 77–83
  cost of, 77
  dew-claws, 139–40
  feeding, 88, 91–3
    by hand, 143–6
  selling, 155–63
  time-table for, 91–2
  training with lead, 100–1
Purgatives, 190
Pymetria, 190

QUARANTINE, 55, 165–6

RABBIT beagles, 61
Rabies, 190
Radnage affix, 60–1
Ravold beagles, 54
Refrigerator, 151
Reynalton prefix, 52
Rheumatism, 190
Ribs, 68
Rickets, 190
Rider, Mrs M., 144

Roboleine, 93
Rochford beagles, 33
Routine, importance, 84
Rowlett, General, 62–3
Royal Rock pack, 32, 33, 63
Rozavel kennels, 54
Runs, 86, 150, 154
Rural Almanack, 26
Russel, James, 31, 35
Rytow prefix, 53

SARCOTPIC mange, 187
Scott, Sir W., 21
Segusian hound, 16
Selling puppies, 155–63
Service, conditions of, 129–30
Shock, 191
Shoulders, 68
Show ring, beagles in, 104
Shows
    equipment for, 173–5
    preparing for, 167 ff.
    procedure at, 169–71
Siddle, Miss, 54, 55
Skeat, Walter William, 18
Skull, 66, 80
Sleeping, 98–9
    benches, 149
Somerville, William, 21
Southover beagles, 24
Sport Sketch Book, The, 22
Sportsman's Cabinet, 22
Sportsman's Library, 29
Spowart, Mrs, 53
Springhill pack, 35
Squire of Low Degree, The, 18
Stallion hound, 107 ff., 116, 117, 118
Stanhurst prefix, 54
Stern, 78
Stewart, J. S., 53
Stings, 191
Stoke Place pack, 34
'Stonehenge', see Walsh, J. H.
Storehouse, 154
Stradanus, Johannes, 20
Stubbs, George, 22
Stud Book of Packs of Beagles, 26
Stud-dog owner, 112–13
Stud fees, 112, 116
Stud service, 115
Surbiton pack, 33, 34

TAILS, 66, 69, 78–9

Tavernmews prefix, 54
Teeth, 81
    care of, 191
Temperament, 109
Temperature, 191
Thighs, 68
This is the Beagle, 111
Thornton, Colonel, 21, 27, 28
Thoughts on Hunting, 21
Throat, 68
Tie, 114
Times, The, 159
Time-table, 85
Tonsillitis, 192
Topsell, Edward, 20
Towpath prefix, 53
Transfers, 163
Travelling, 126–8
Trimming, 169
Trinity Foot beagles, 35
Tripe, 89
Turner, Allen, 33, 34

ULVERSTONE beagles, 33
U.S.A.
    beagles in, 61–5
    imports of beagles from, 55–6

VETERINARY surgeon, when to call, 177
Vetzyme yeast tablets, 93
Vionite, 93
Virol, 93
Vomiting, 192
Vyse, Howard, 34

WALSH, J. H. ('Stonehenge'), 23, 24,
    25, 30, 61
Weight, 67
Wellshot beagles, 54
West Surrey pack, 34
Whale meat, 90
Whelping, 132–5
Whelping kennel, location of, 154
Whitney, George D., 111
Whitton, Miss, 53, 54, 55
Whitwell, Mrs D. F., 54
William III, 21
William the Conqueror, 17
Wilmshurst, Miss, 53
Wilmshurst, Mrs, 54